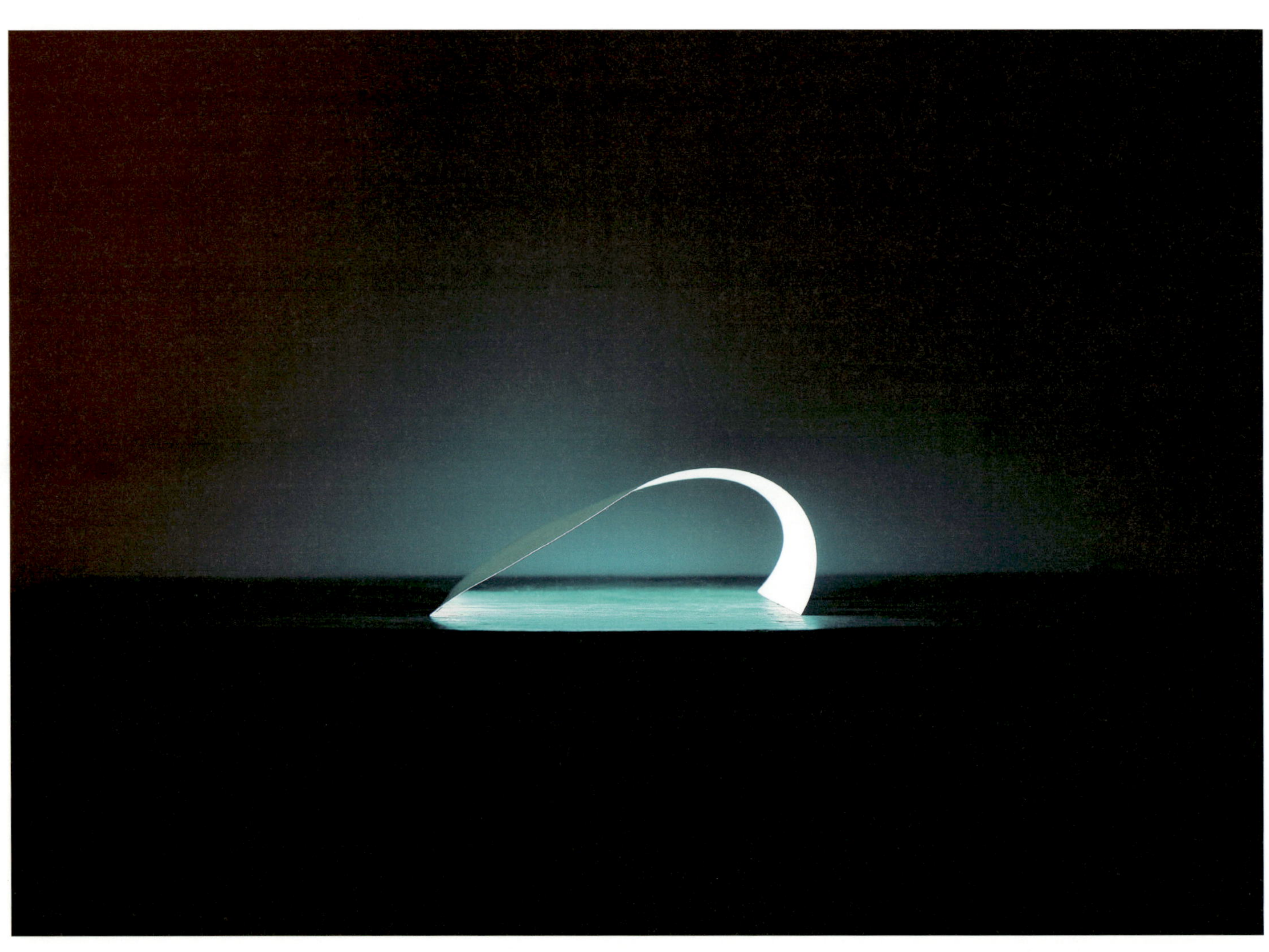

JIANG PENGYI Everything Illuminates "Every single thing has a moment of sanctity, as a flash of divinity, during which its own properties and attributes sound like a prayer." - Born in Yuanjiang, Hunan Province in 1977, Jiang Pengyi graduated from the Beijing Institute of Art and Design in 1999. He received the Tierney Fellowship Award from The First Annual Three Shadows Photography Award in 2009, the Jury Grand Prize from the Société Générale Chinese Art Awards in 2010 and the Aletti Art Verona Prize for Photography in 2011. He was invited to participate in the Helsinki Photography Biennial 2012 and is nominated for the Prix Pictet 2012. He recently had solo shows in Shanghai (Aike-Dell'Arco Gallery) and Hong Kong (Blindspot Gallery.) His works are in some of the most prestigious international collections: Fondazione Banca Aletti, Italy; Artnow International Inc., USA; Frac des Pays de la Loire, France; The Tierney Family Foundation, USA; UniCredit Art Collection, Italy and Germany. Jiang Pengyi currently lives and works in Beijing, China.

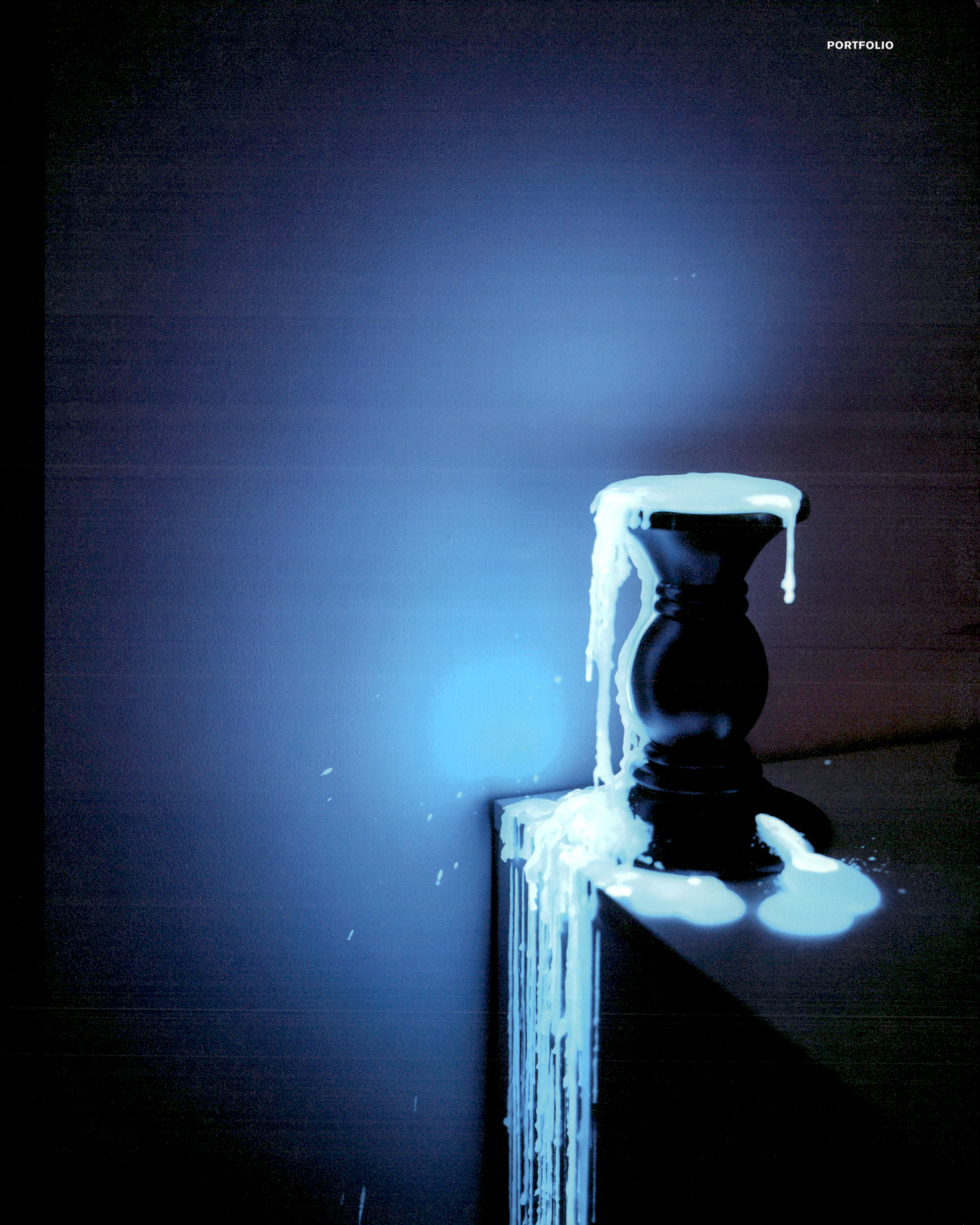

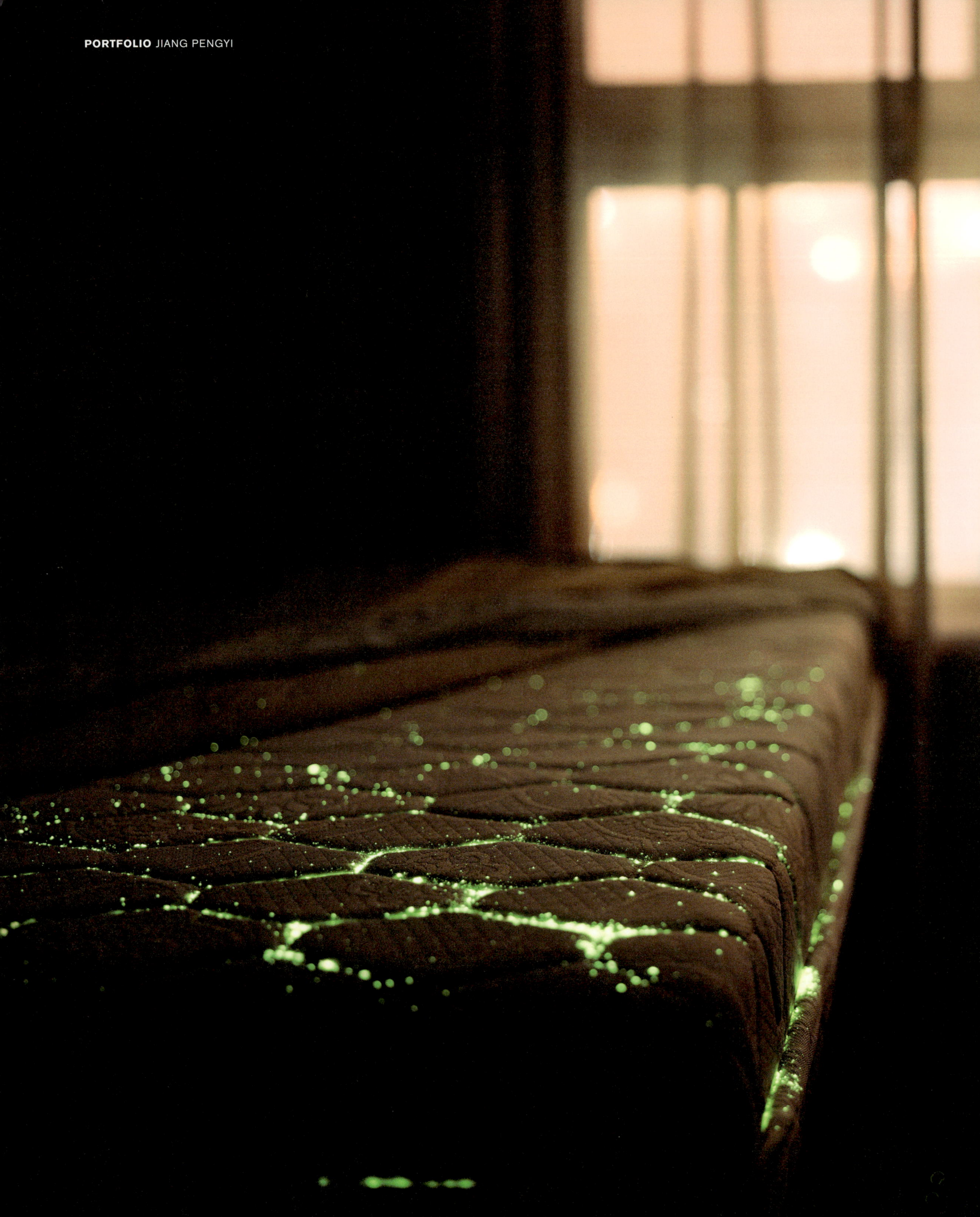

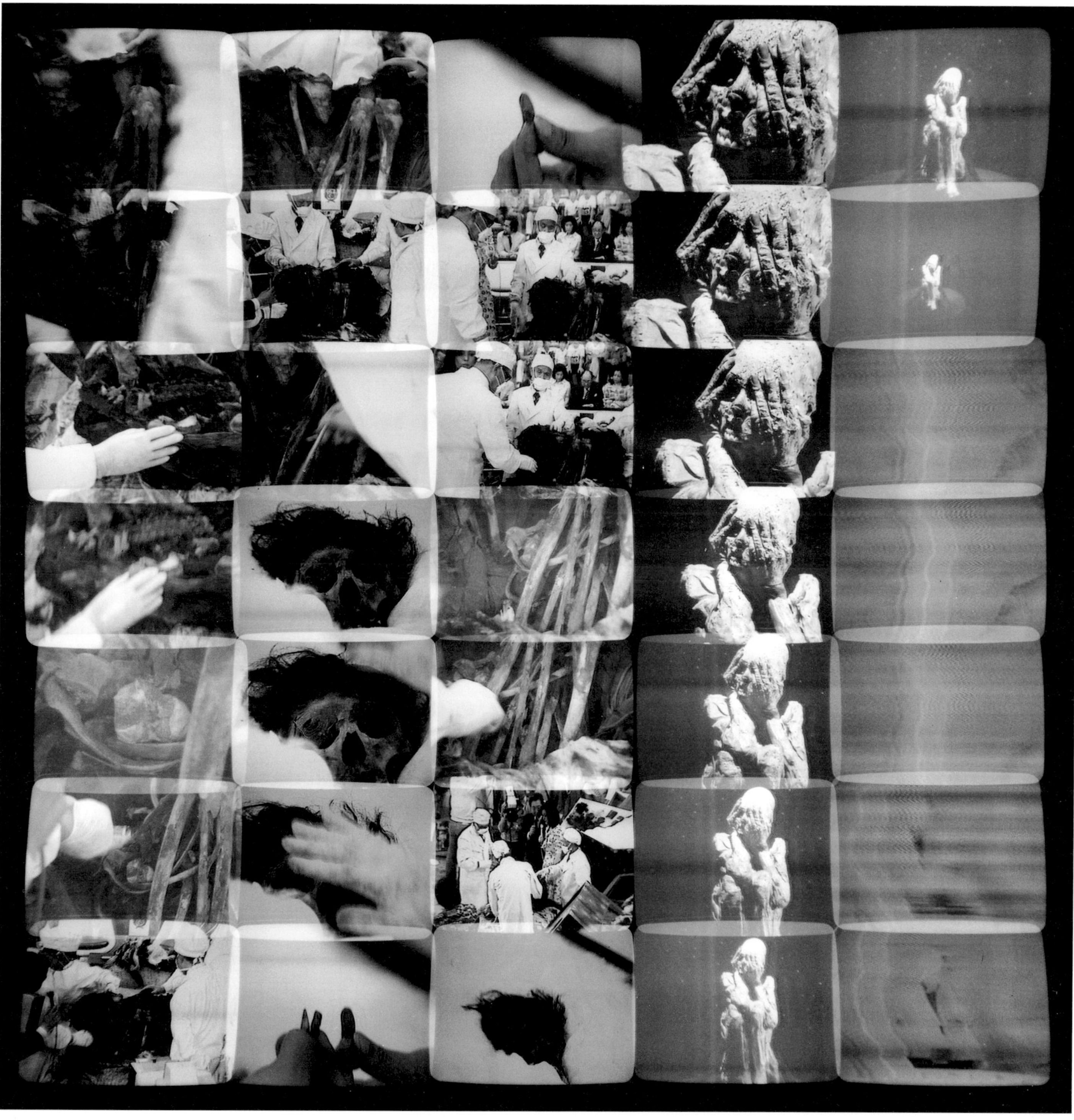

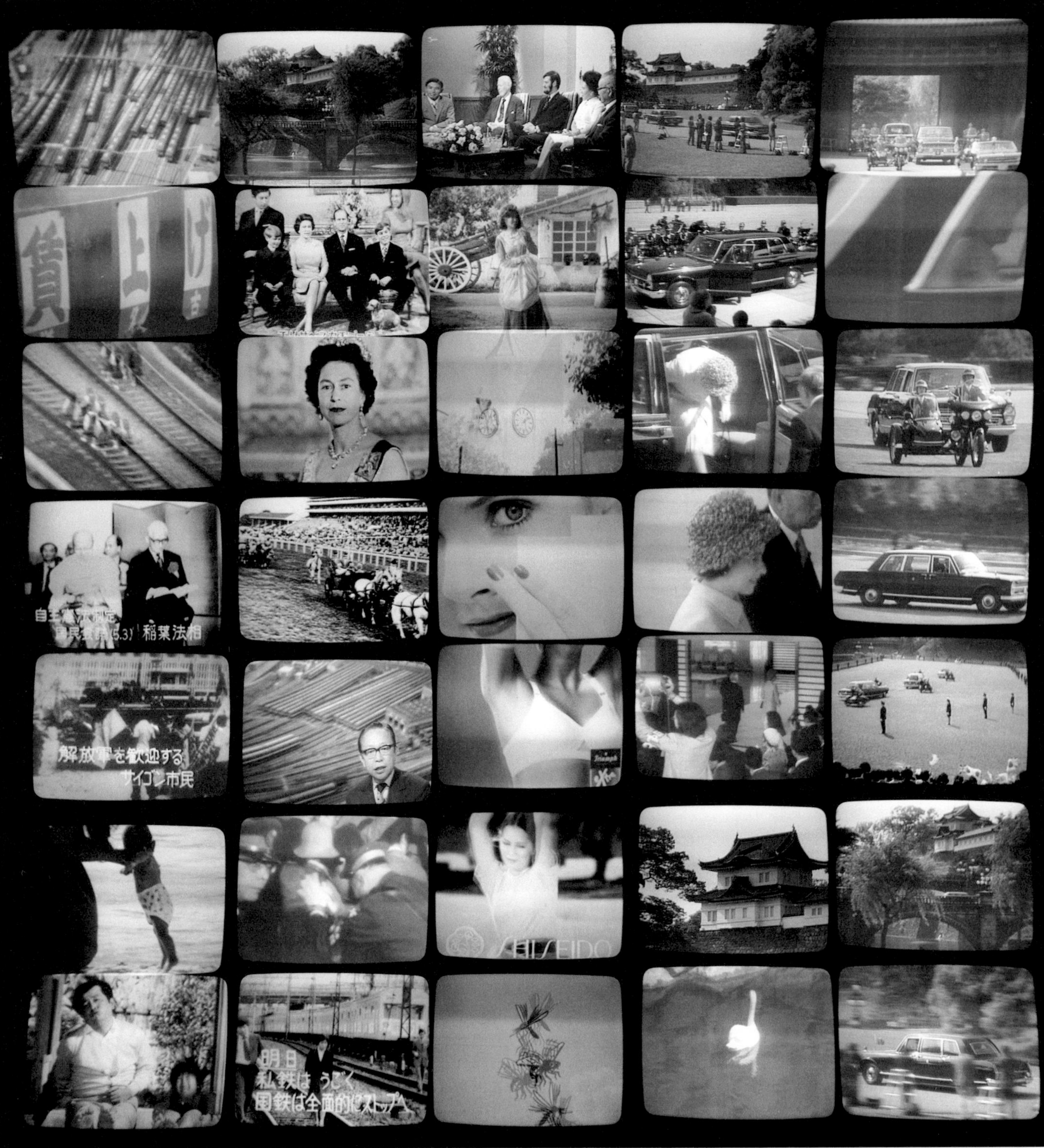

MASAO MOCHIZUKI
TELEVISION
introduced by his gallerist
François Sage

When I met Masao Mochizuki for the first time I was surprised by the beauty of his face and the softness of his eyes. They were the eyes of youth, eyes taken back to childhood by the illness he had contracted, even though his body was moving towards old age.

He is my elder but both of us discovered television when we were children, when it came to inhabit a singular place in our lives. Television opened our eyes, our hearts and our consciousness to many themes, people, things, countries and events that, until then, we had rebuffed perhaps or simply overlooked. It was, at that time of our rather dull existence, a magnificent, strange, radical revealer, a revealer of us. We are the children of television as others have been of the train, electricity, radio, cinema and the airplane: children that cried when John F. Kennedy died; marveled at Yuri Gagarin's space travel; cheered jubilantly at Mohammed Ali's victories; and watched, bemused and amused, at the visit of the Queen of England. It punctuated our otherwise dreary lives and transformed our evenings. Thanks to television, we felt alive.

Mochizuki was passionate about television and he was equally circumspect about its meaning. The artist ingeniously modified his Mamiyaflex C-2 twin lens camera so that he could fix multiple images produced by his television "set thirty five to be exact" in one picture frame. By manipulating his camera in the same way, again and again, he captured continuously the endless outpouring of images from the television. He then organized them to record and recreate how those moments of history are imprinted in the memory of a viewer.

The inventive, genial and always delicate photographer transformed television into an object that reveals the sequential images we keep as memory. Not the continuous frame-by-frame sequencing that results in the moving image but rather the discontinuous snapshots that our minds keep of an event to remember it. Thanks to him, photography has laid its hands on television, has it under control, dissected it, made it an object of reflection, and his thoughtful images relate not only to those moments of history but they change the status of television itself. Mochizuki's photographs of television are memory streams as powerful as Proust's madeleine dipped in tea.

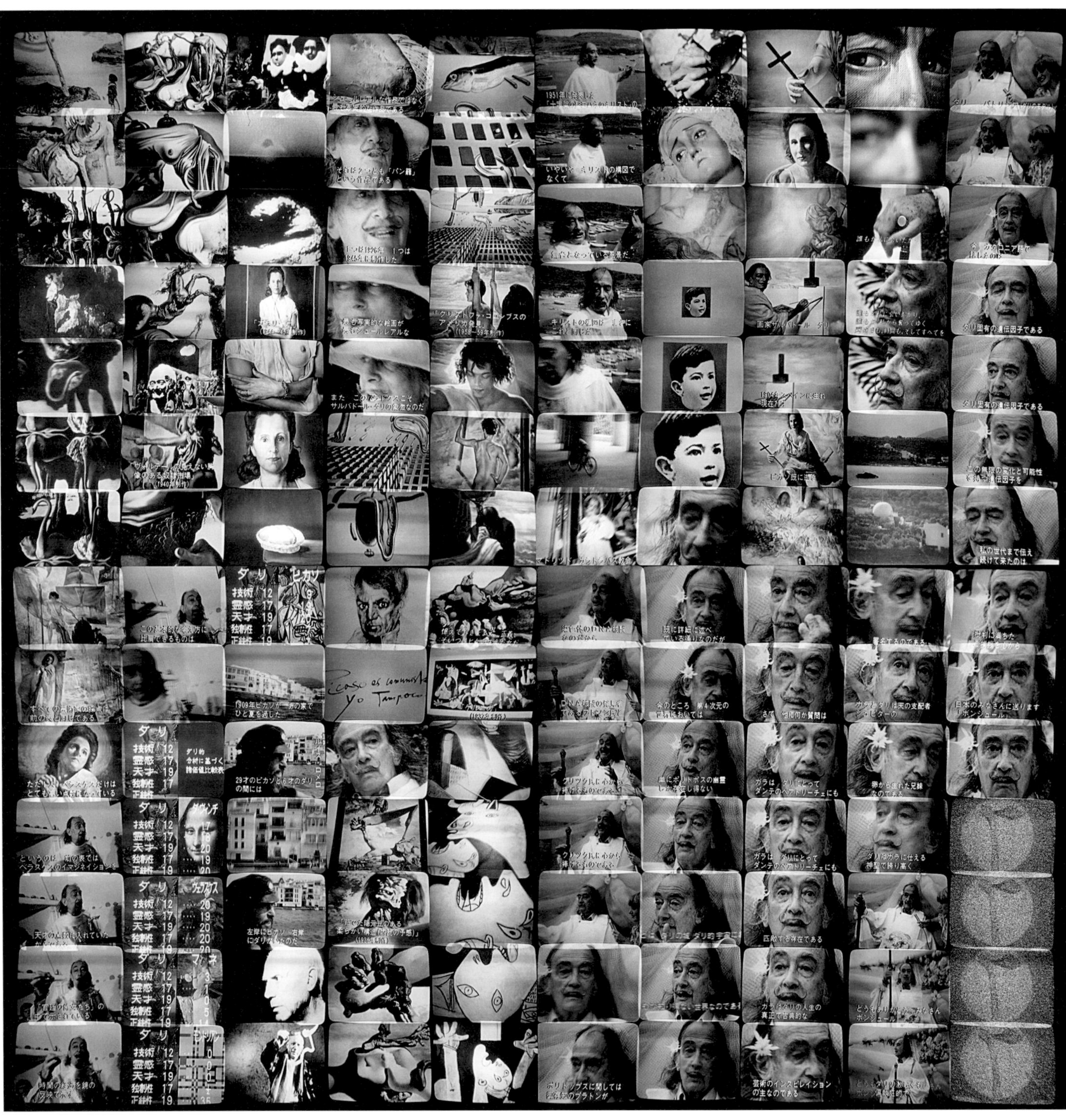

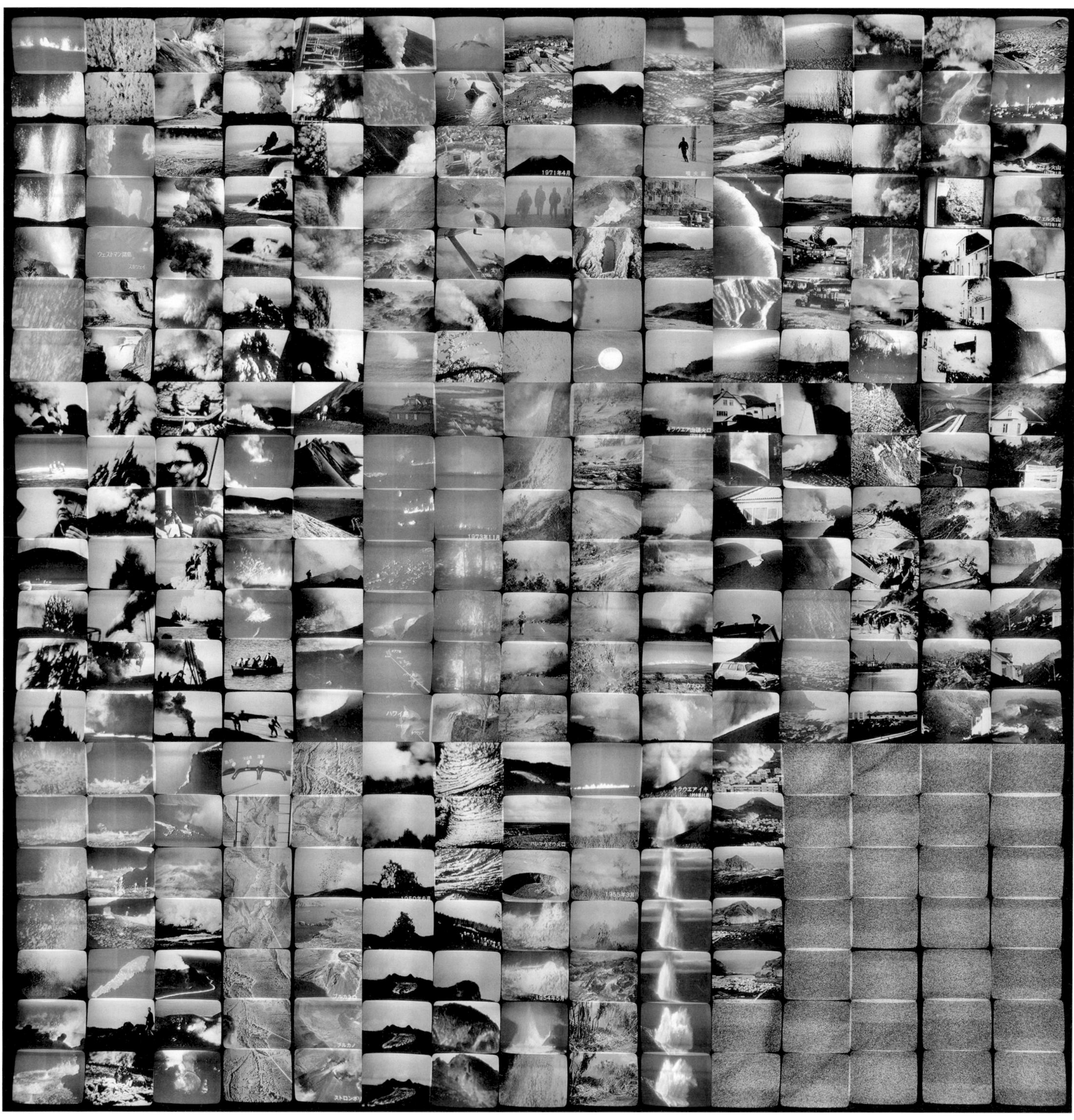

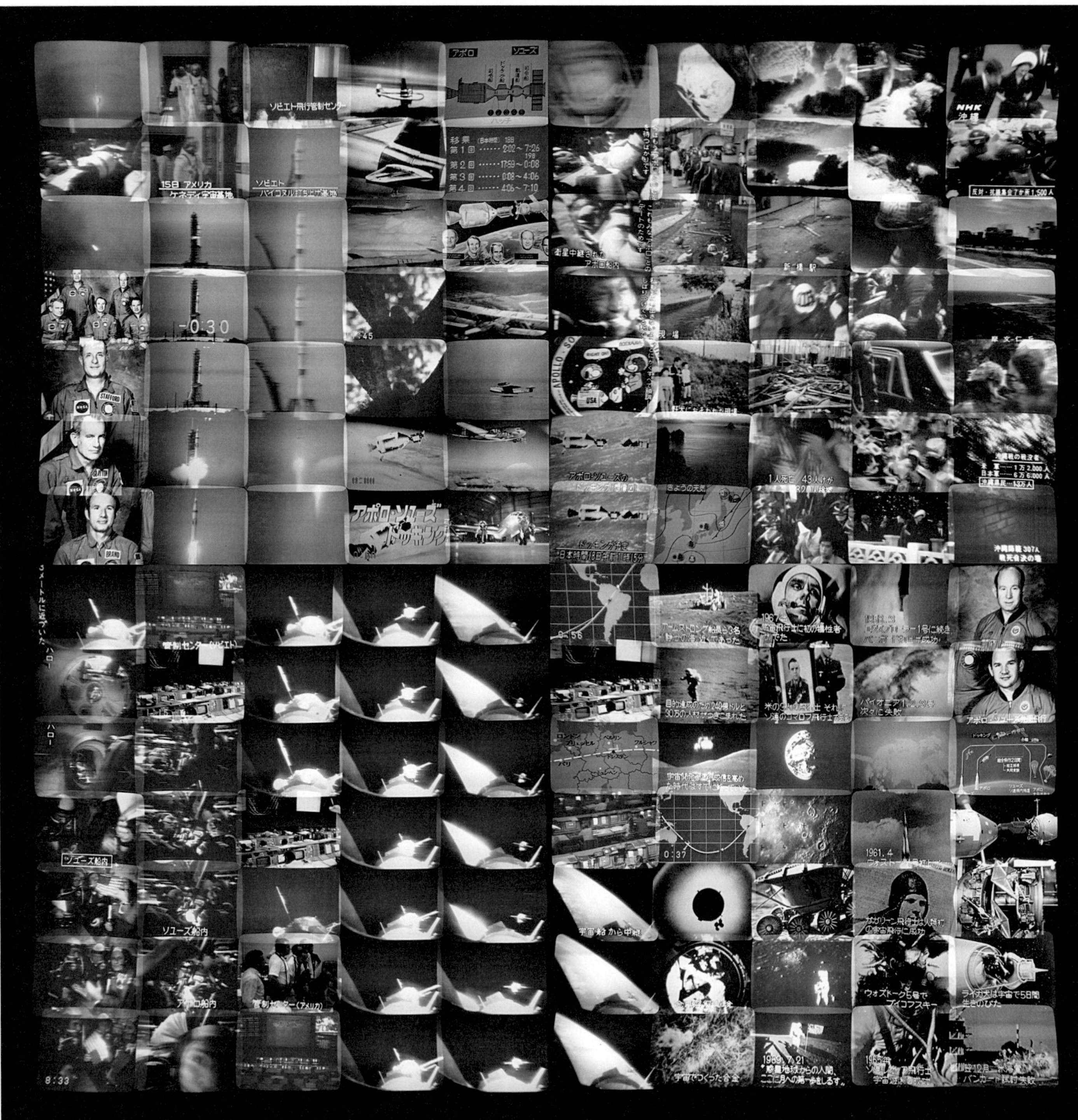

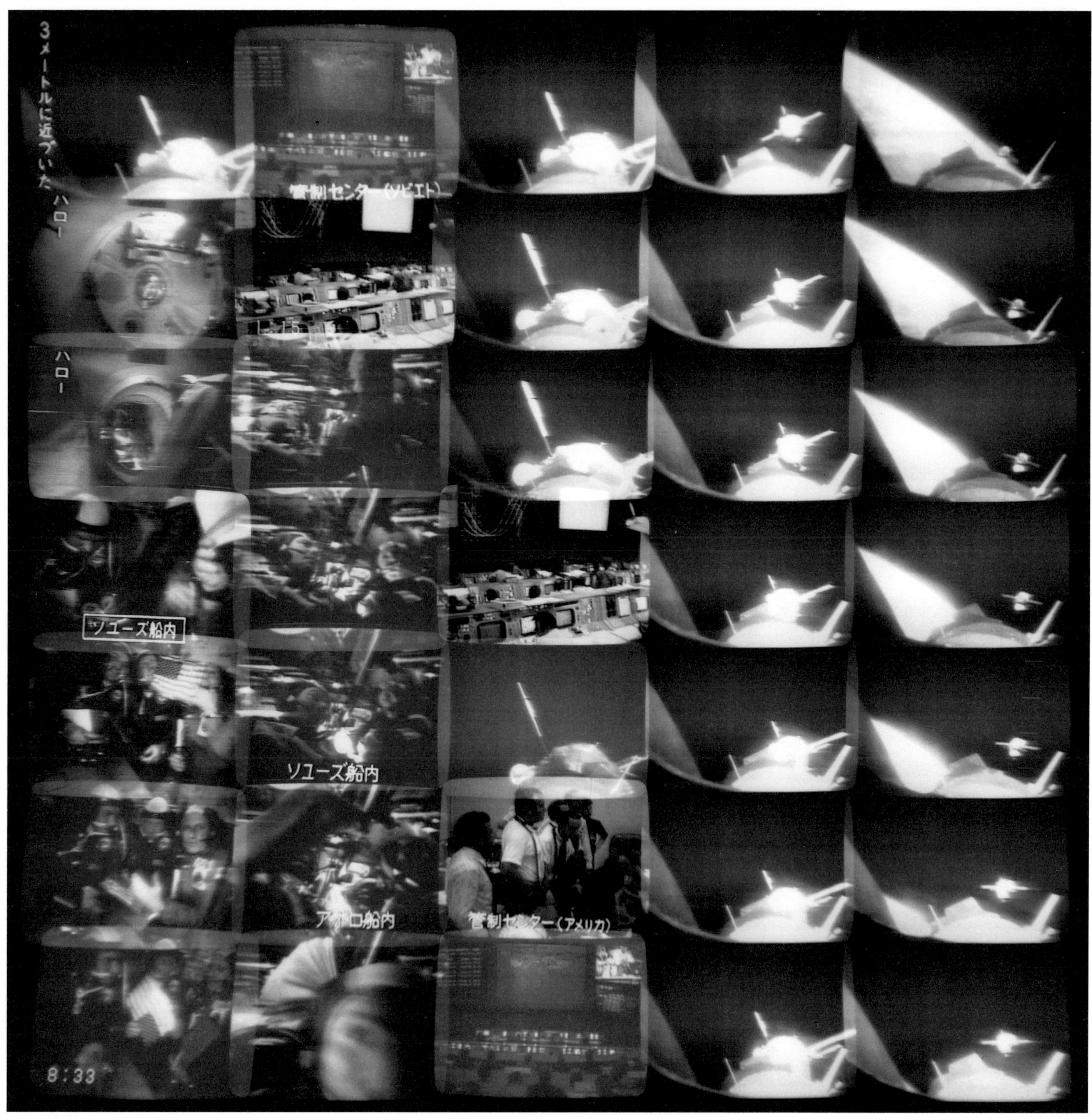

Page 7 The Mummy from Peru, July 10, 1975, **NTV,** *1 frame. Page 8* HRM Queen Elizabeth in Tokyo, May 7, 1975, NTV, *1 frame. Page 10* The World of Salvador Dali, December 19, 1975, NHK, *4 frames. Page 11* The Great Sakata Fire, October 30, 1976, NHK, *4 frames. Left* Apollo Soyuz docking, July 17, 1975, NHK, *4 frames. Above* Apollo Soyuz docking, July 17, 1975, NHK, *1 frame. Following spread* Ali vs Lyle, May 16, 1975, NET, *6 frames. All images © the artist and Sage Paris, Courtesy Sage Paris*

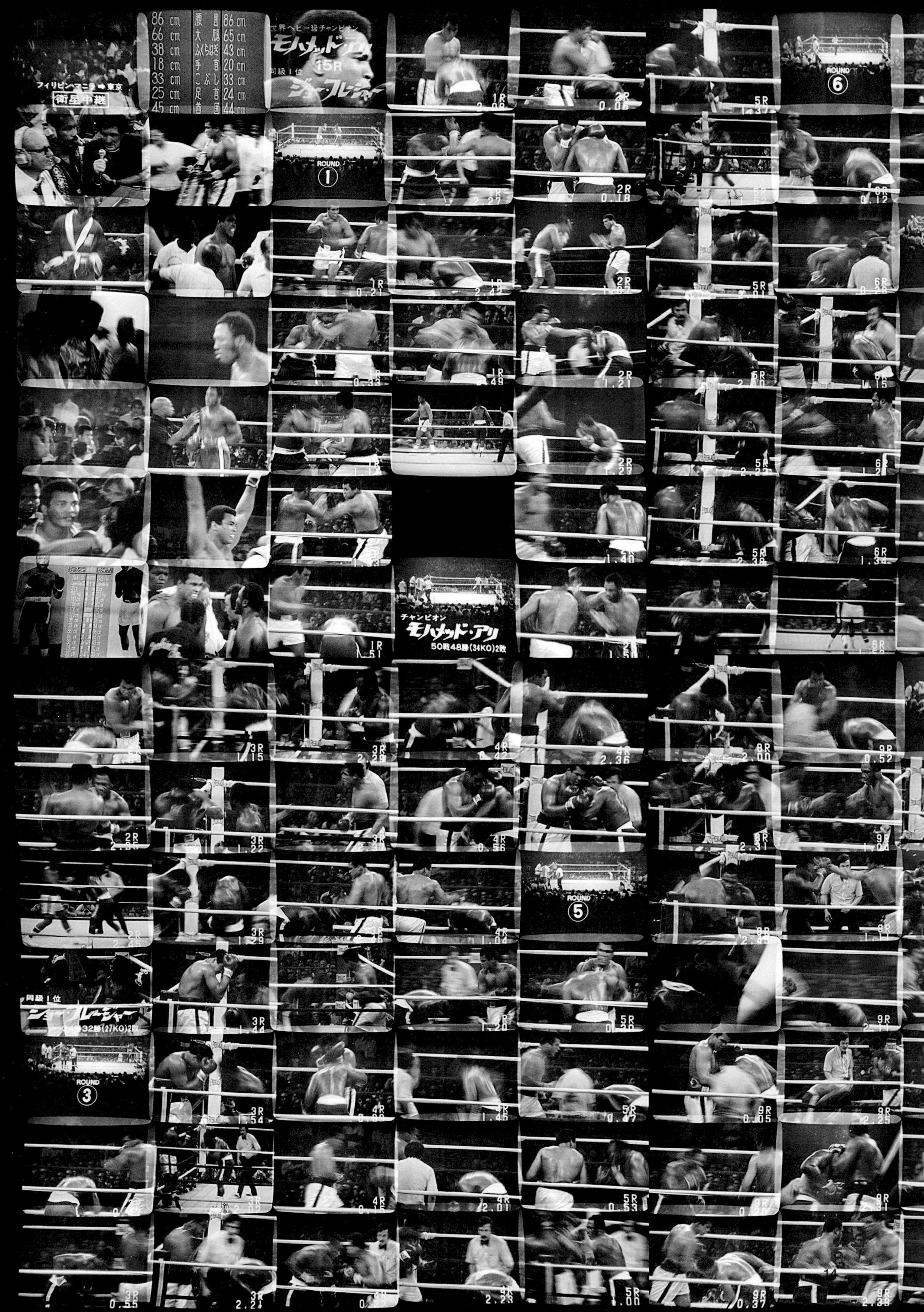

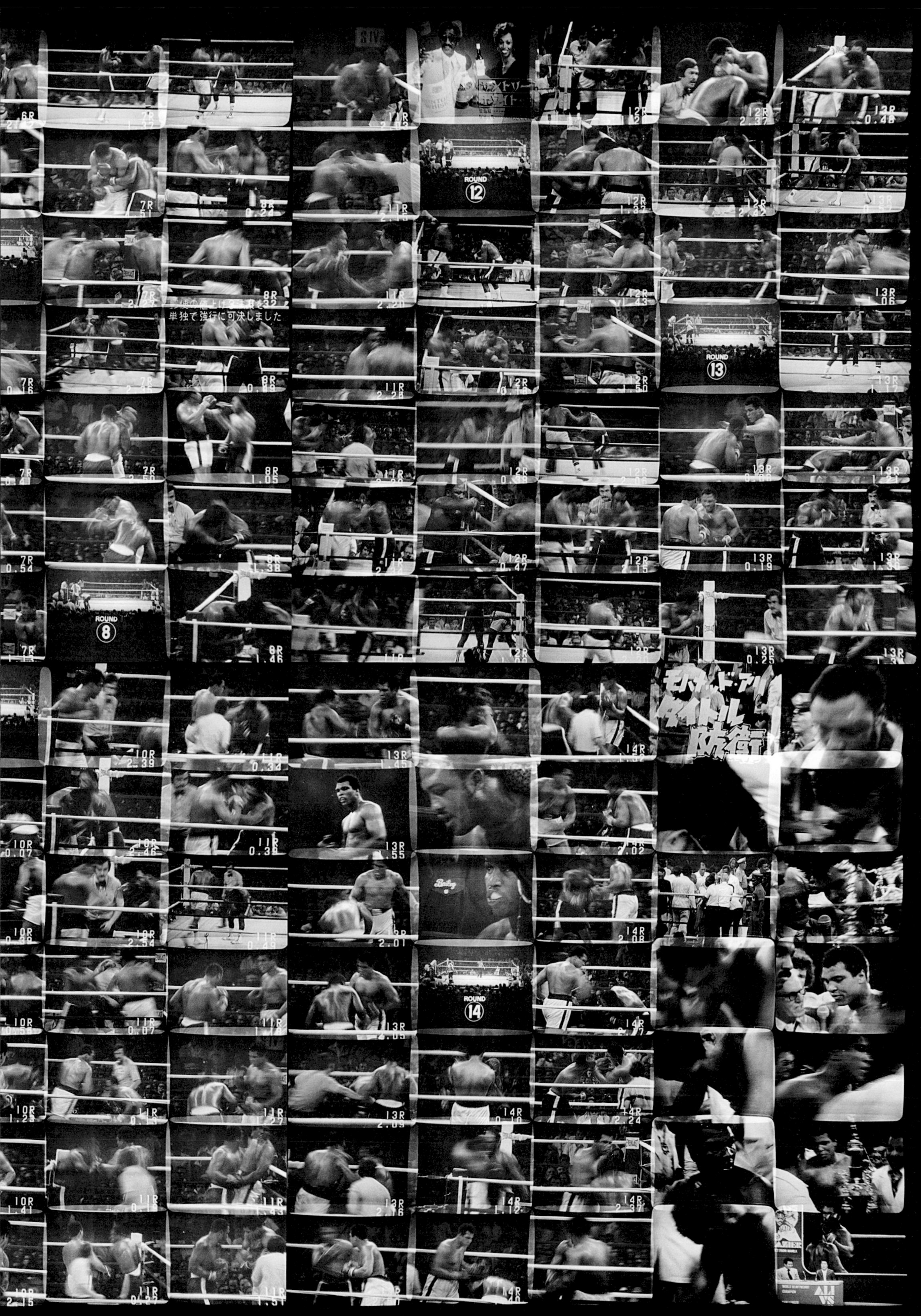
単独で強行に可決しました
モントリオール
タイトル
防衛
ROUND 8
ROUND 12
ROUND 13
ROUND 14

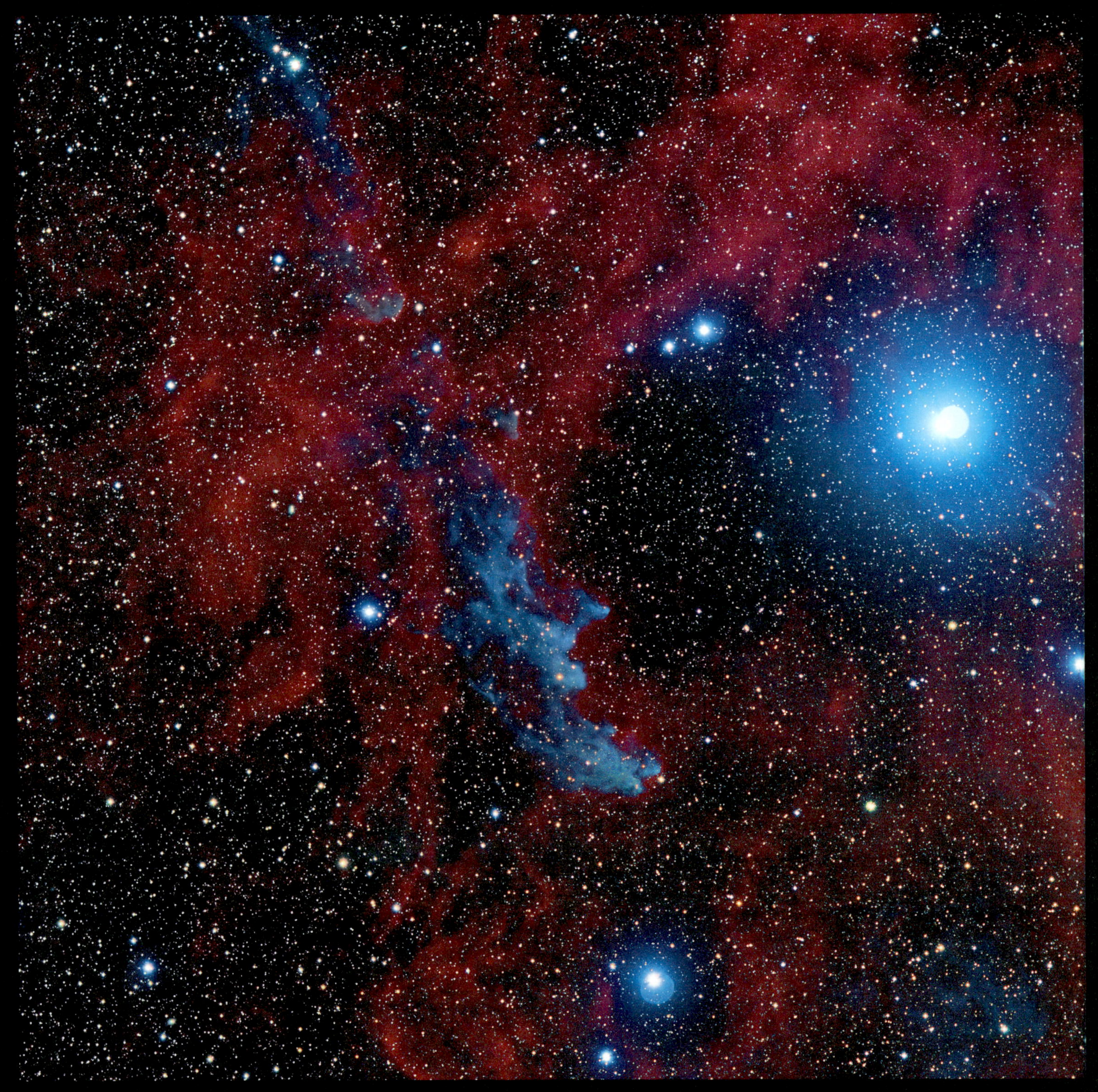

The Witch Head Nebula
Warrumbungle Observatory, Coonabarabran, NSW, Australia

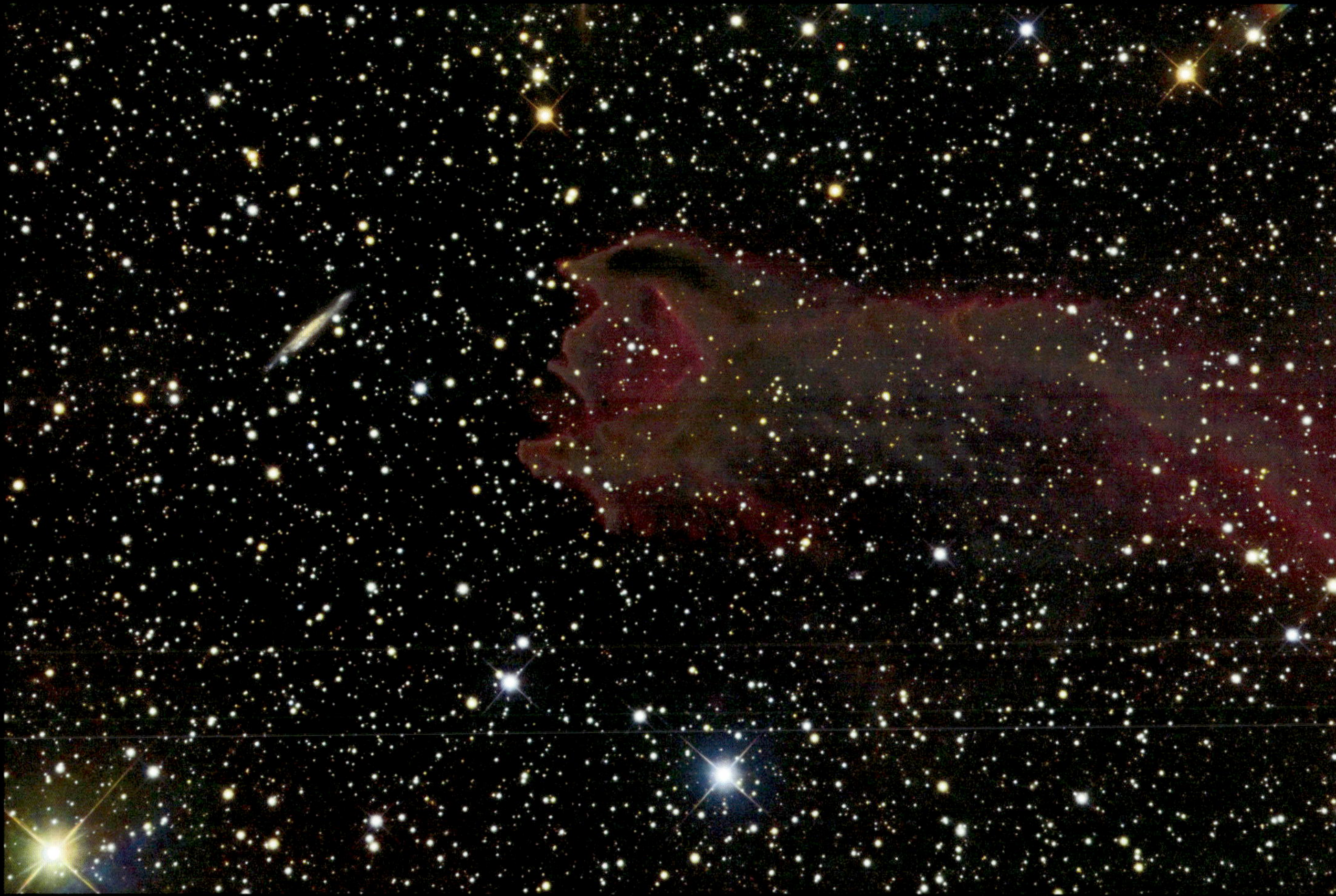

The Hand of God (CG4)
Pingelly, WA, Australia

Marco Lorenzi
ASTROPHOTOGRAPHY

To photograph the night sky is to photograph time, light, and the origins of both. In a sense, astrophotography is the final frontier; a relatively unknown realm invisible to the naked eye, a spectacle of what is literally 'otherworldly.' Is the motivation to discover something new, something unknown, or as physics would suggest, to photograph something that is old, that has passed and that will continue passing long after our own existence.

Perhaps it is the very notion of the unobtainable that so endears us to these images, for instance in the case of urbanites, where light pollution restricts one's ability to experience the cosmos; the corollary of time and life that has existed for billions of years are now revealed in the present. Perhaps it is also the discrepancy between the timelessness of the galaxy versus the moment of its capture on film. But camera technology (and its advancement) is key here, the means to experience a sliver of space, and still solely on a visceral level; unlike an image of a flower or a vase, there is no way to touch the universe.

An astrophotographer must usually travel to remote locations to capture images of the deep sky, in order to allow for long exposures without the film or detectors being obstructed by stray light. "When I have chances I travel to dark sites in Canary islands, Namibia and Australia," says Lorenzi, "to enjoy the glorious view of the Universe from those pristine skies."

All images © Marco Lorenzi

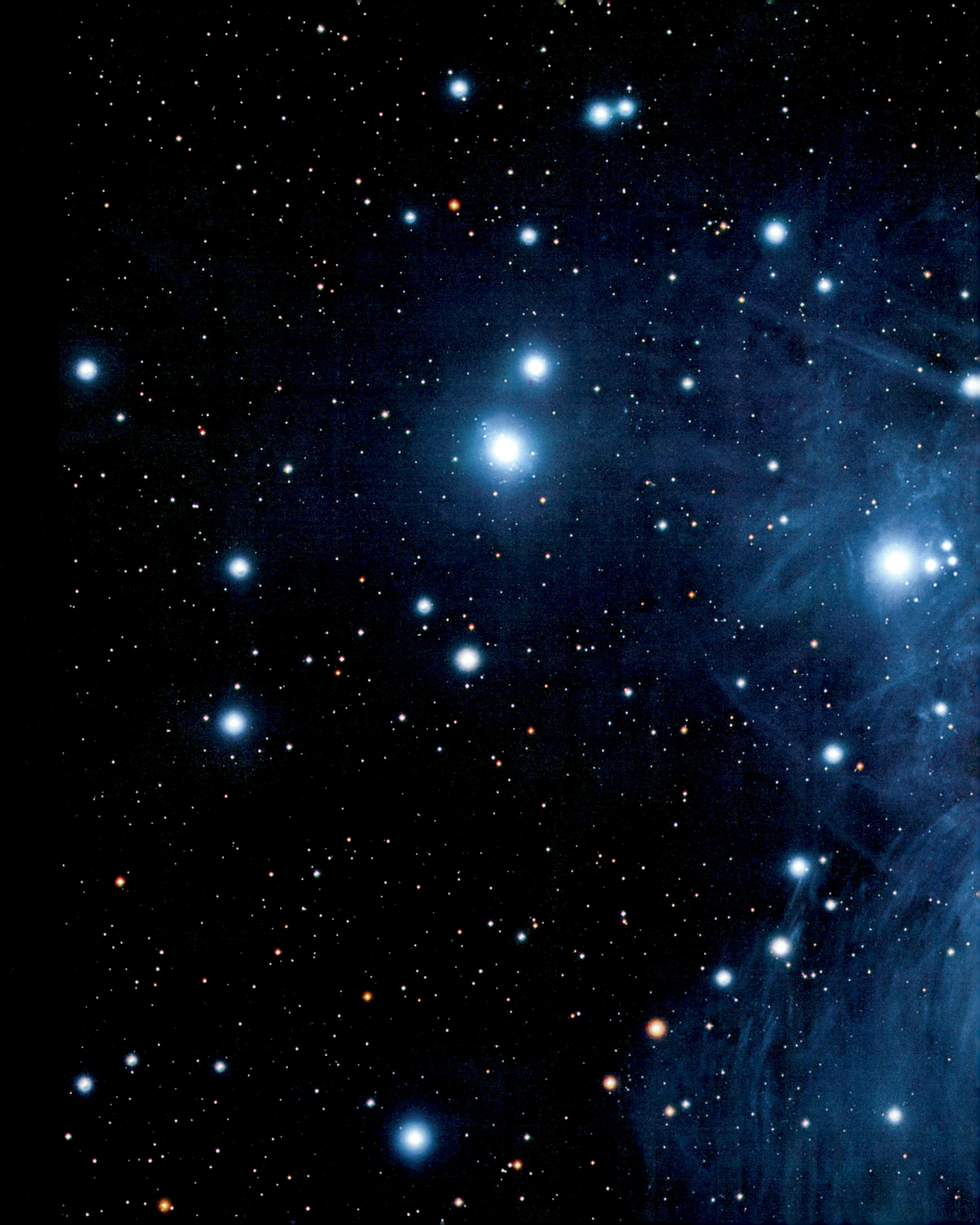

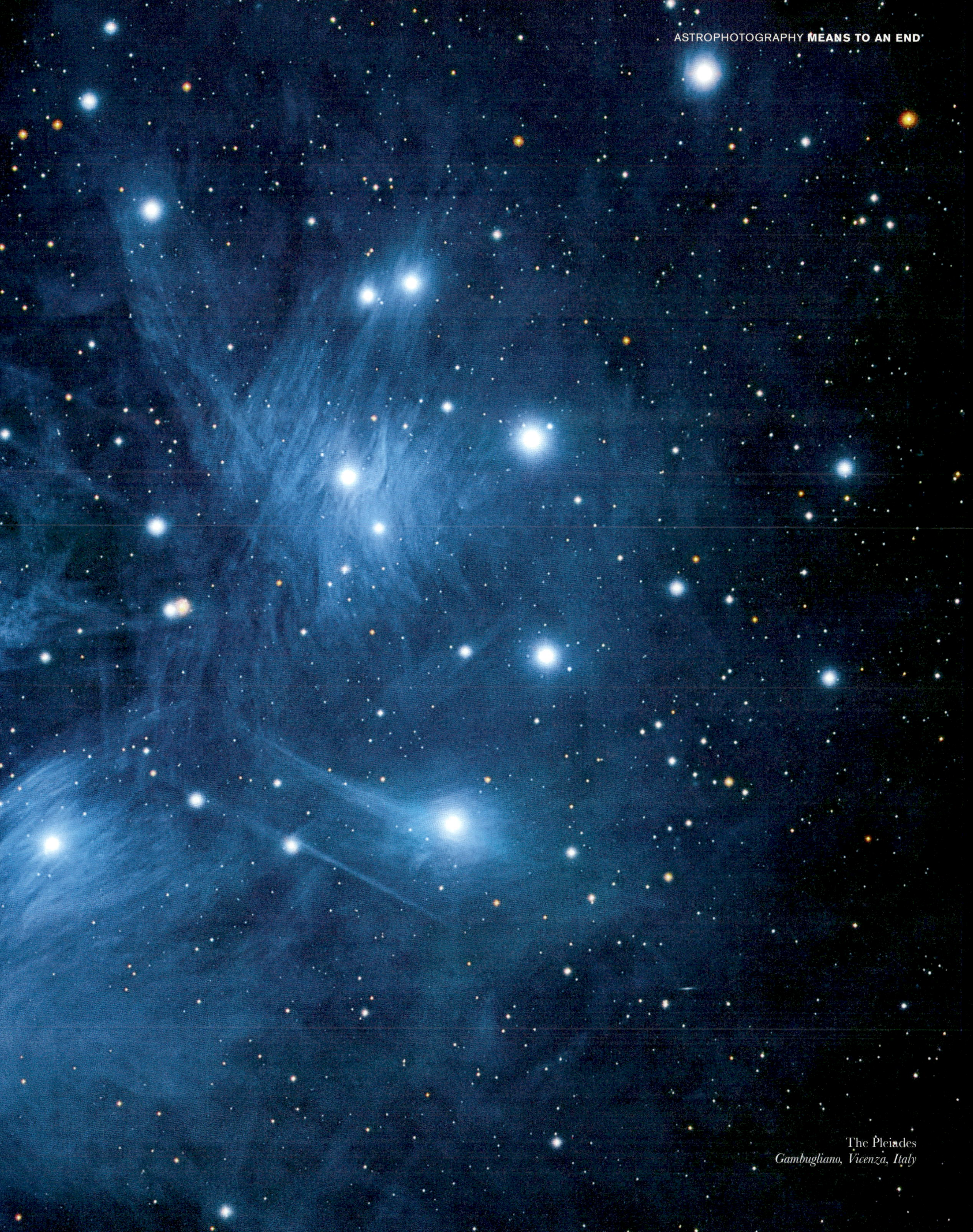

The Pleiades
Gambugliano, Vicenza, Italy

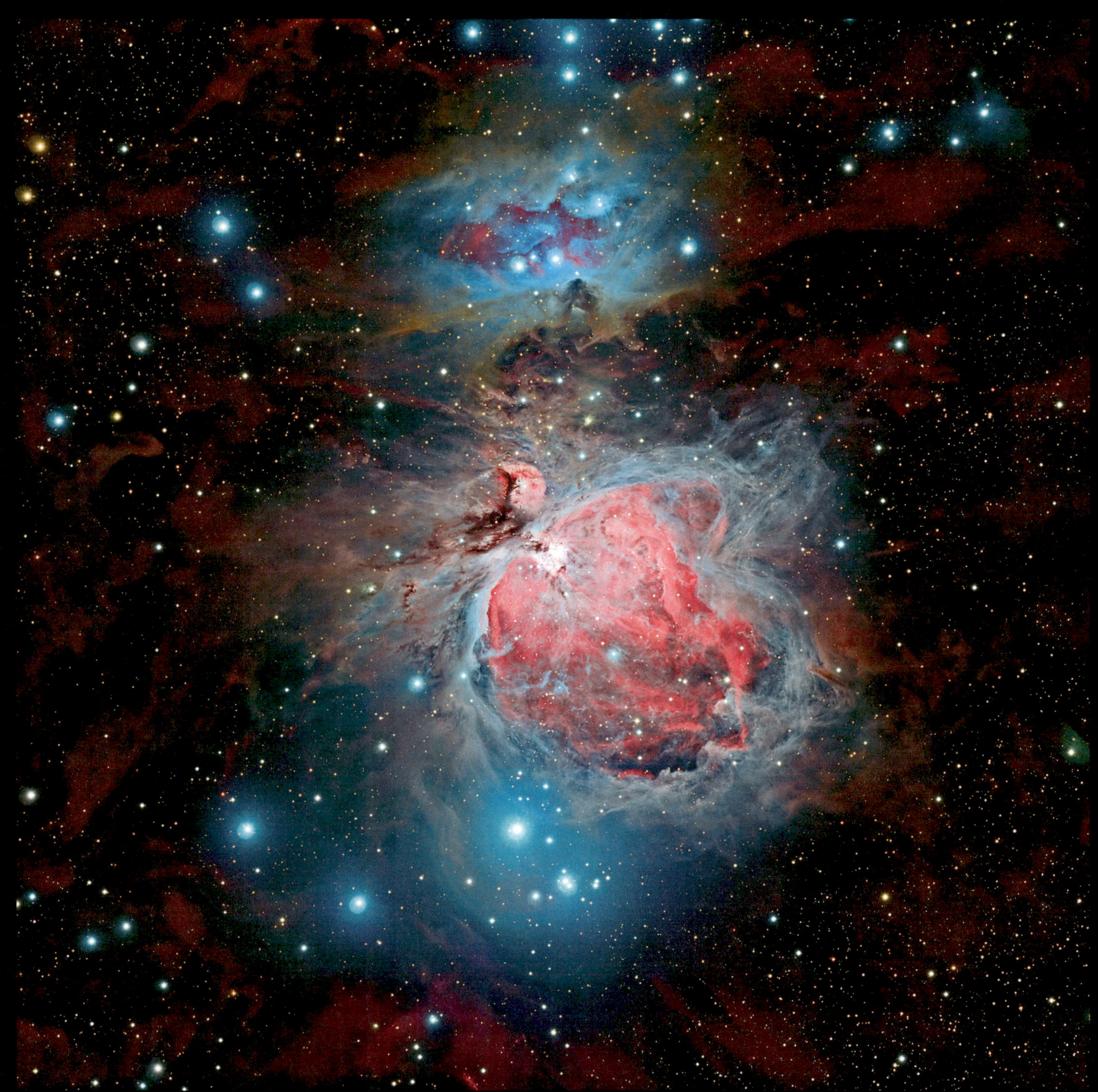

Orion Nebula (M42)
Warrumbungle Observatory, Coonabarabran,
NSW, Australia

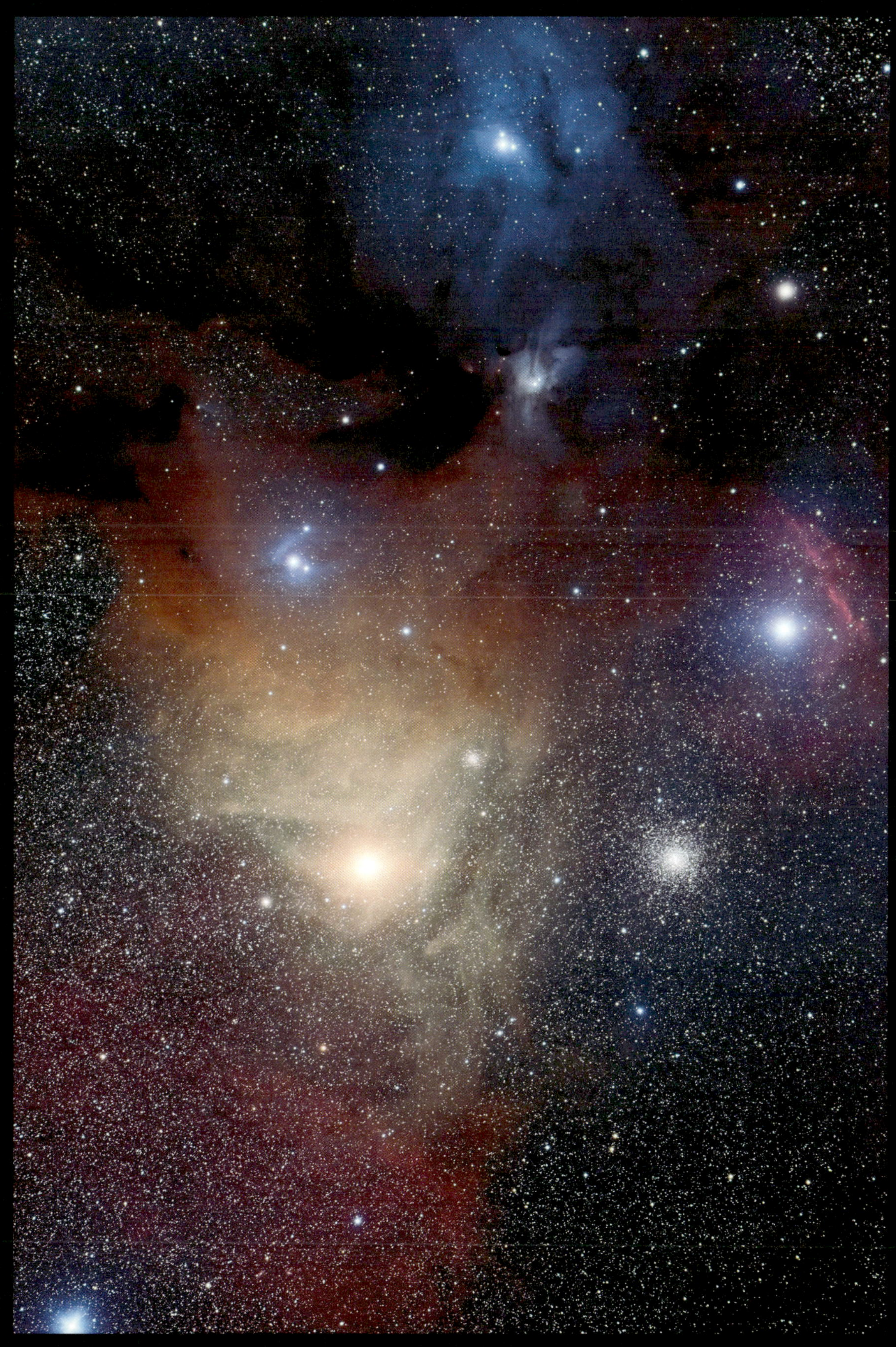

Antares & Rho Ophiuchi
Mt. Magnet, Western Australia

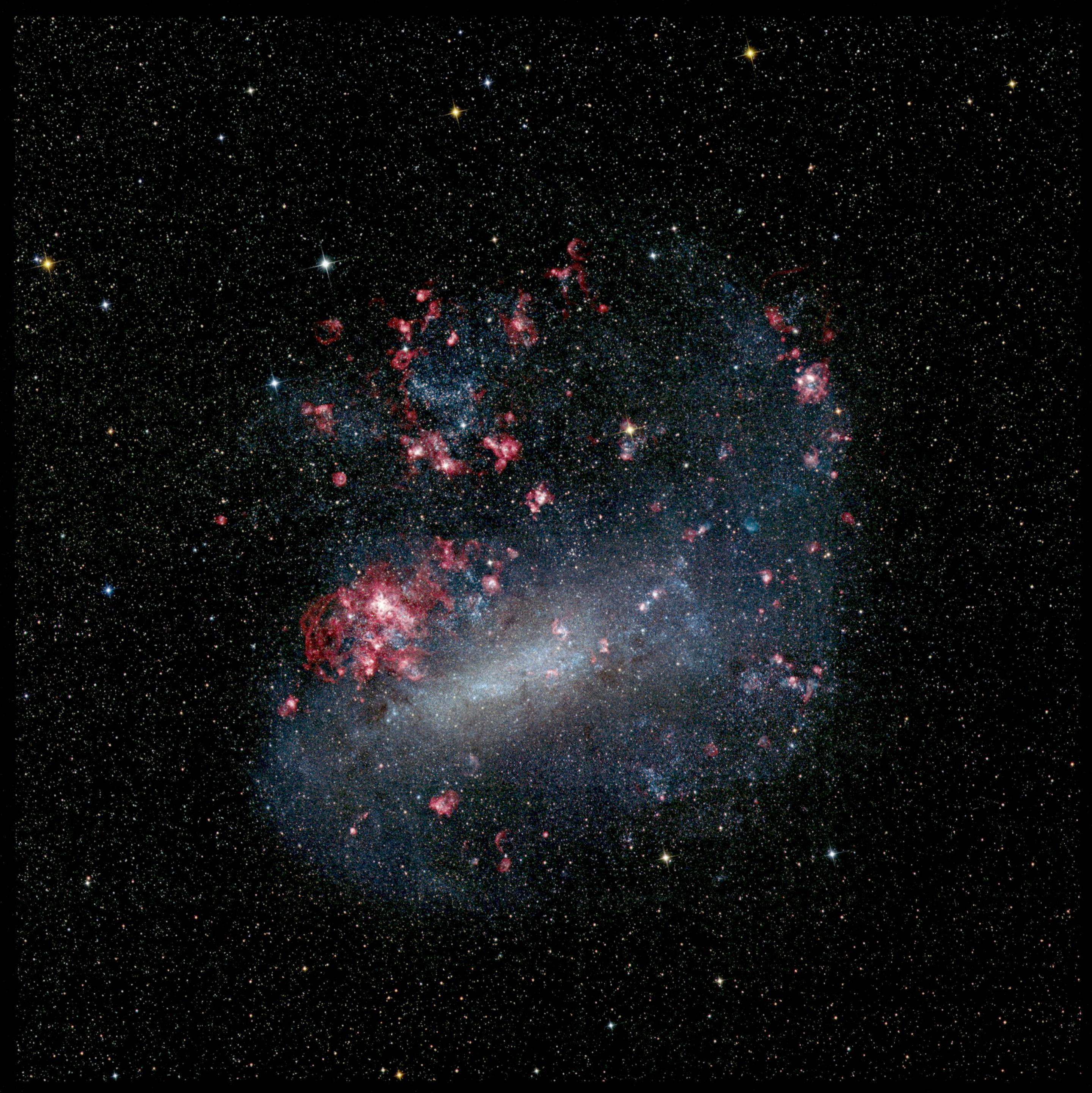

The Large Magellanic Cloud
More than 73 hours of total exposures went into this 4 panels mosaic covering about 140 square degrees of sky.
Warrumbungle Observatory, Coonabarabran, NSW, Australia

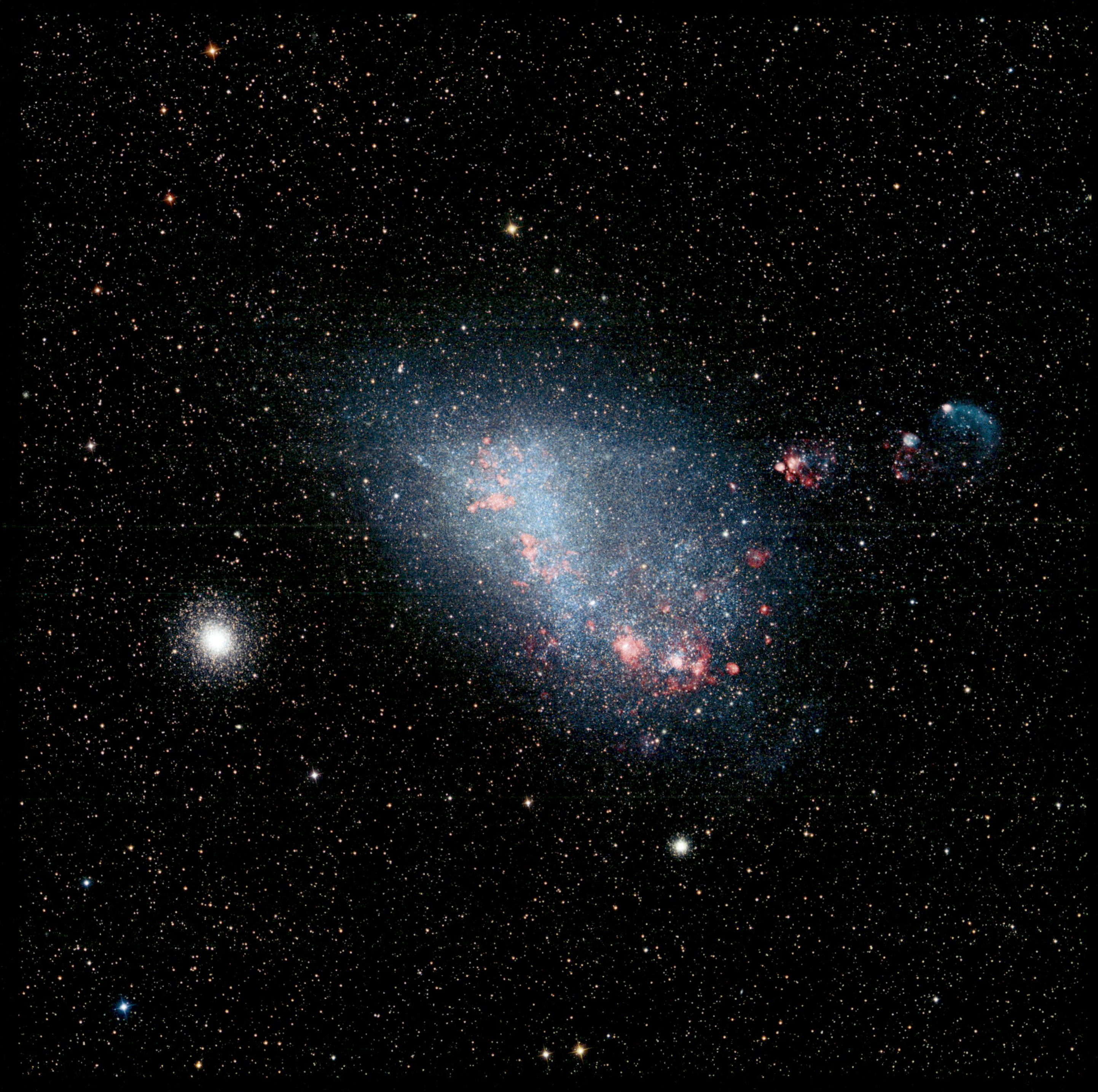

The Small Magellanic Cloud (SMC)
Warrumbungle Observatory, Coonabarabran, NSW, Australia

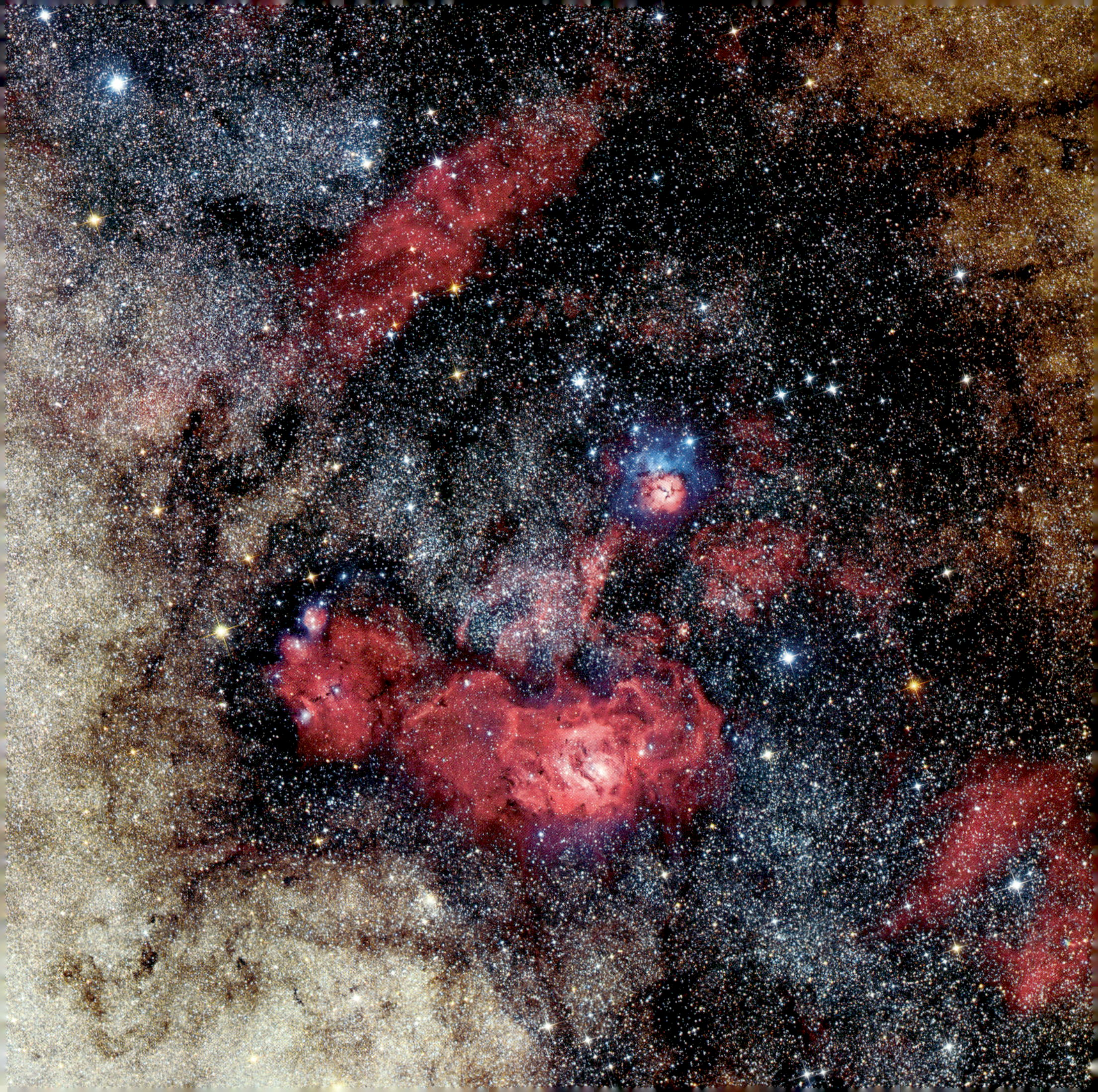

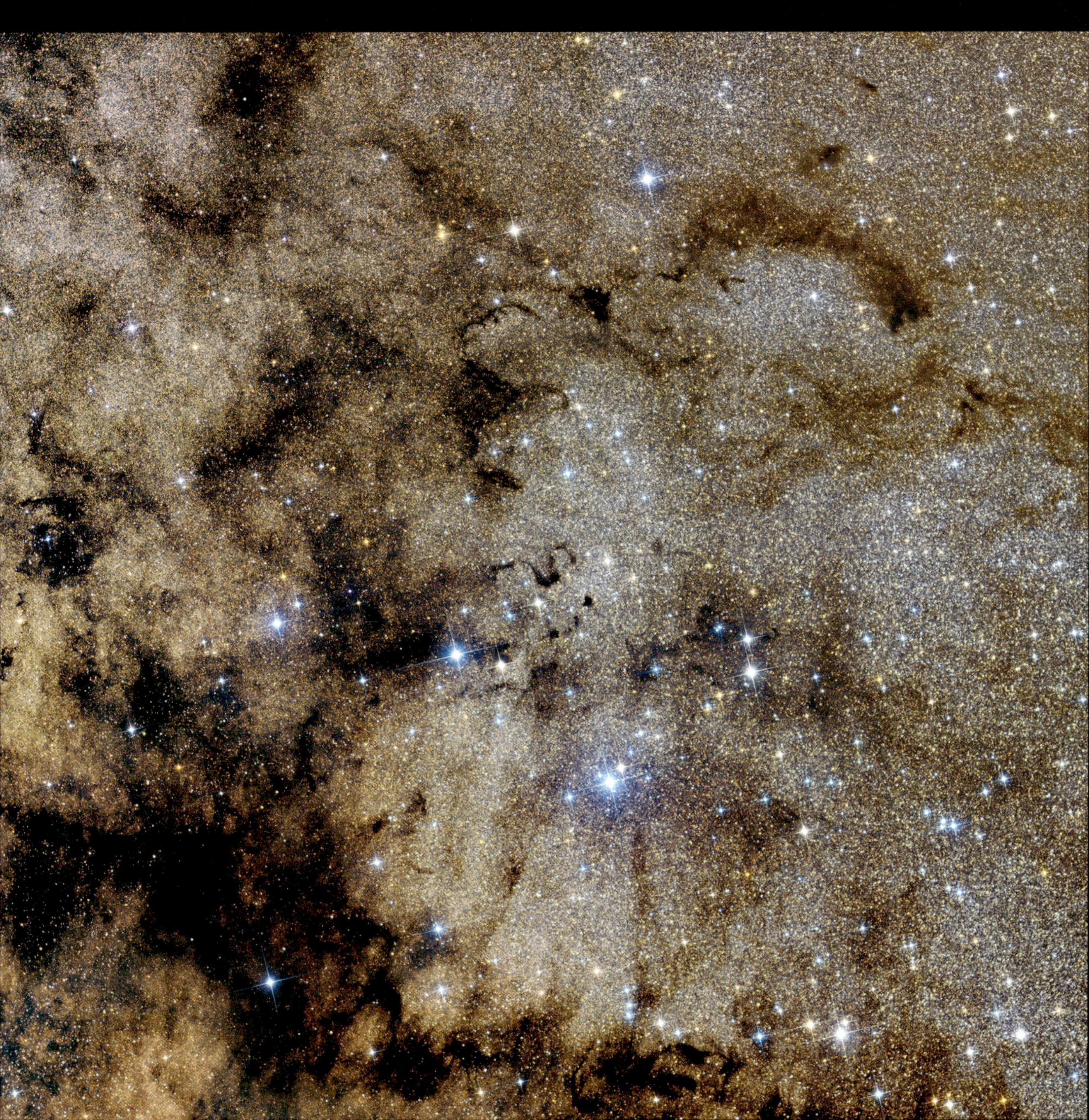

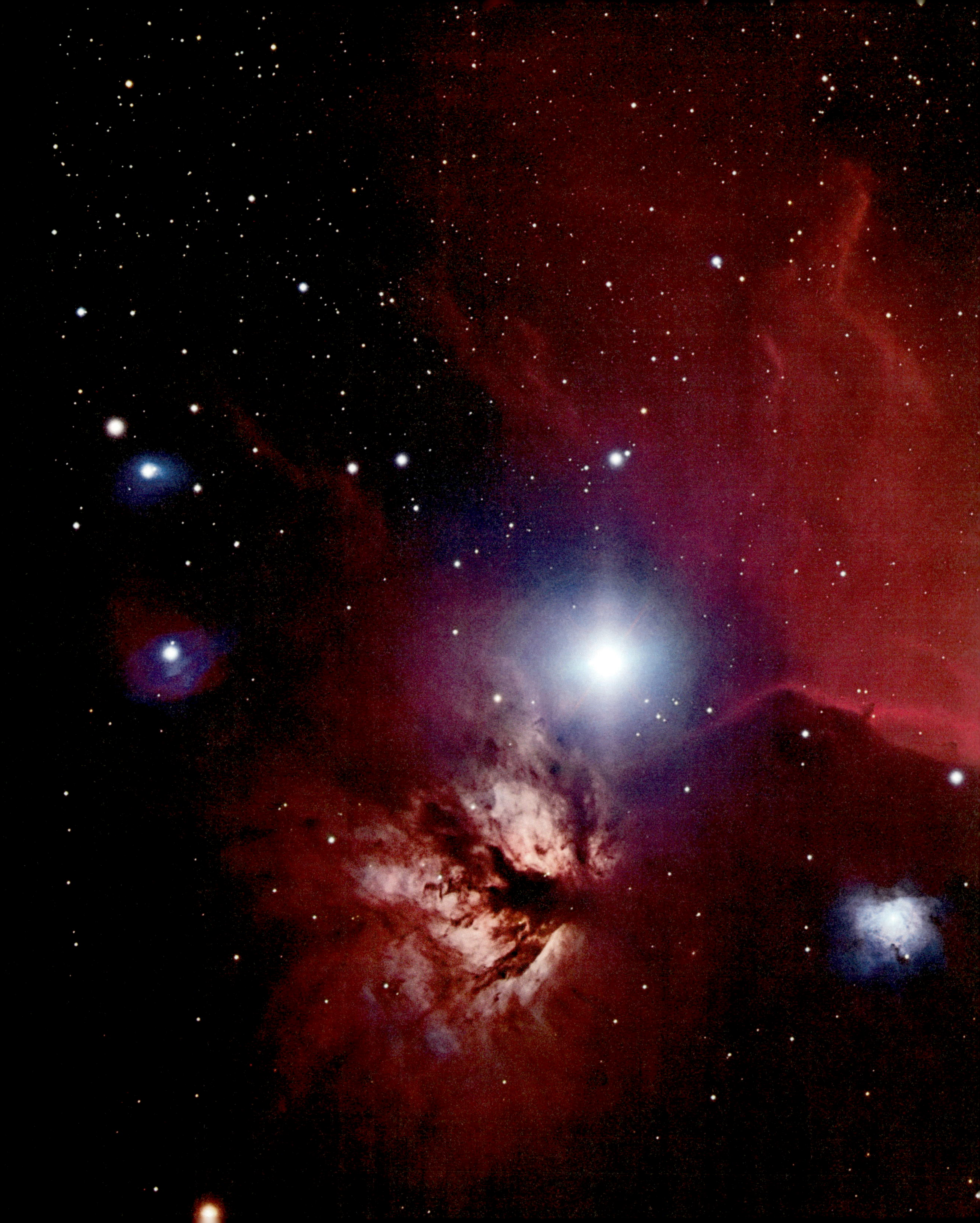

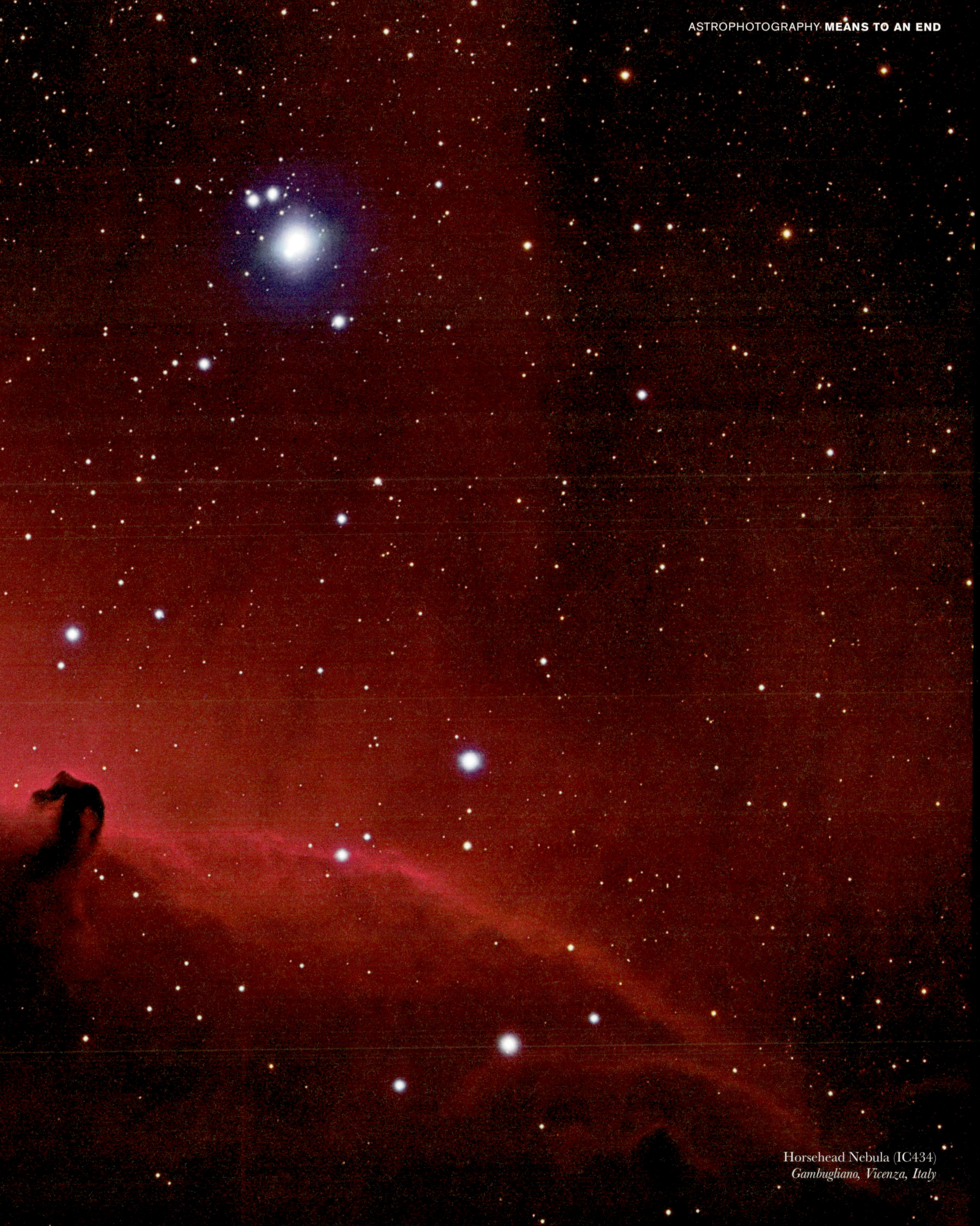

Horsehead Nebula (IC434)
Gambugliano, Vicenza, Italy

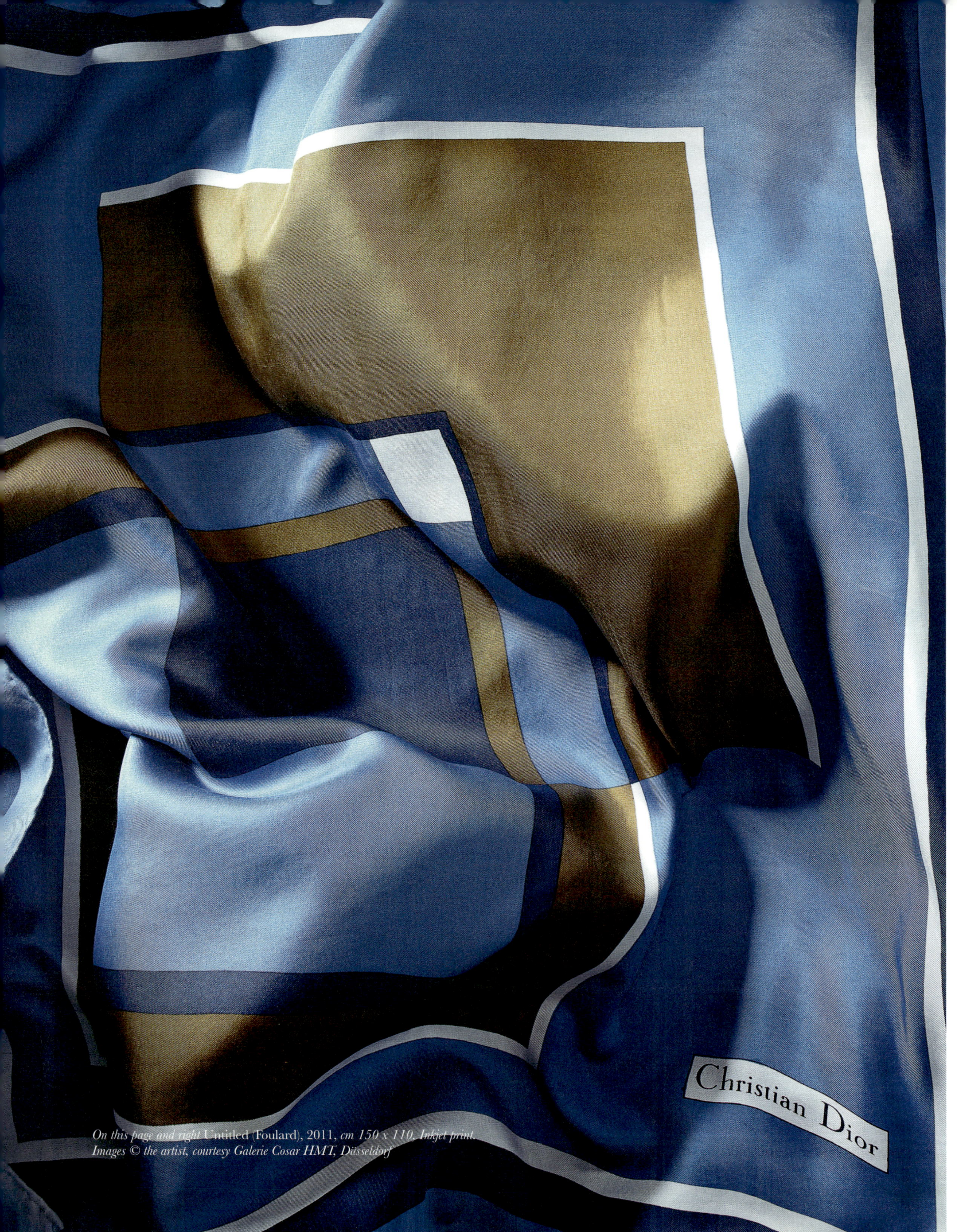

On this page and right Untitled (Foulard), 2011, cm 150 x 110. Inkjet print.
Images © the artist, courtesy Galerie Cosar HMT, Düsseldorf

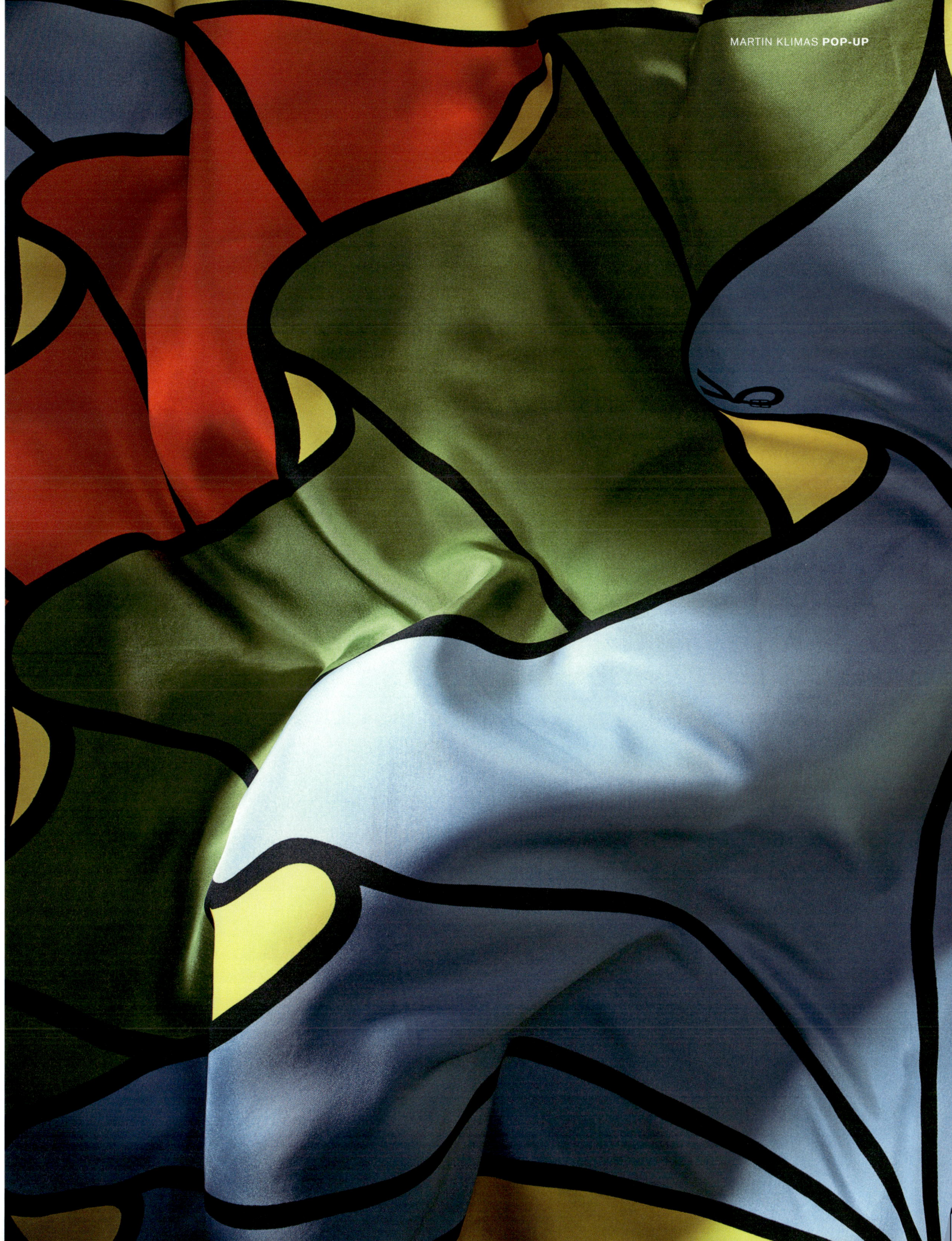

MATTHEW MONTEITH Guardare Between 2008 and 2009, Matthew Monteith spent a full year in Italy as recipient of the Abigail Cohen Prize at the American Academy of Rome. While in Europe, he began focusing his attention on the relationships between people and the works of art they encountered in places like museums, churches, archeological sites and around the street. His main subject became the precise moment when viewers come into contact with artworks through vision and instantly react as a result of their personal interpretation. "How art is viewed is highly subjective to an individual at a moment in time," says Monteith, "but my Caravaggio is not yours, which makes it all the more beautiful." *Guardare* is thus a subtle investigation on the act of seeing itself and on the countless contextual issues that influence the reading of every single artwork, whether it regards depicted observers, the photographer, or each of us in front of his pictures. - A native of Howell, Michigan, Matthew Monteith is lecturer at the Yale University School of Art and Hunter College, as well as Instructor at the International Center of Photography in New York. His book *Czech Eden,* published by Aperture, won the PDN Photo Annual Award in 2008. His work, exhibited in numerous solo and group exhibitions in America, Europe and Japan, is a constant meditation on the ways we perceive the objects we use and the places we inhabit.

Right Notation Boxed, Rome, Italy, 2008. *Page 32* Roman Forum, Rome, Italy, 2009. *Page 33* Feet, Santa Maria Maggiore, Rome, Italy, 2009. *Page 34 Above* Arm, Centrale Montemartini, Rome, Italy 2009 *below* Notation, Aphrodite, Rome, Italy, 2009 *Page 35* Finger, Galleria Borghese, Rome, Italy, 2009. *Page 36* Capitoline Museum, Rome, Italy, 2009. *Page 37* Carmela & Bill with David, Galleria Borghese, Rome, Italy, 2009. *Page 38* Notation Uffizi, Florence, Italy, 2009. *All images © the artist*

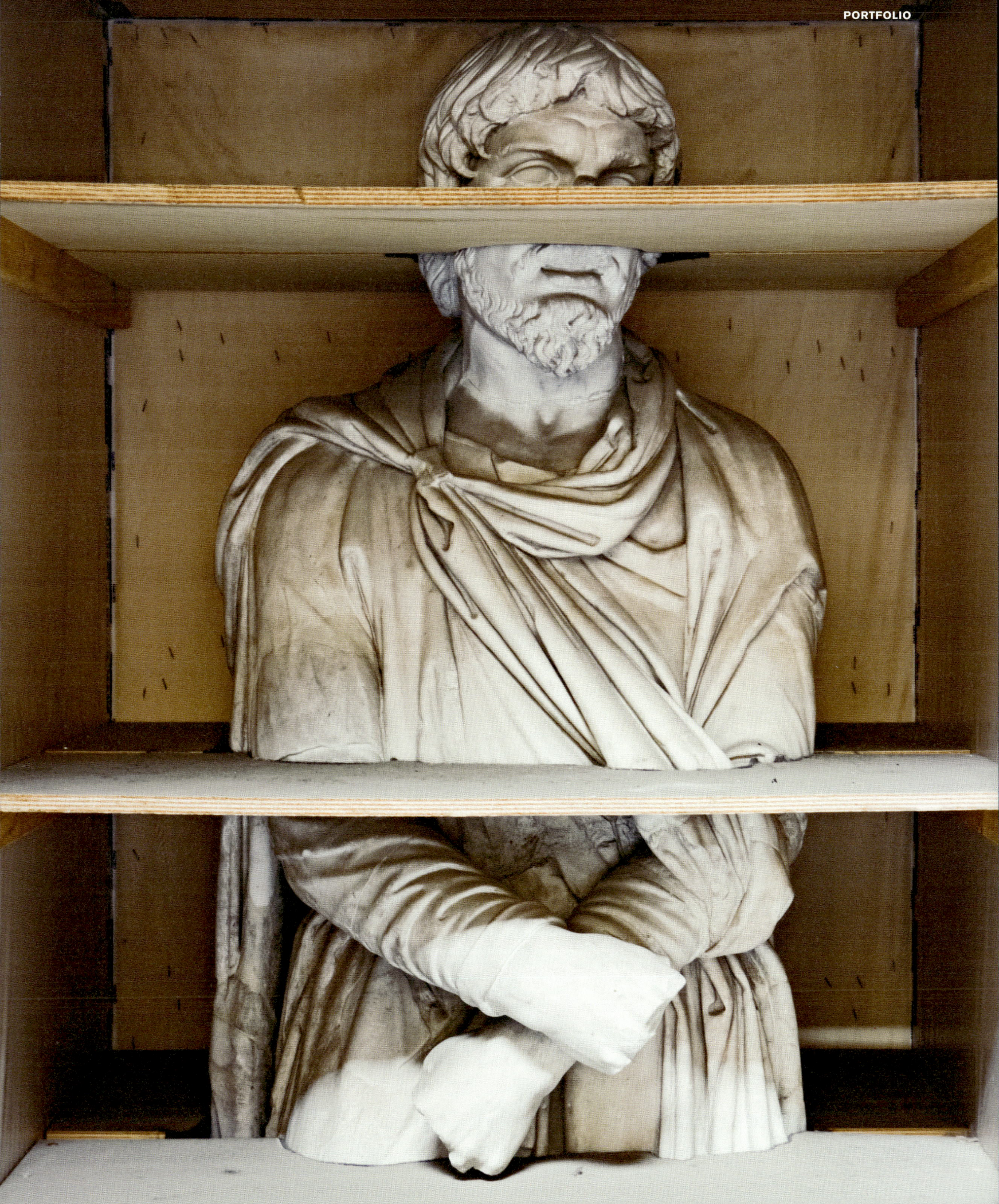

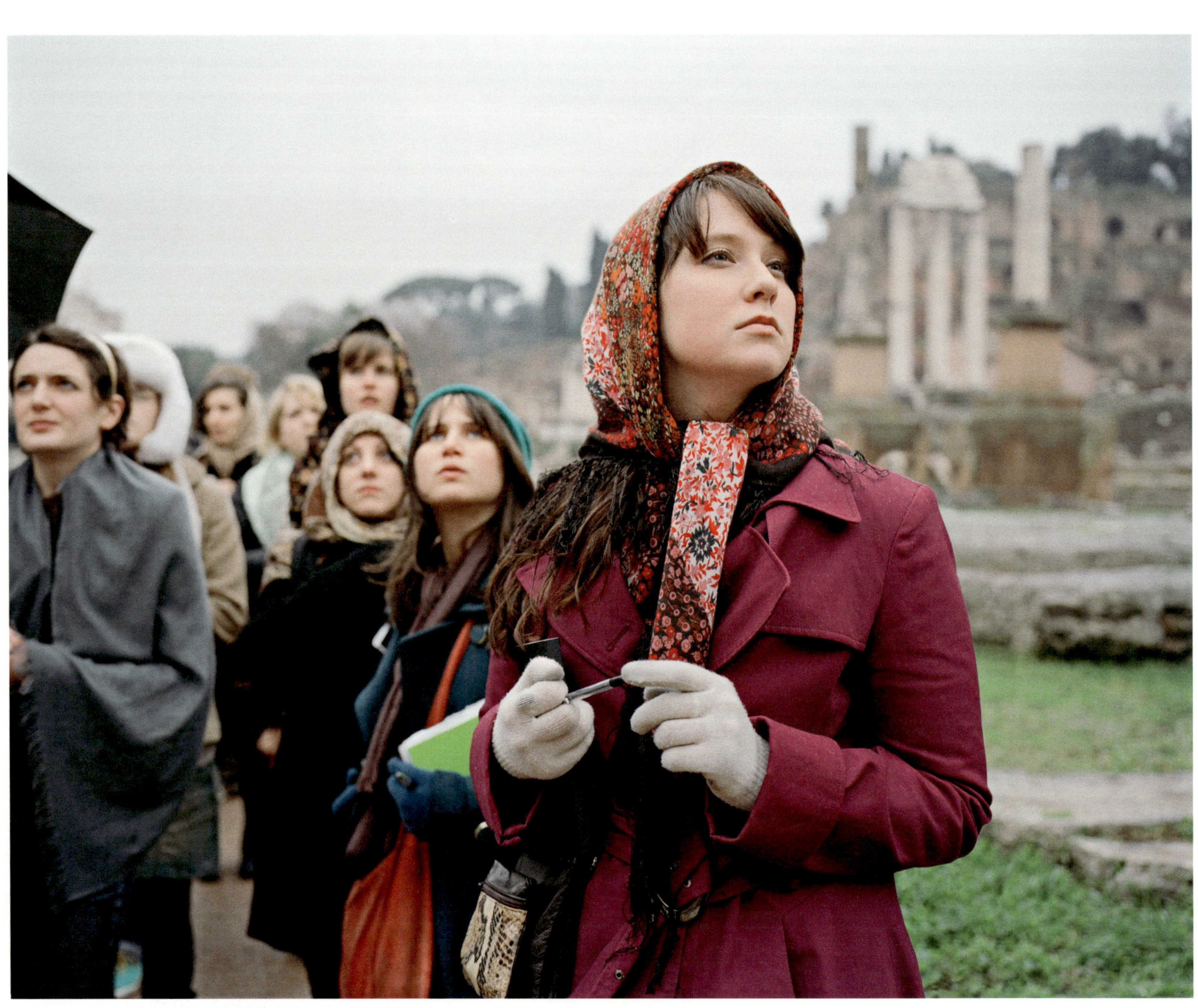

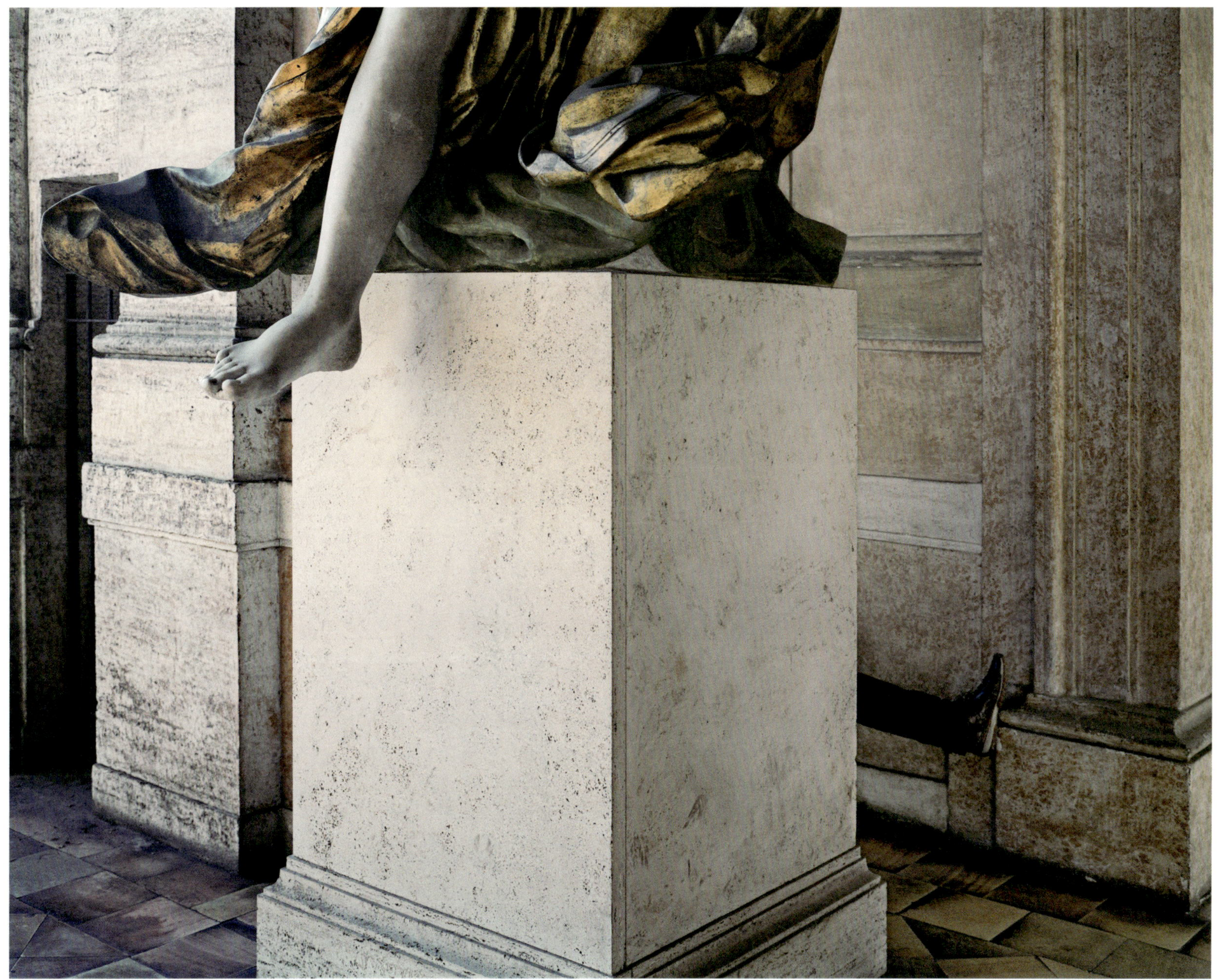

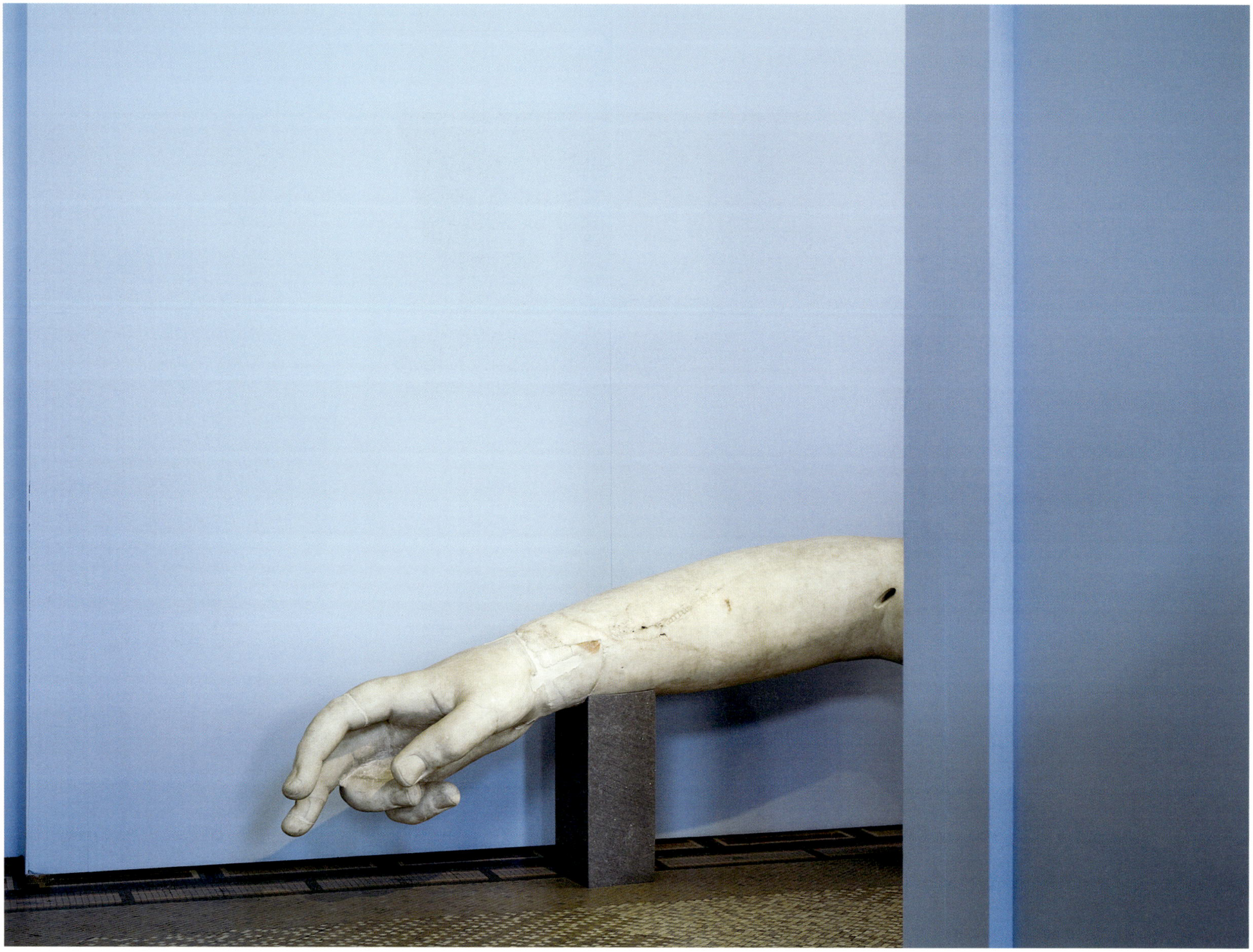

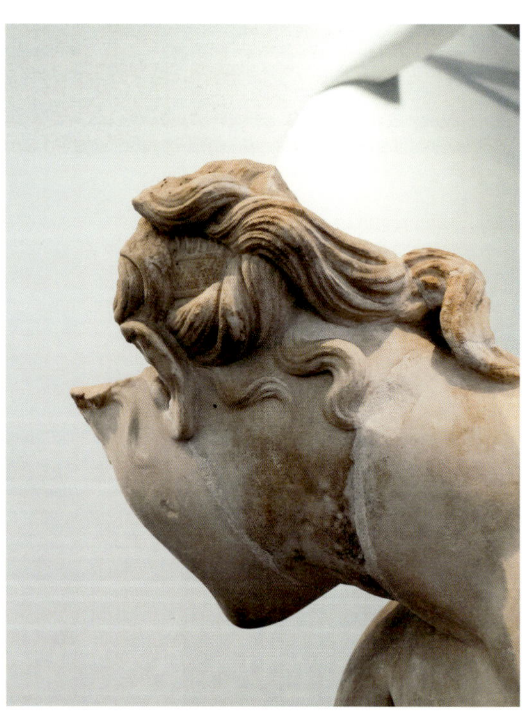

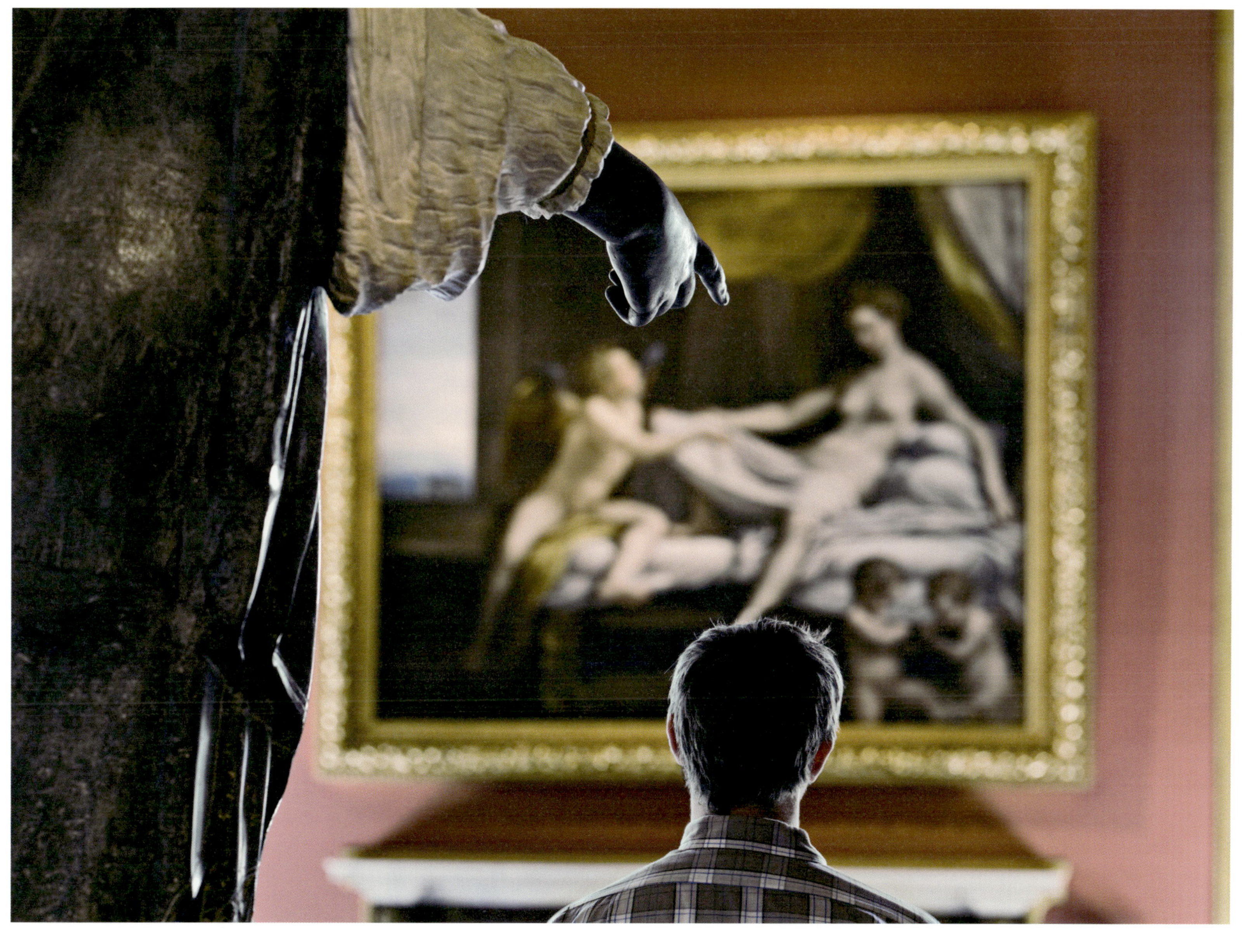

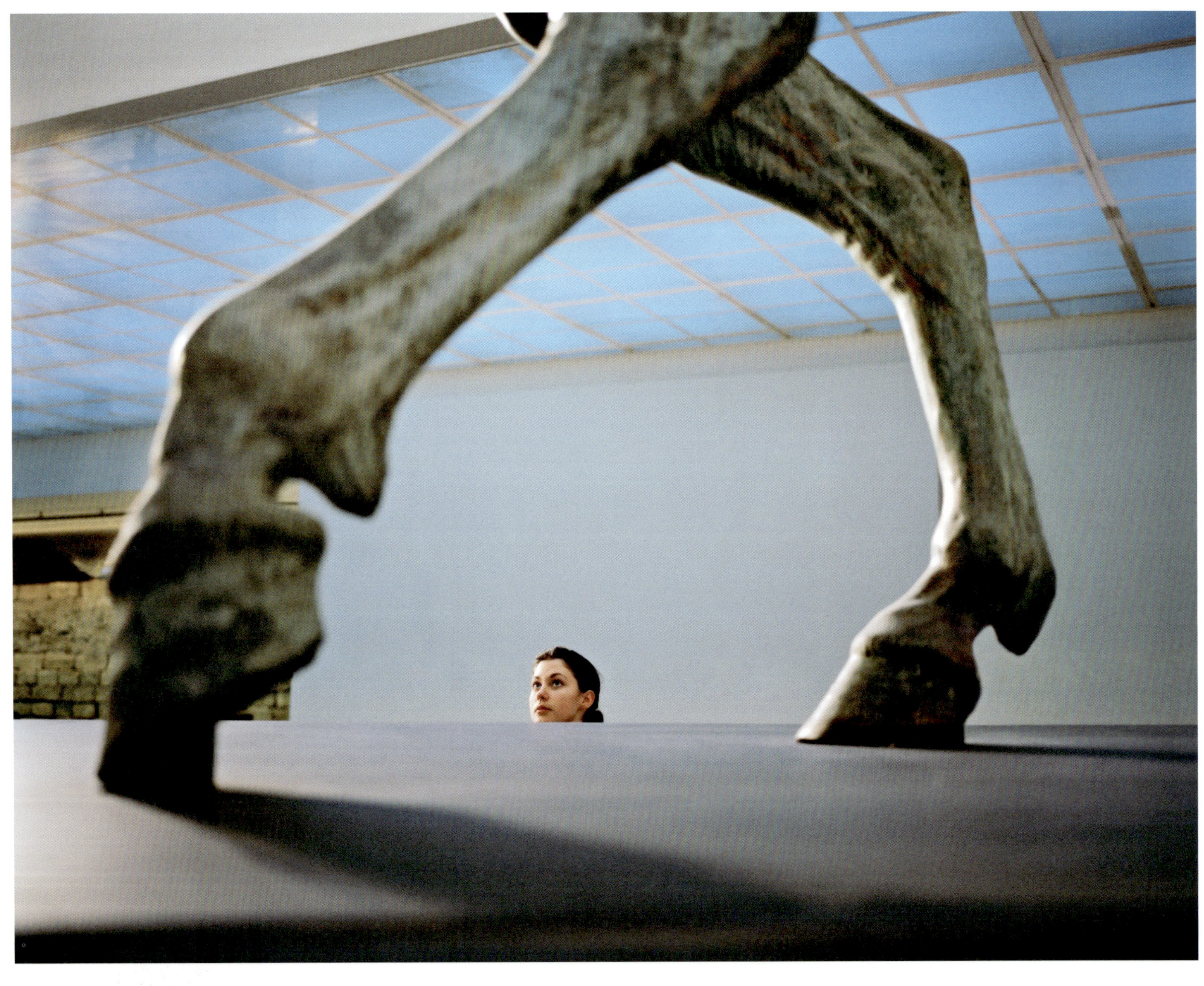

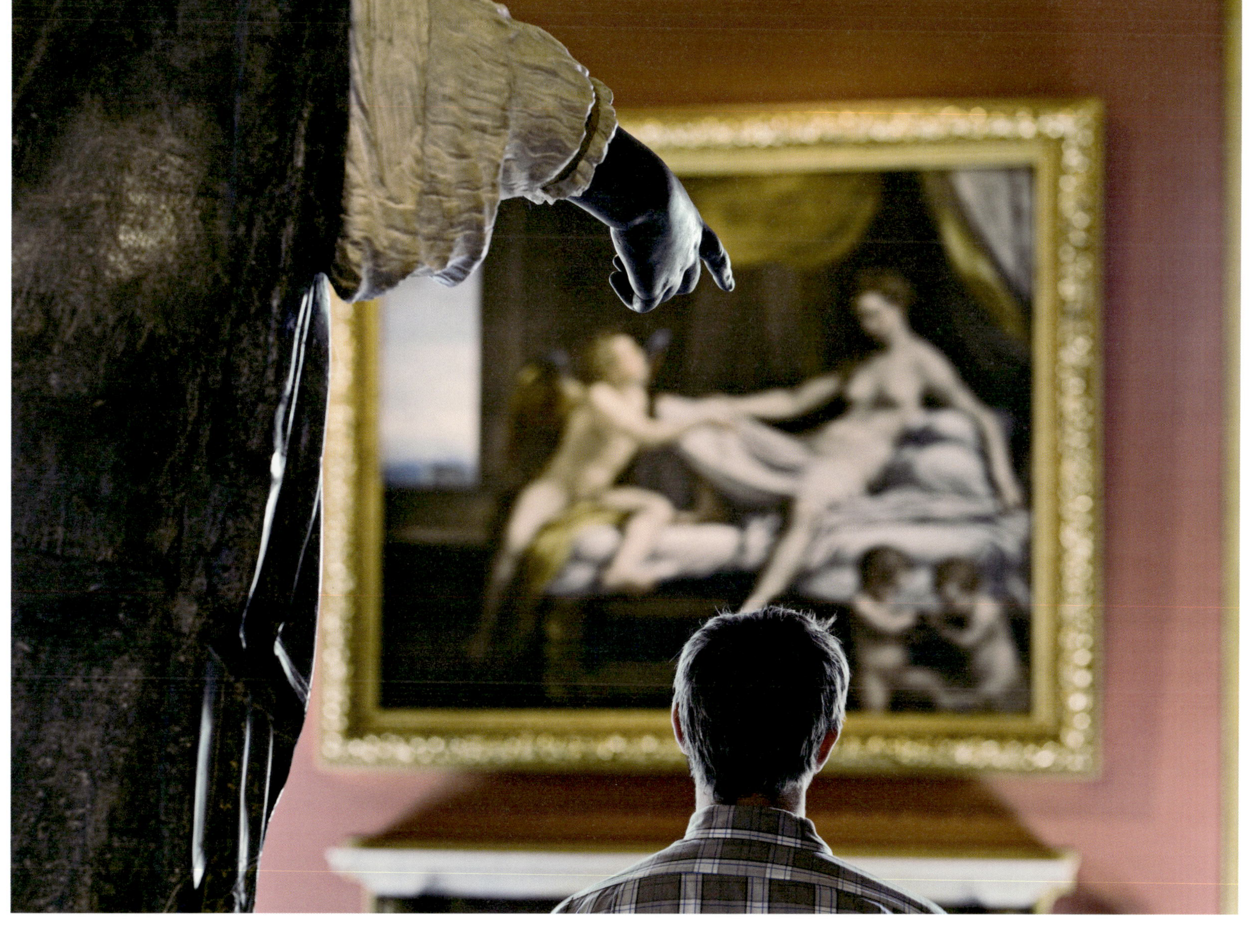

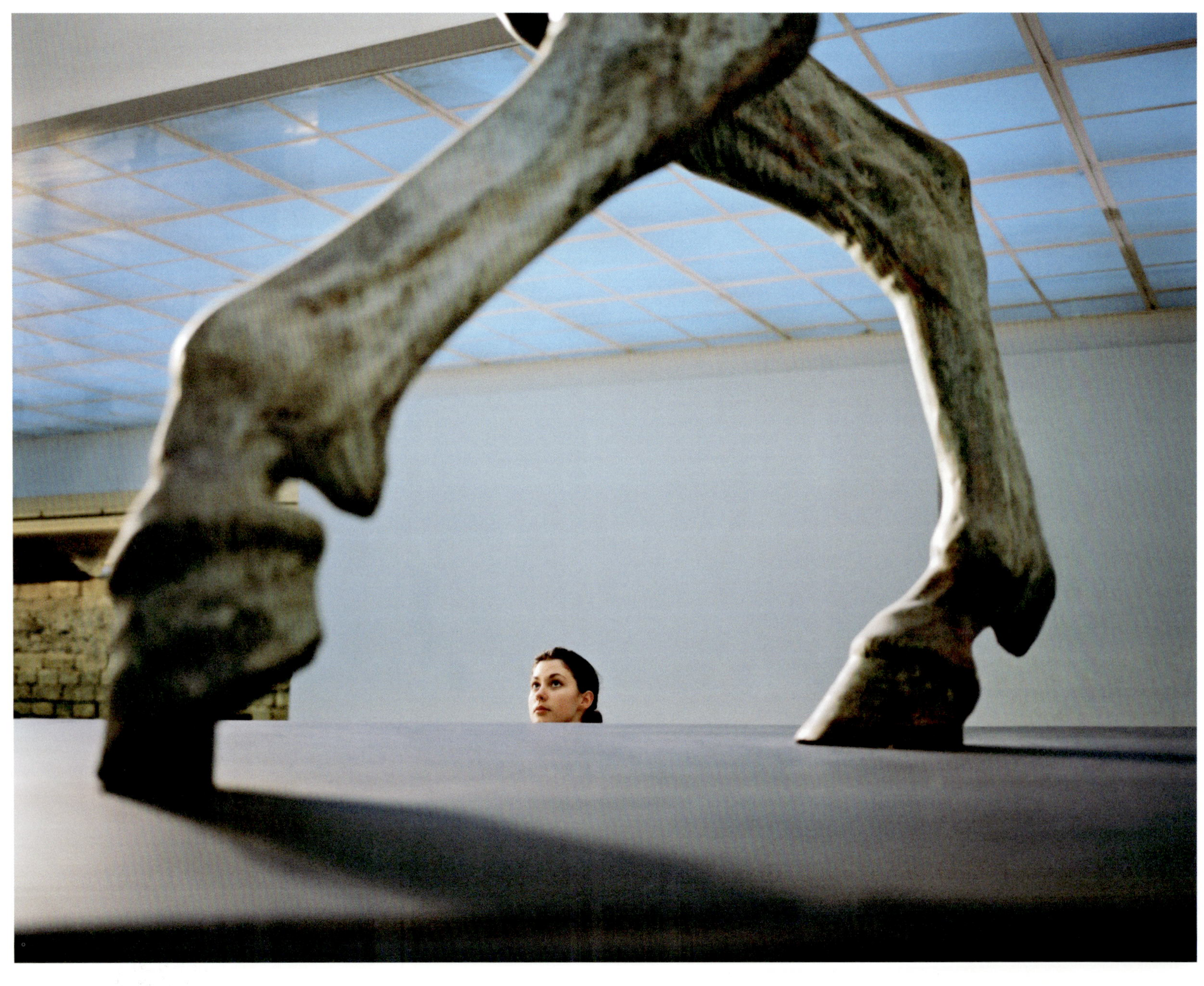

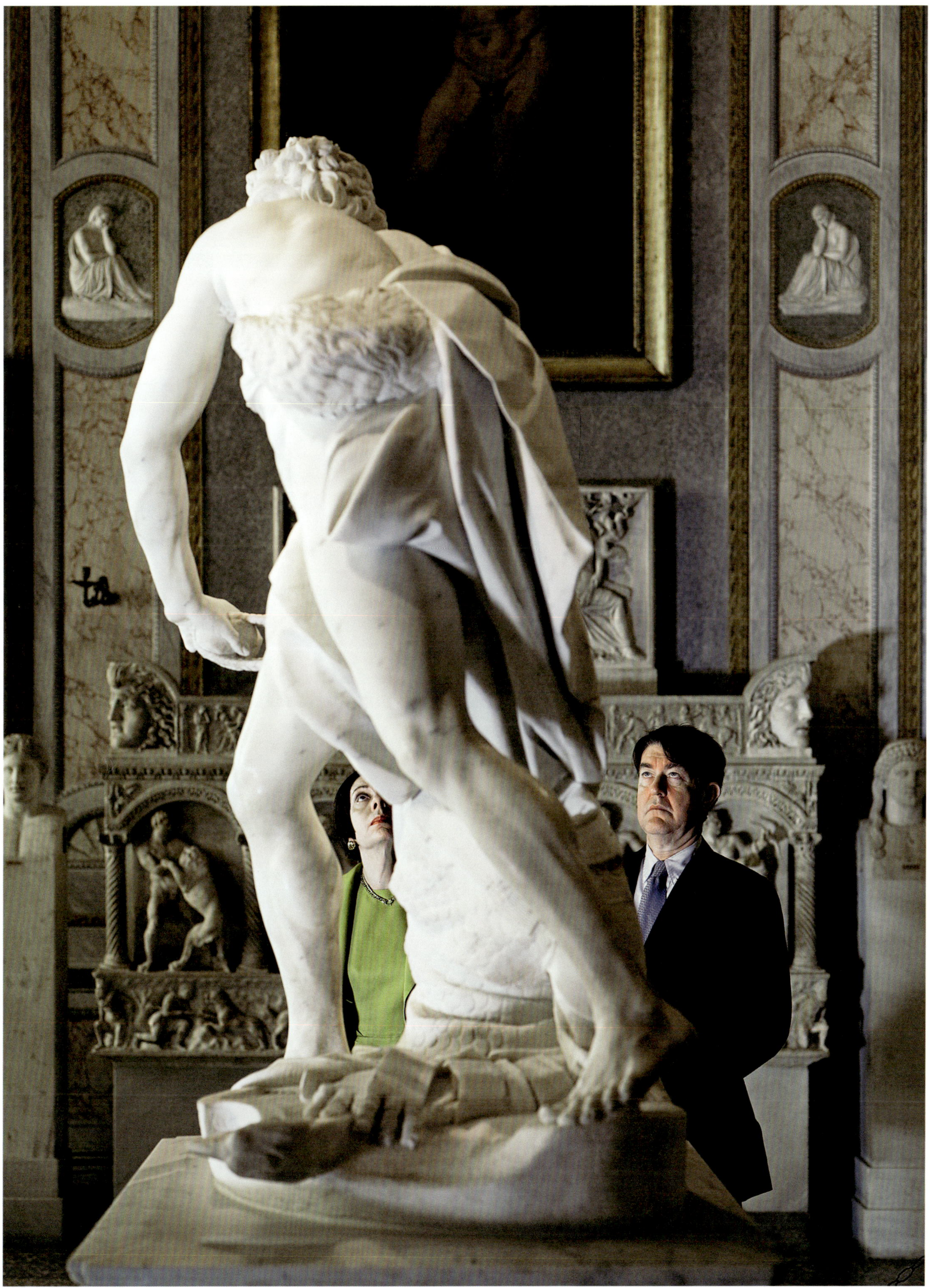

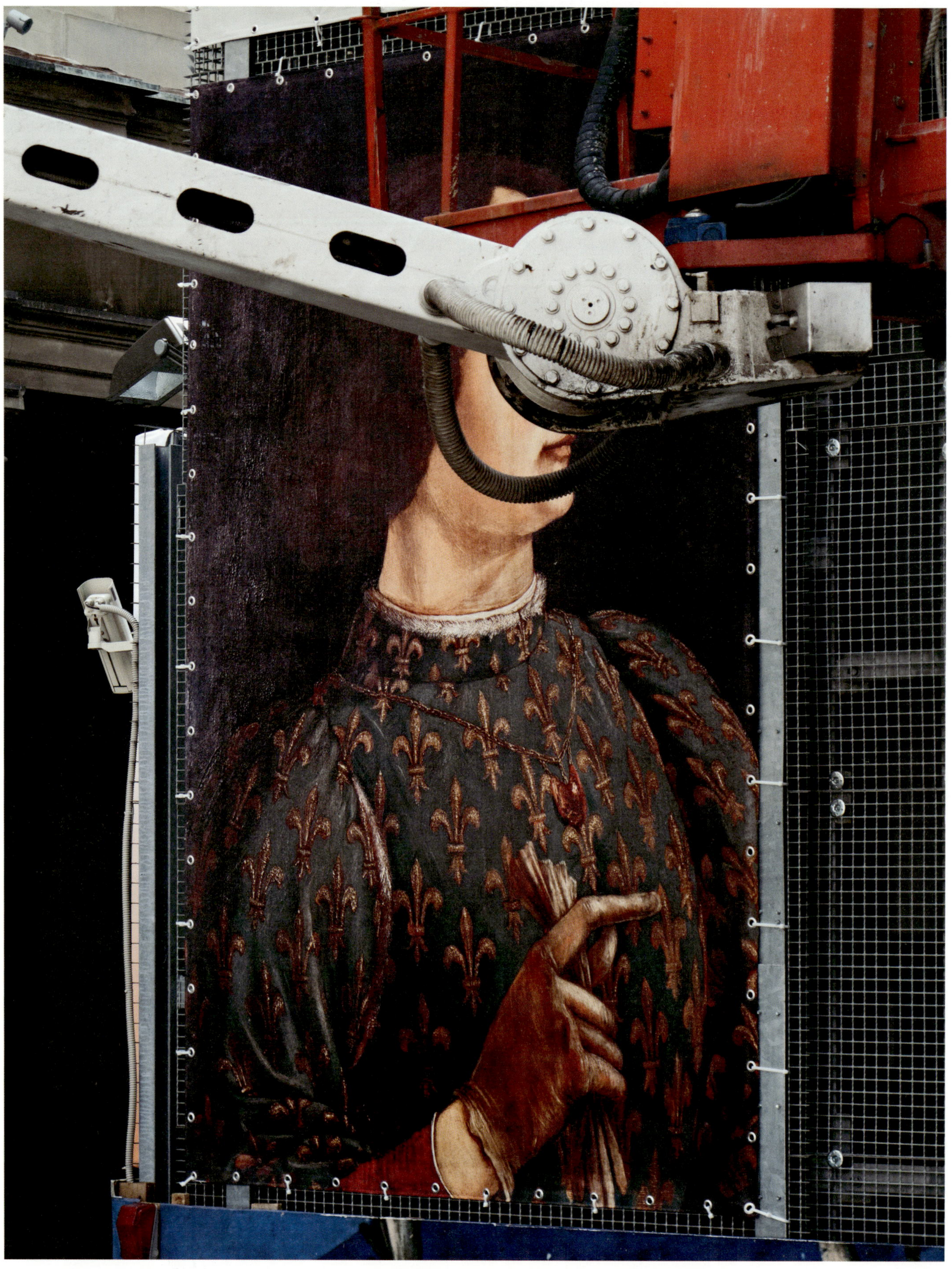

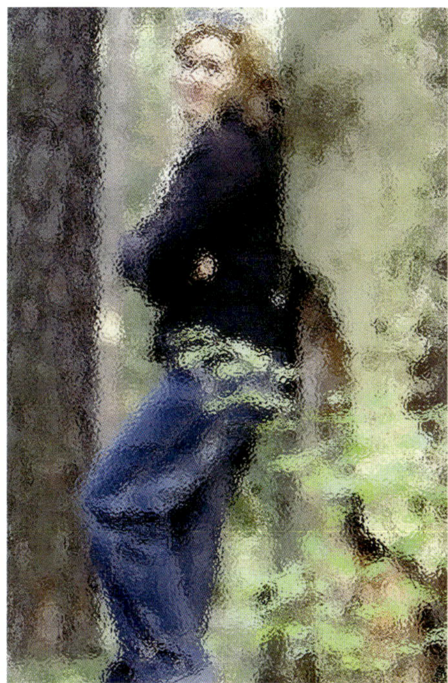 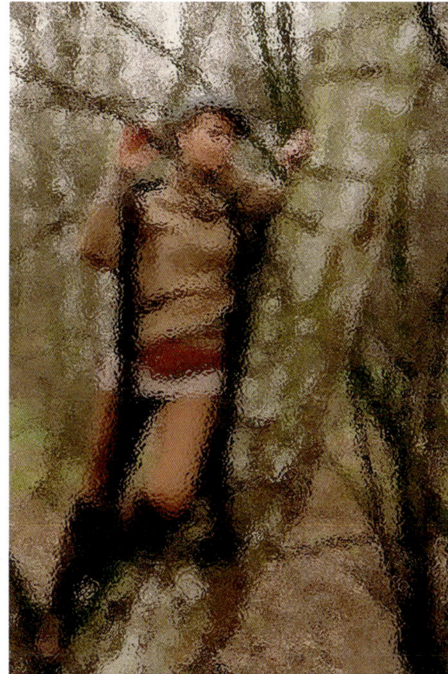 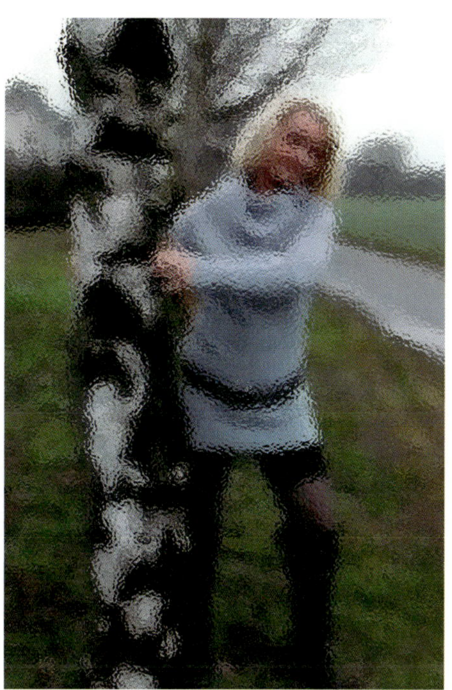

PETER PILLER
PHOTO SOURCE INTERNET

Peter Piller collects sociologically from the Internet to reveal in numbers and patterns the character of a visually similar group.

In the 21 pigment prints contained in *Hintergrundfarbe* (Background Color), Peter Piller's interest is directed at a particular moment, that appears briefly in the live stream of a sex webcam, a scene that can only be made visible by being captured technically as a still picture. Conventionally, Internet strippers leave the frame of the view finder to change outfits after contact is made with a customer. It is during this split-second before the 'service provider' returns to the screen, that Piller captures the uninhabited interior, which he translates into a coarsely pixilated color surface – what his exhibition statement calls "visual synonyms of spatial non-information."

In Piller's related recent body of work entitled, *Frau Baum* (Miss Tree), 2012, the artist culls from an online dating service images of women leaning on tree trunks or perched in tree branches. To protect the identity of his borrowed source (i.e. the person pictured) and to emphasize the similarity of gesture and behavior, he applies an archaic tool from Photoshop called the 'Frosted Glass-Effect.' With this blurriness, an apparent second layer of distance, Piller emphasizes the at-hand voyeurism and the common use of digital media to obscure identity.

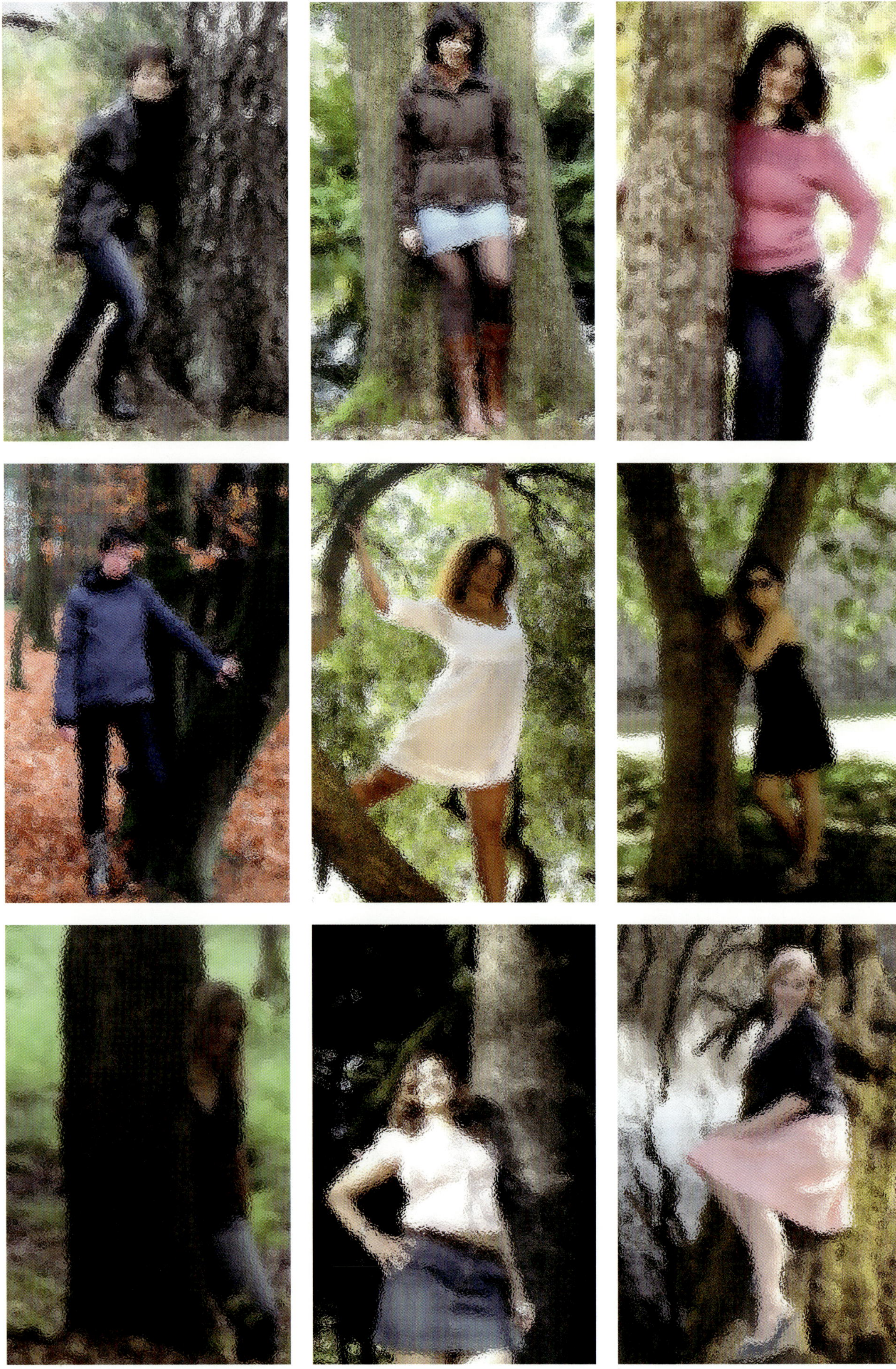

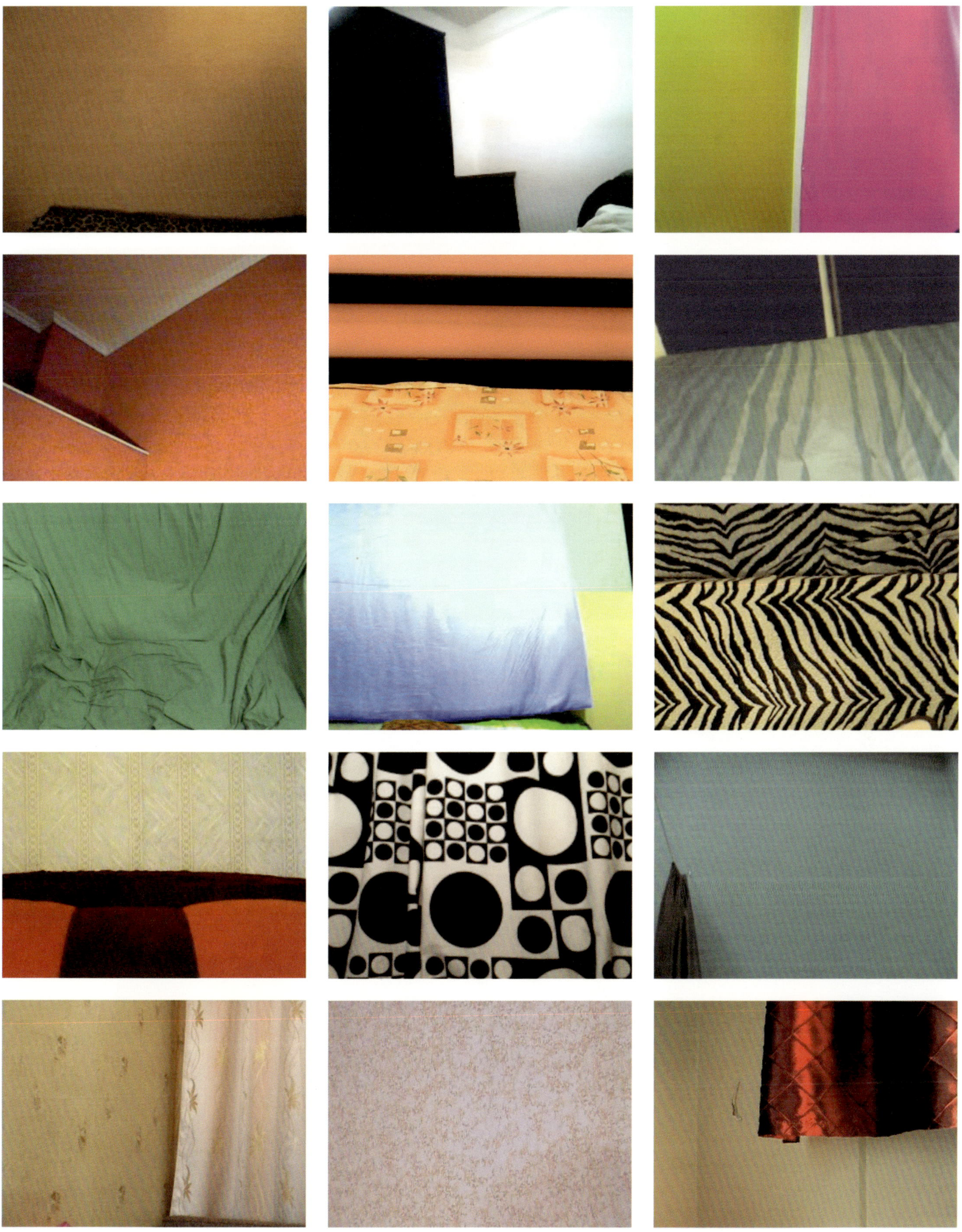

Pages 39 left Woman, tree, 2012, *pigment print, cm 45 x 30. Above* Hintergrundfarbe, 2010, *20 archival pigment prints, cm 57 x 75. All images © the artist, courtesy Andrew Kreps Gallery, New York*

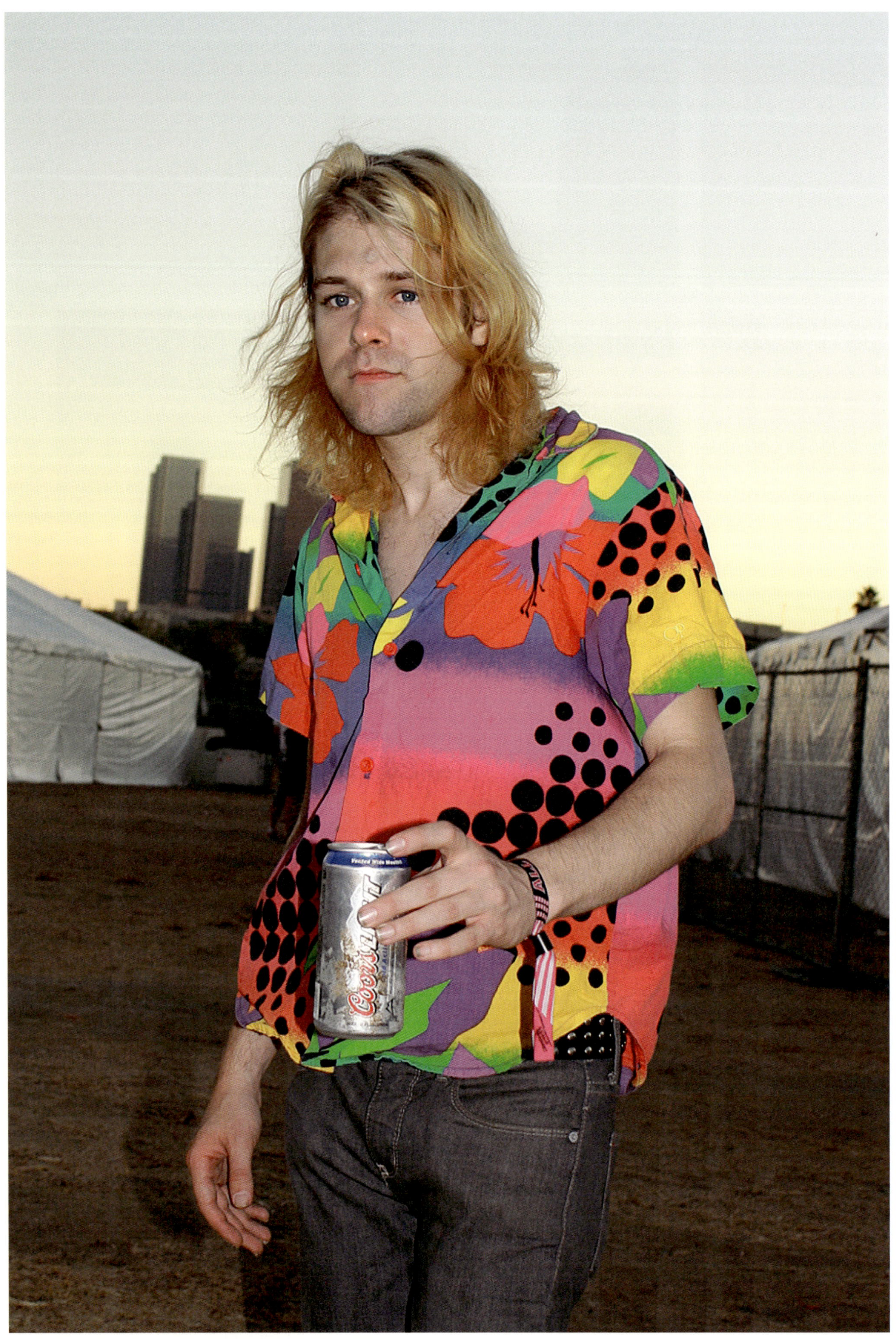

JOSH KLINE
by Alex Gartenfeld

When Josh Kline started making composites of celebrity headshots in 2009, he was an amateur at using Photoshop, which was appropriate for an artist whose work takes on questions of labor and leisure. This body of work has evolved along with the vernaculars it mined.

Critique of authenticity is at the heart of all of Kline's images. With Citizen Dick/Hurl Jam/ Guess Jeans (2010,) Kline shaves contours and pushes together the flesh of Matt Dillon and James Franco, two hunky brunette actors who came to fame playing disaffected tough guys. The resulting generically handsome mutant has flushed cheeks, a ratty goatee, and cowlicks atop a prominent forehead.

By virtue of the resemblance to both actors, the image cleaves, creating a kind of compare-and-contrast. Kline condenses the men's roles in movies and in 'reality,' suspending them in a professional, real-life situation (one with pathetic depths) - in front of a Guess Jeans step-and-repeat.

Kline's images are awash in the Nineties, a decade currently popularly packaged as retro-authentic, in spite of now four decades of post-modern critique.

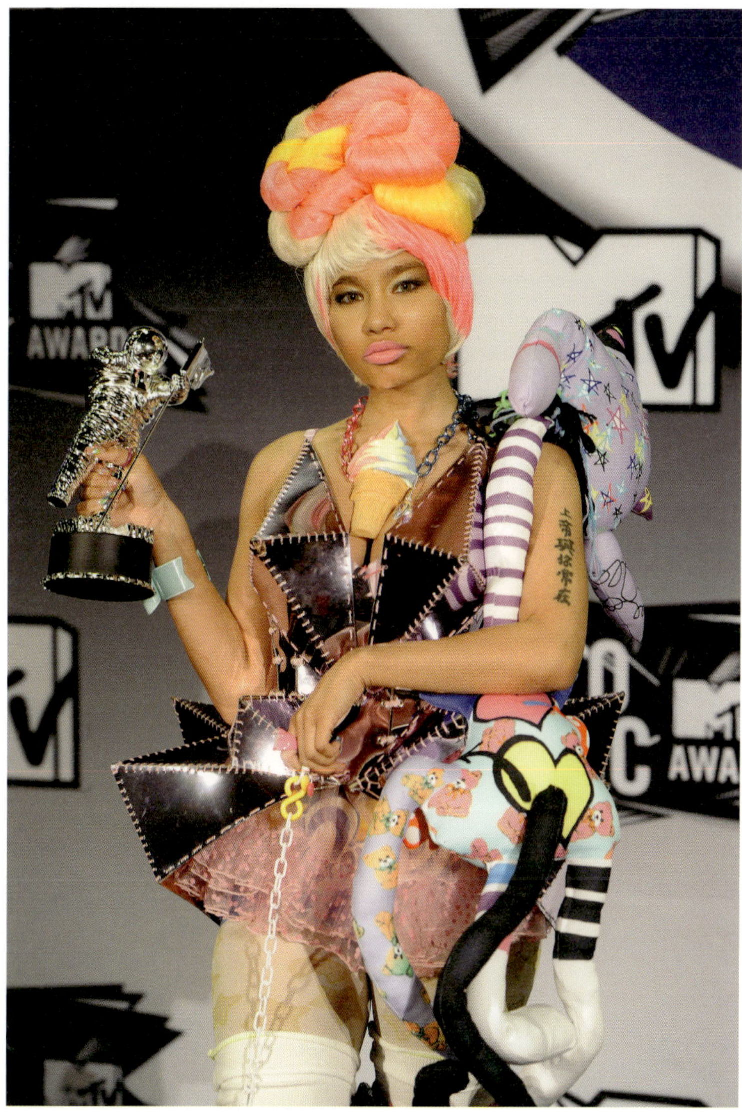

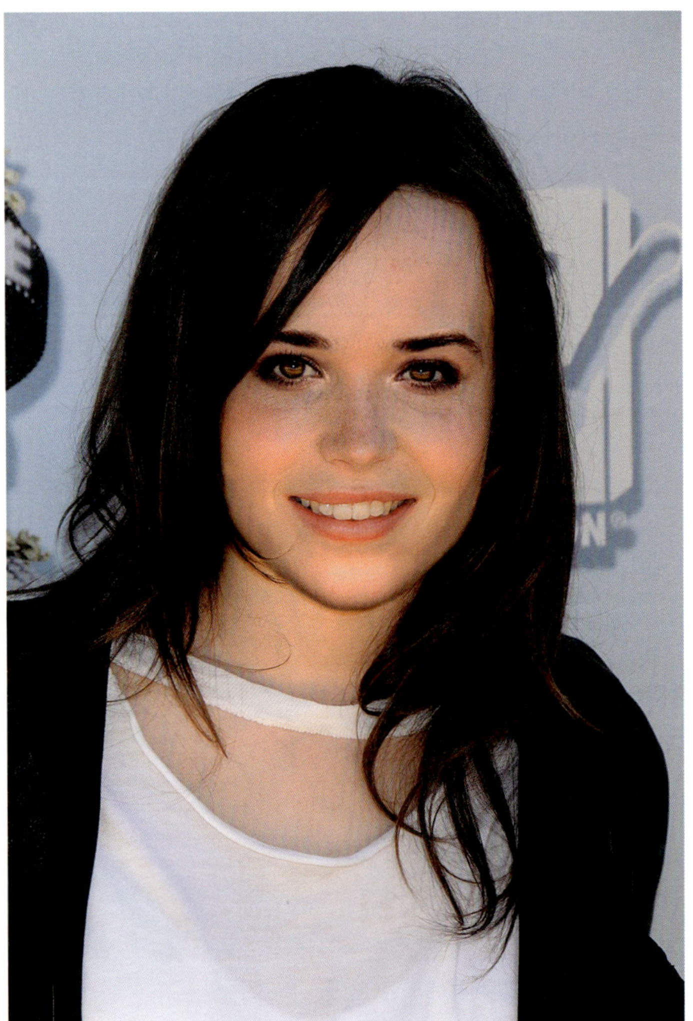 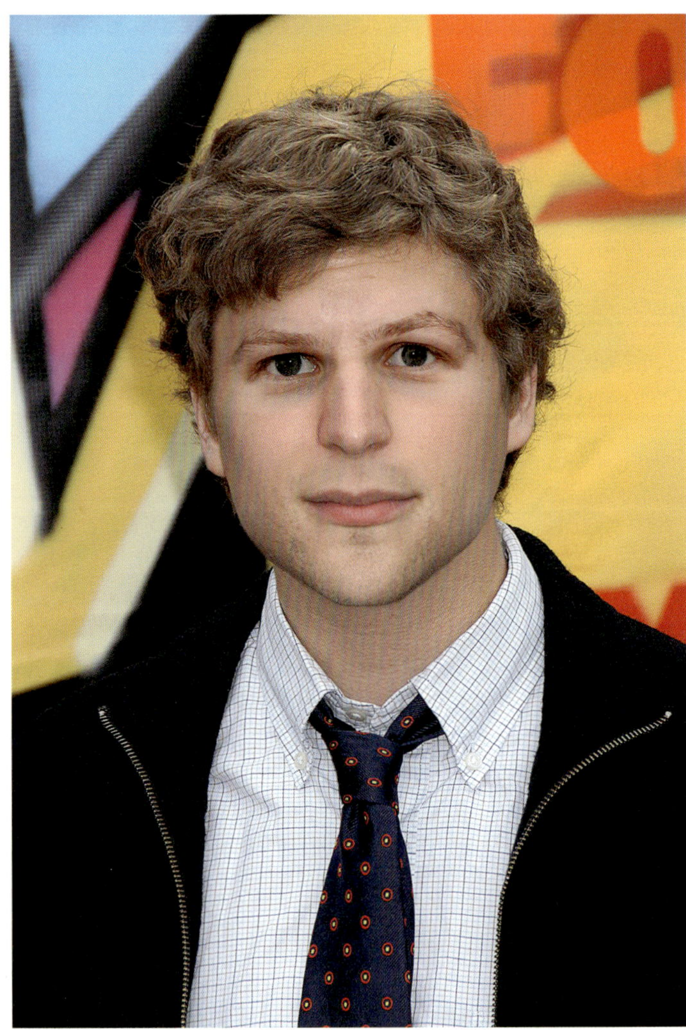

Page 42 Haunted Deodorant, 2011. *Page 43* Absorbing the 90s, 2011. *Above* Canadian Brunettes, 2010,
Facebook Friends, 2010. *Right* Dress Jeans, 2011, Actress/Shoplifter/Psychology Major, 2011.
All images cm 76,2 x 50,8 © the artist, courtesy the artist and 47 Canal, New York

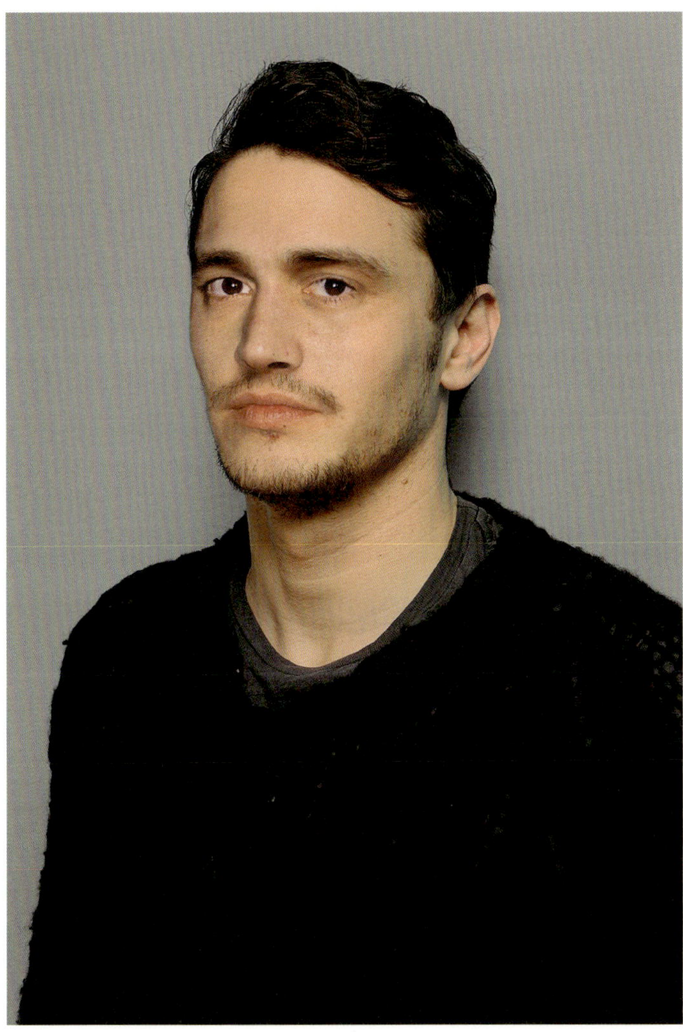

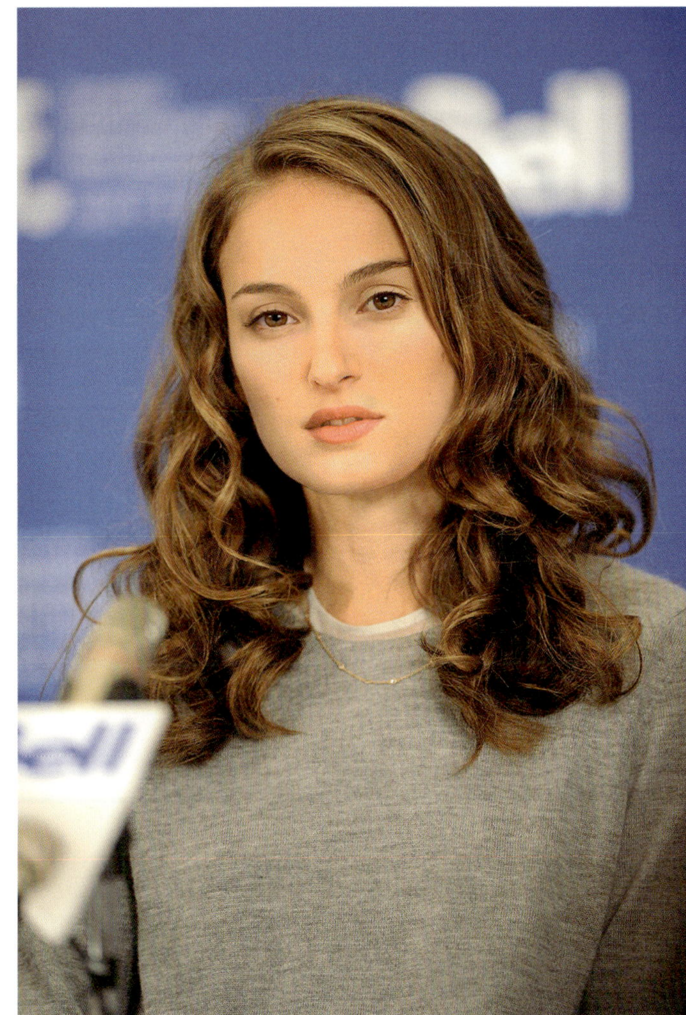

The artist unpacks the Gen-X slacker cliché in *Dress Jeans* (2011,) when he revisits Franco's face and splices it with Johnny Depp's. Though Depp is very famous and has a long public history, he shares with Franco an emphasis on masculine seriousness. Depp, like his allegorical and star-making turn in the television series *21 Jump Street,* the young man too darn pretty to be taken seriously, supplements his aura of authenticity by intermittently disputing fame. For Franco, seriousness equates with ceaseless cultural production, embodied somewhat interestingly in his admiration for the role of the artist.

When Kline's collage manipulation is evident, it evokes détournement, what Guy Debord and Gil J. Wolman called the language of contradiction, unmasking popular branded headshots as scripted performances. This critique is not a simplistic thwarting of media, as Debord wrote in the Situationist International: "far from aiming at arousing indignation or laughter by alluding to some original work, will express our indifference toward a meaningless and forgotten original." Kline deploys these contradictions to extrapolate on the singularity we anticipate in the faces of celebrities, as they endlessly step-and-repeat.

Increasingly, Kline's images don't appear as collages, but as an entirely new person. His combination of Winona Ryder (the girl too smart to be a Heather[1]) and Natalie Portman (the Harvard graduate who nearly gave up acting) surprisingly resembles *Gossip Girl* second fiddle Leighton Meister. The new creation invokes post-human anxiety of plastic surgery or cloning, while referencing the way collage has, as Charlie White describes, normaliz[ed] as an everyday experience.

The subtle shift in Kline's technique over the last year, from crafting Frankensteins to new, fully synthesized human beings, coincides with a change on many web sites, including Facebook. In the new 'timeline' platform, a user-created profile is synchronized fluidly with feedback from other users. Collage and détourné are foundational to this poly-vocal logic, which creates multiple simultaneous and potentially conflicting histories - identities based in declaration, description, inscription and hearsay. The result is a subject who's truly a composite.

1. *Heathers,* dir. Michael Lehmann, 1988

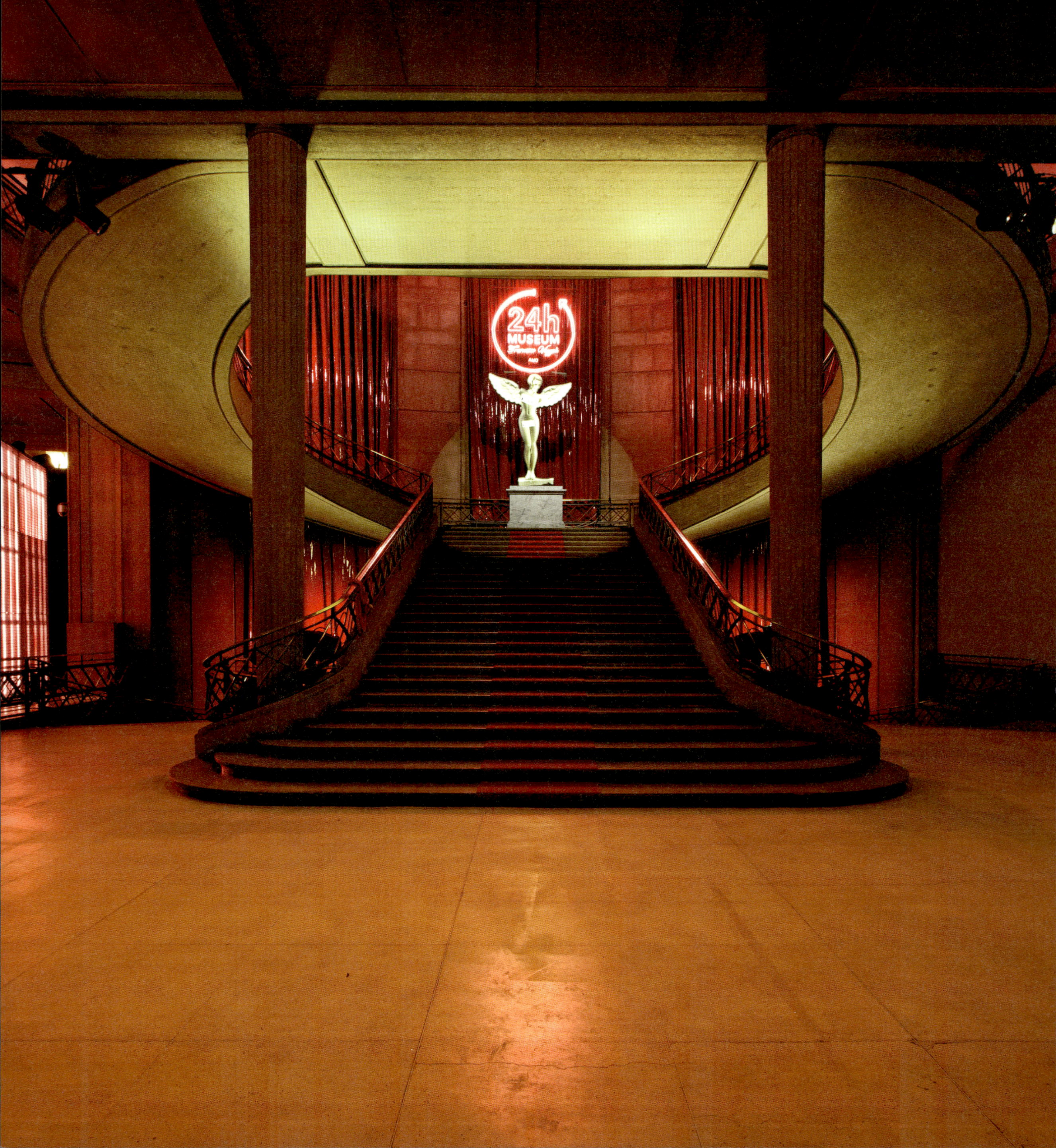
24h
MUSEUM
AMO

Fleeting, fake, and not always for sale

Appearance is clearly, or rather, upon reflection, not reality!

FRANCESCO VEZZOLI 24 HOURS MUSEUM
PHOTOGRAPHED BY ADRIAN GAUT AND TOLD BY CAY SOPHIE RABINOWITZ

On a much anticipated winter eve in Paris, fashionable figures and figureheads flocked with their calligraphy inscribed hard copy invitations in hand, to Palais d'Ilena, a historical batiment which currently house of the French economic, social and environmental council. To most residing around this 19th arrondissement building, the line of chauffeured cars was likely to suggest one of the seasonal runway shows commonly scheduled during the city's fashion weeks. But the encounter revealed itself to be something else.

The reason for being there was a mise en abyme of extreme conceptual rigor: Francesco Vezzoli's 24 Hours Museum.

A reflexion of the artist's engagement with the conventions of fashion and art. A play on the artist's affiliations with the elite crowds and with the formats in which art and fashion are presented. A query on who and what makes art; a wrench into the means of production and distribution. Earlier that day photographer Adrian Gaut was invited by Vezzoli to capture his installation for Fantom. Since the fleeting museum would remain intact only for 24 hours, photography would play a key role in the legacy of his work.

Vezzoli was decisive about letting Gaut record his intervention independent of any artistic direction. He did not want the reproductions usually required by museums or galleries or the party pictures of the event, knowing of course that in the weeks to come his guest list of actresses, designers, models, publishers and collectors would have inevitably flooded magazines and blogs. Even in the absence of persons, the space of the palais designed in Greek revival style by August Perret in the mid 1930 revived with Vezzoli's *gesamtkunstwerk* was not lacking in drama. These pictures are a conversation of objects in space. A dialogue that did not last long.

Cars arrived to deliver the most photographed faces to a cocktail reception and dinner served on Miuccia Prada's personal china - she is a long time associate of Vezzoli and the whole project was sustained by her eponymous fondazione. Embroidered linens on long banquets outlined a central space surrounded by walls of pink neon. Collectors ogled actresses, editors querried designers, artists captivated business executives. Kate Moss' bare legs atop a white fur failed to cause a significant stir when she arrived well into the 3rd course. We all seemed to be method acting a play staged around impervious architecture and the constant gaze of fragmented eyes that Vezzoli had collaged onto full scale lightbox versions of antique bodies.

Just as dessert was served, sound became muted by masses of people: next tier VIPs, who began to surround us. We were fully illuminated. The space suddenly seemed more like a cage than an area of privilege. It was not just the guest list or the off limits location that made the scene an attempt to make art challenge the way we see things in the world. As a metaphor, the operation stands for the way meaning cannot be affixed to a static set of conventions, especially regarding public institutions and the public which institutions serve. The occasional art curator or critic would dismiss *sotto voce* the scene as mere decadent spectacle but s/he would be missing the point, mistaking appearance for reality, sidetracked by the smooth surfaced cheekbones, the neon sculptures and the champagne service. Vezzoli uses synthetic, glittery, reflective surfaces to make nothing in the space a singular point of focus or contention.

What looks like marble is made like stage props of wood and plastic, what looks like sculpture is photographic, what looks like a party is a performance where the most exclusive guests don't yet know that they will be captivated.

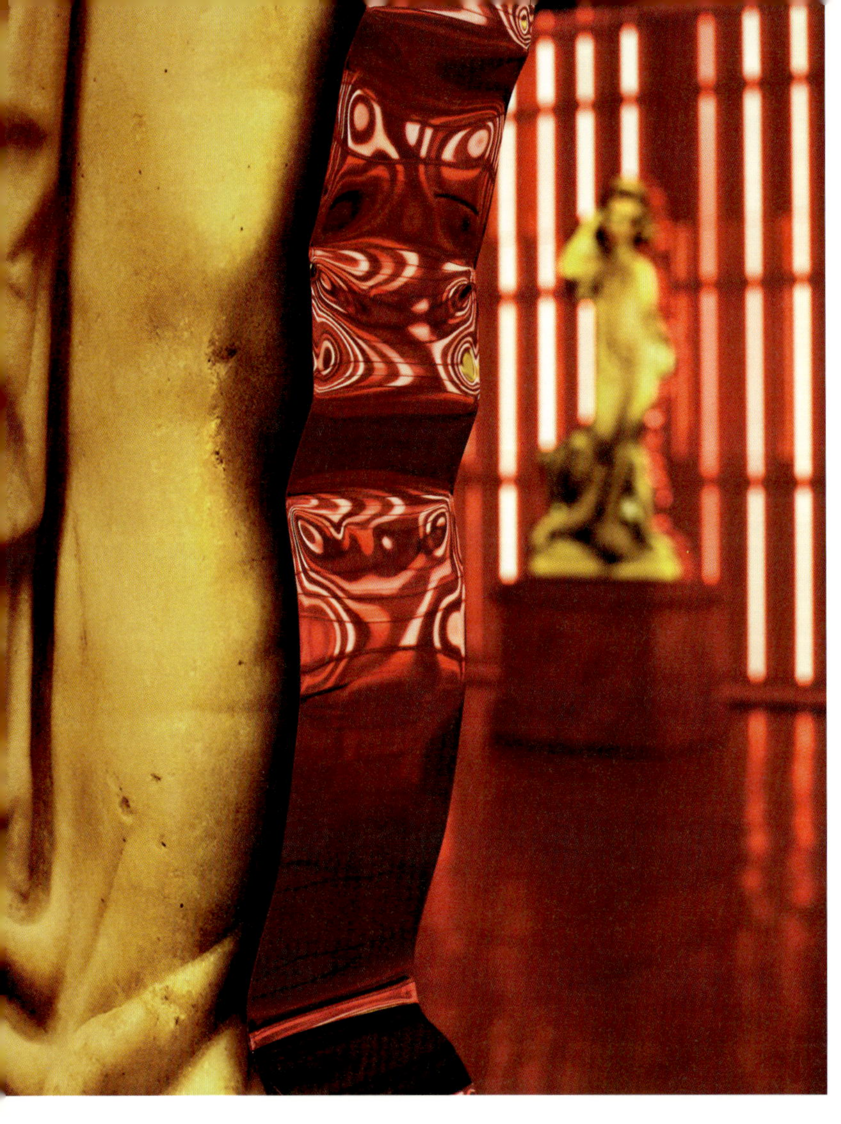
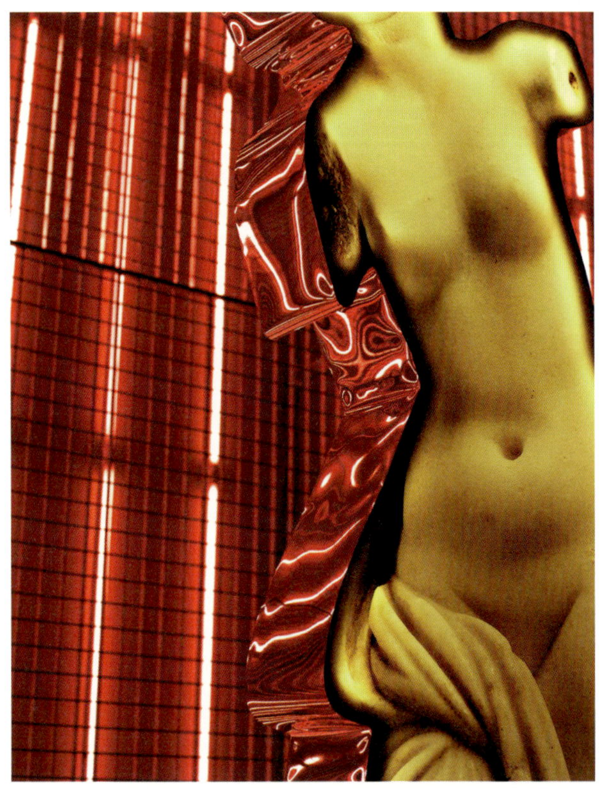

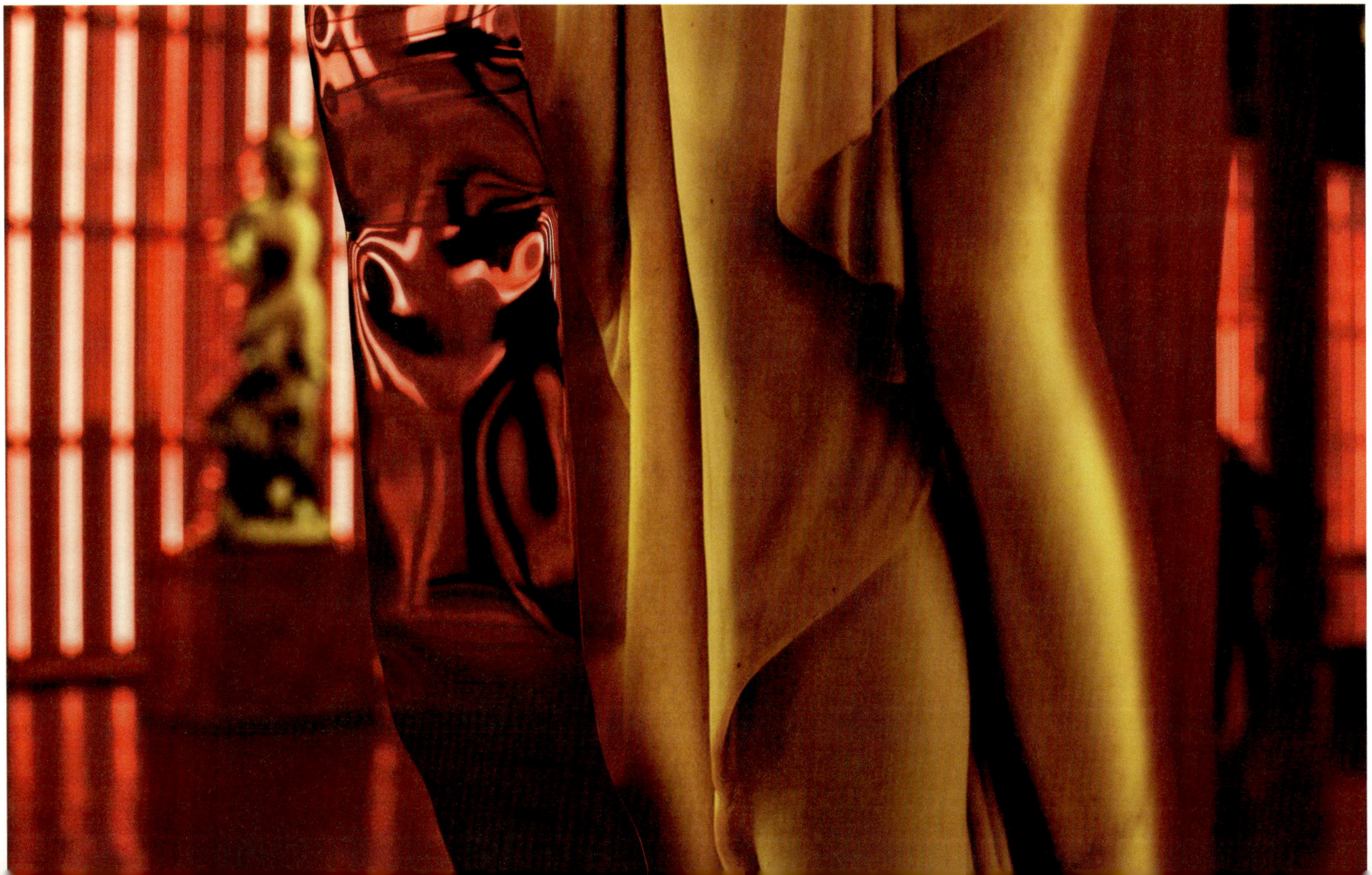

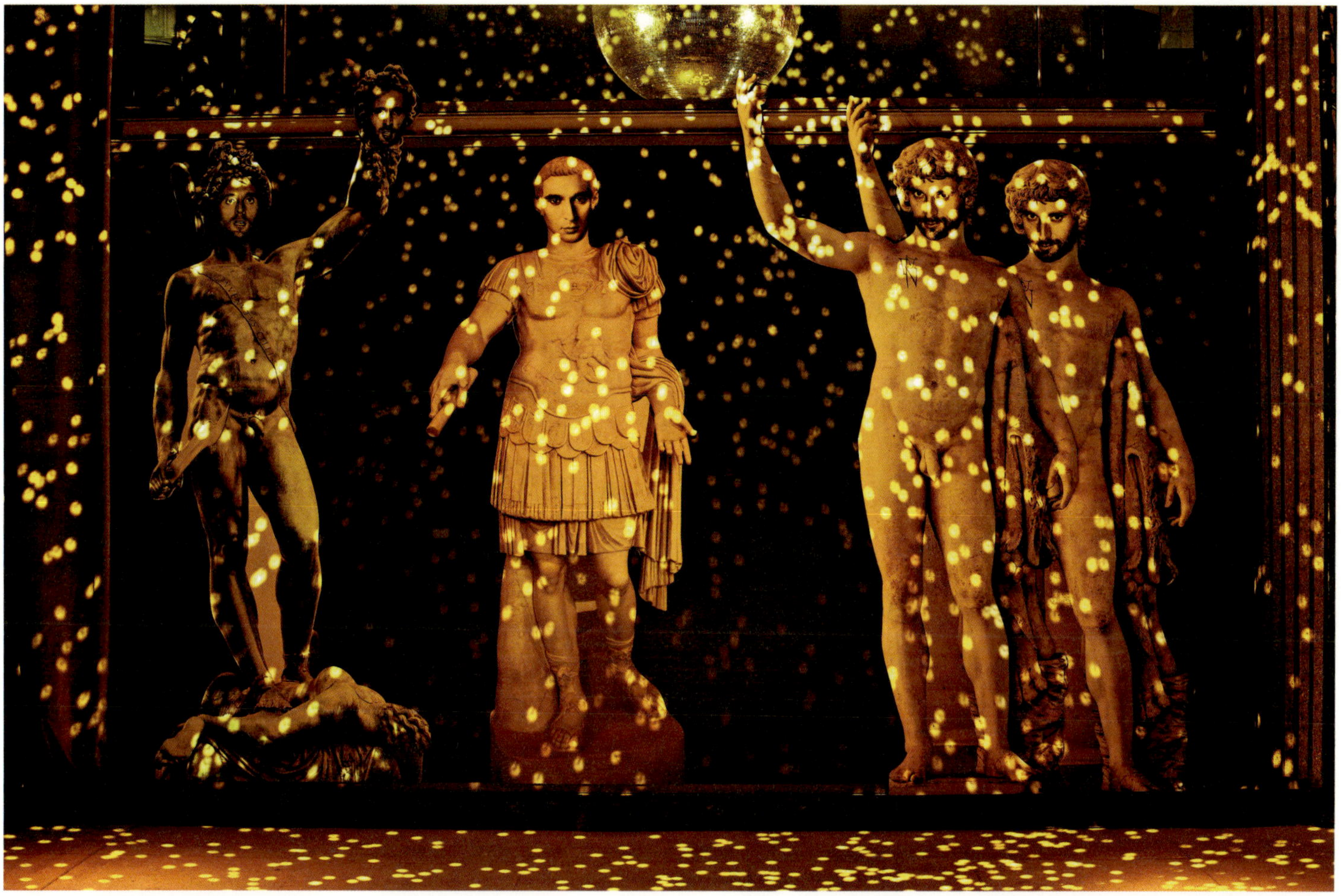

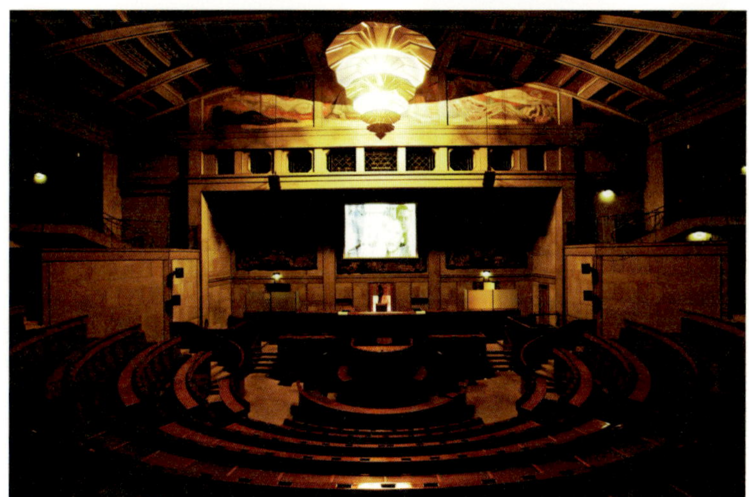

All images: Francesco Vezzoli 24 Hours Museum, Paris, 2012.
Photo Adrian Gaut © the authors

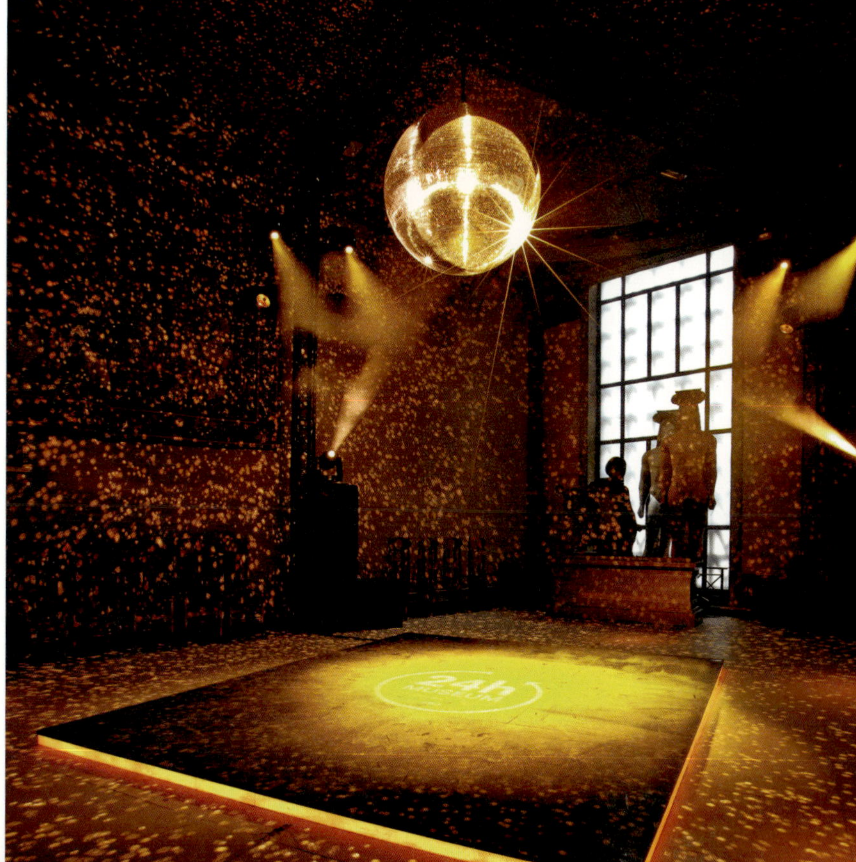

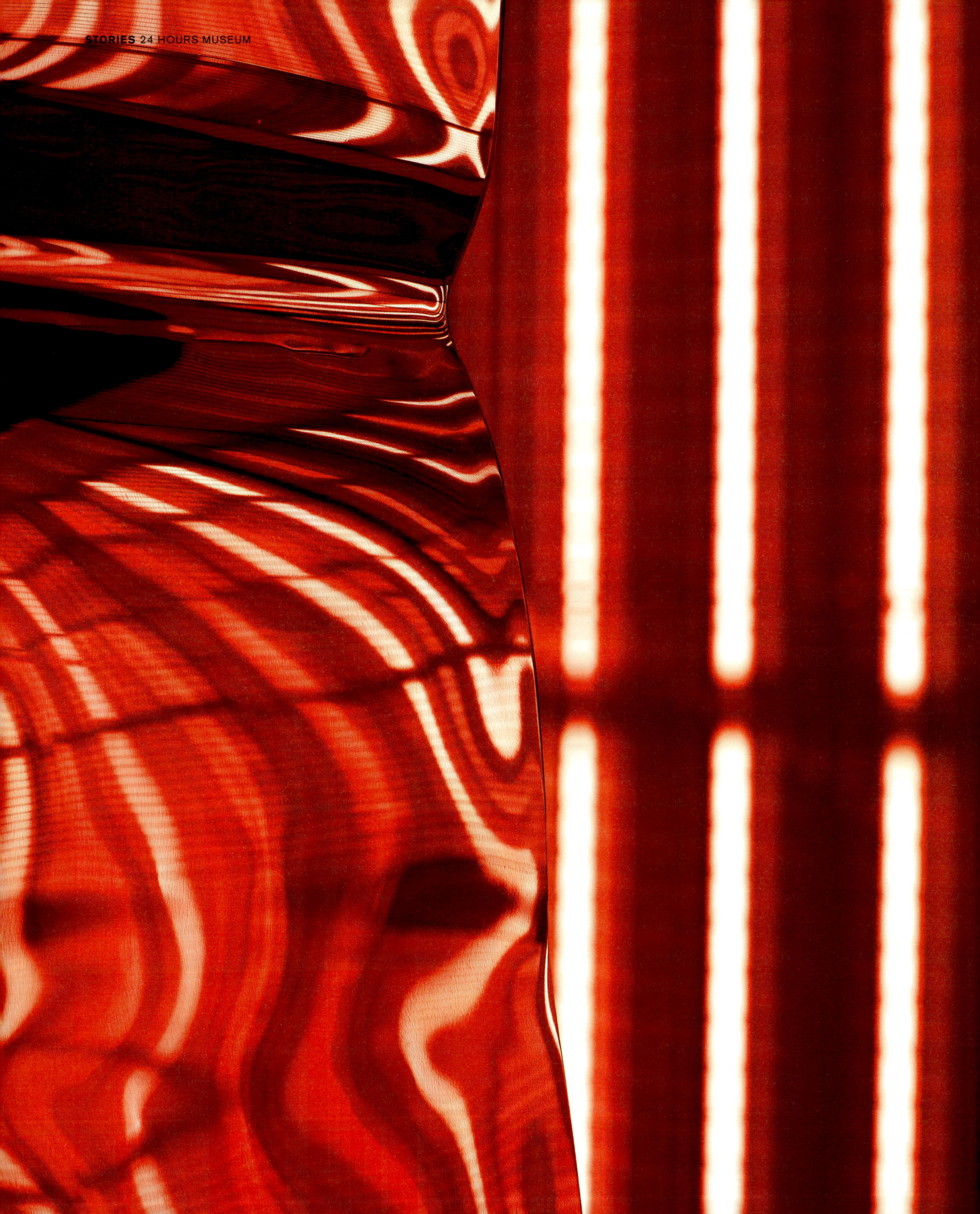

K8 HARDY
BECAUSE SHE SAYS SO
by Anna Papier

K8 Hardy is no stranger to unusual fashion photography. For her zine *FashionFashion* **(2009) the artist played dress-up in the most outrageous combinations of thrift store-found and otherwise assembled ensembles reminiscent of biker chicks, goth hippies, frolicking tube sock-wearing gymnasts, and drag queen performers, among others. In one memorable image, she sits spread-eagle showing her dollar sign-patterned underpants soiled with menstrual blood. And while each image underscores the radical shifts in tone and style, mood and temperament of her heroines, neither image is so spot-on that it might derail into the perfect stereotype; in other words: K8 Hardy doesn't do cliché. She is not interested in the interpretation of her images as a critique of a particular group dress code or gender role, or as a way to identify with marginality, mass culture, or the exclusivity of hipster subsets. Don't mistake these images for a rejection of sharp dress codes, of looking good, of sartorial hotness. They just might not at first appear to conform to conventional ideas of what looking sexy in one's clothes might mean.**

Lesson No. 1: K8 Hardy's pictures are not a critique of fashion photography as a dry, lifeless lesson in gender roles, objectification, and commodity fetishism. Rather, they are a celebration of the transgressive curiosity that arises when every item of clothing is so over-determined and their combinations so 'wrong' that our stories of what might arouse their wearers become loopy, outlandish, endless riffs on desire, individualism, and joy.

The format in which Hardy chooses to circulate her images is also to be considered: her zines are true to form; center-folded, staple-bound, colored papers embrace the notion and conventions of the self-made, yet the clean lines of one image per page, sometimes repeated in different sizes across the fold, sometimes accompanied by a blank opposite page adorned with a snappy quote, or artfully overlaid with a collage of another image (but never too much), and the slightly bleached, cool tones of her saturation suggests a keen awareness of the well-made simplicity you might find in magazines such as *apartamento* or the unbearable cuteness of Australian magazine *Frankie* (except, of course, that Hardy's photos are neither simple nor cute.) I am sure the next J. Crew catalogue will have stolen a page or two from K8 Hardy. Which brings us to lesson No. 2: K8 Hardy's images are not 'unprofessional.' They are not about the inability to produce industry-level standard, or the rejection of composition, craft, and production value. They simply don't share the same idea of where value is located, and instead establish an aesthetic that has already taken hold in the more outlying regions of hip mass culture, albeit with more radical implications.

All this is helpful when we consider the most recent series of K8 Hardy, which premiered at this year's Whitney

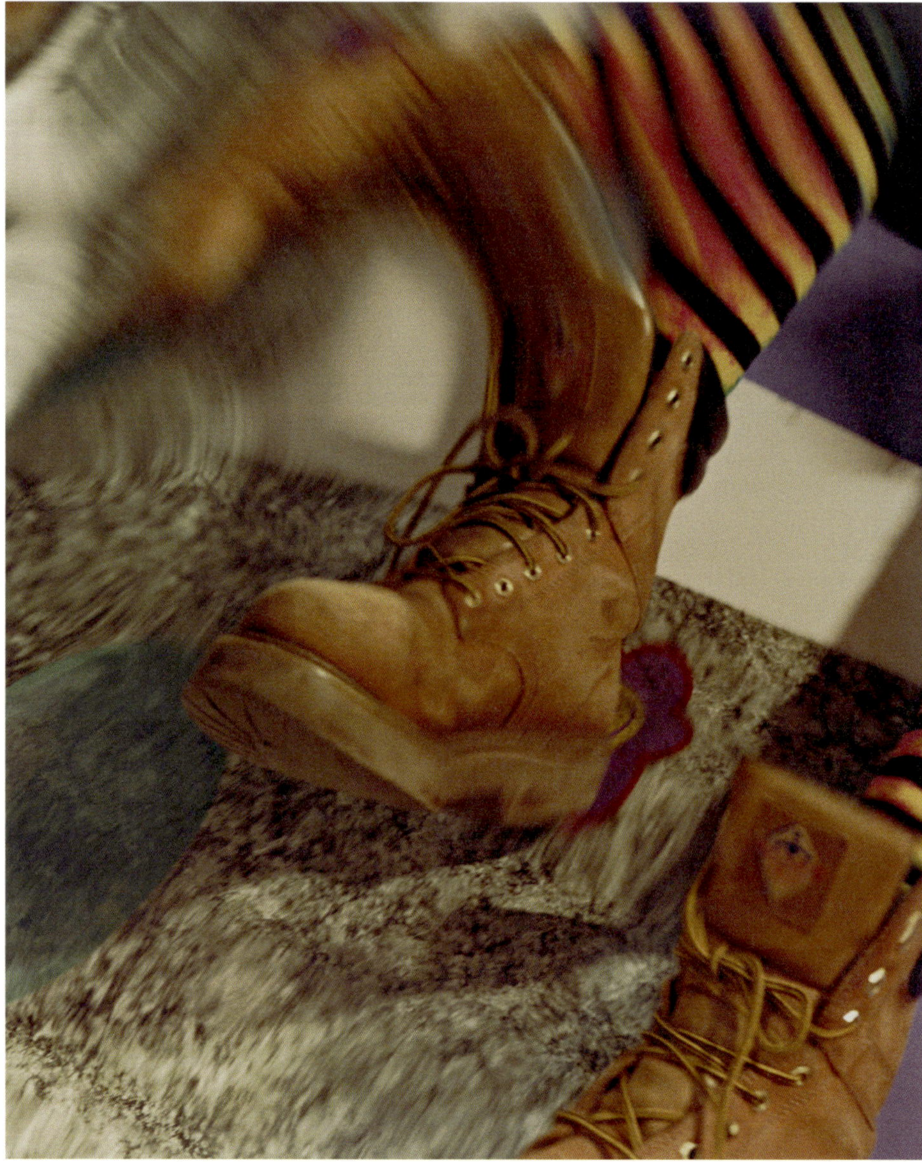

Biennial in New York. Her installation consists of an "abstract shoe campaign" hung salon style on a long main wall in the Whitney and occasionally interrupted by sculptural assemblages fashioned from hairpieces, the odd single shoe or dismembered (mannequin's) foot. The images cover the basic footwear genres high heels and pumps, boots, ballerinas, platforms, sneakers, and rubber sandals are all well represented and are all modeled by the artist herself. In some

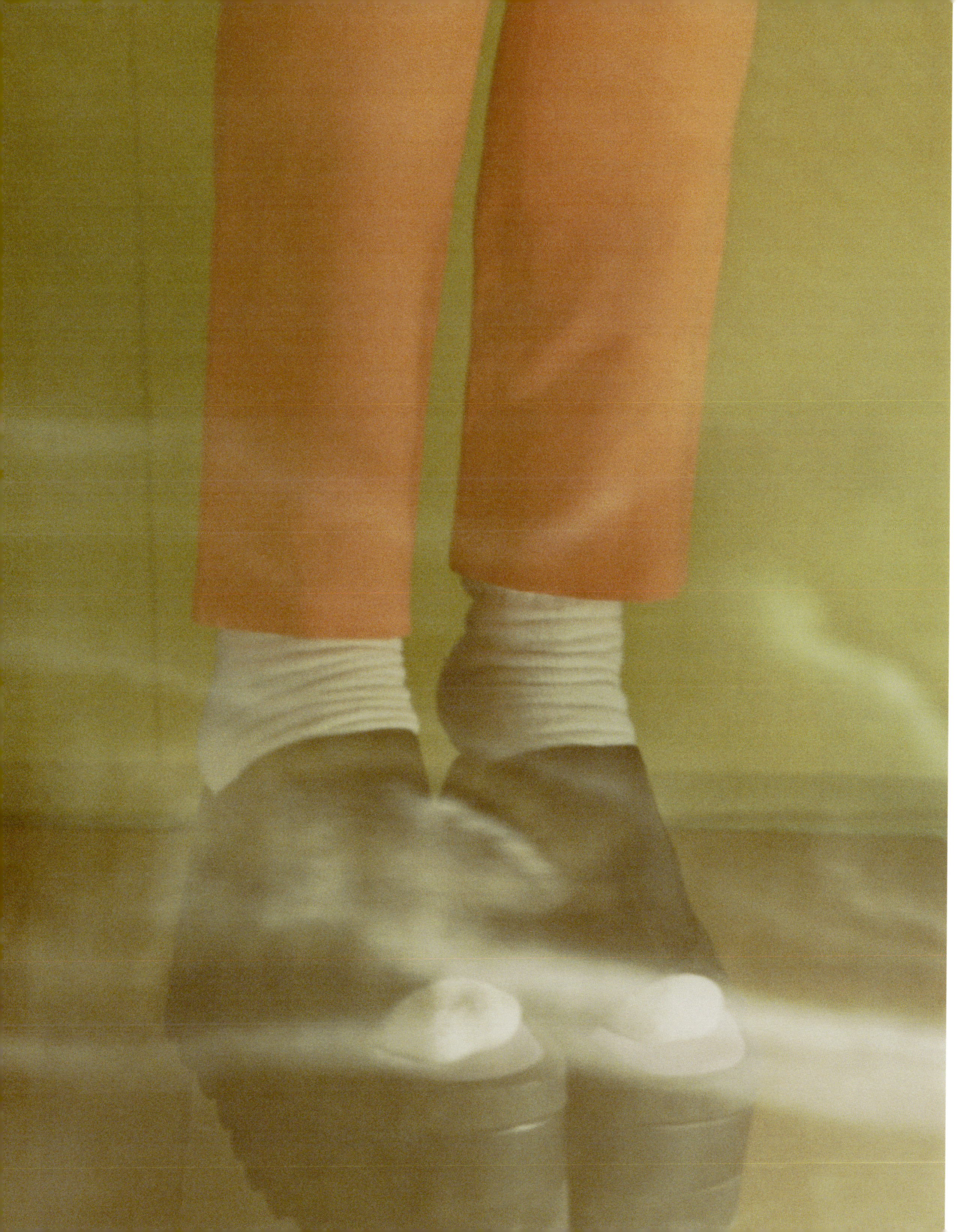

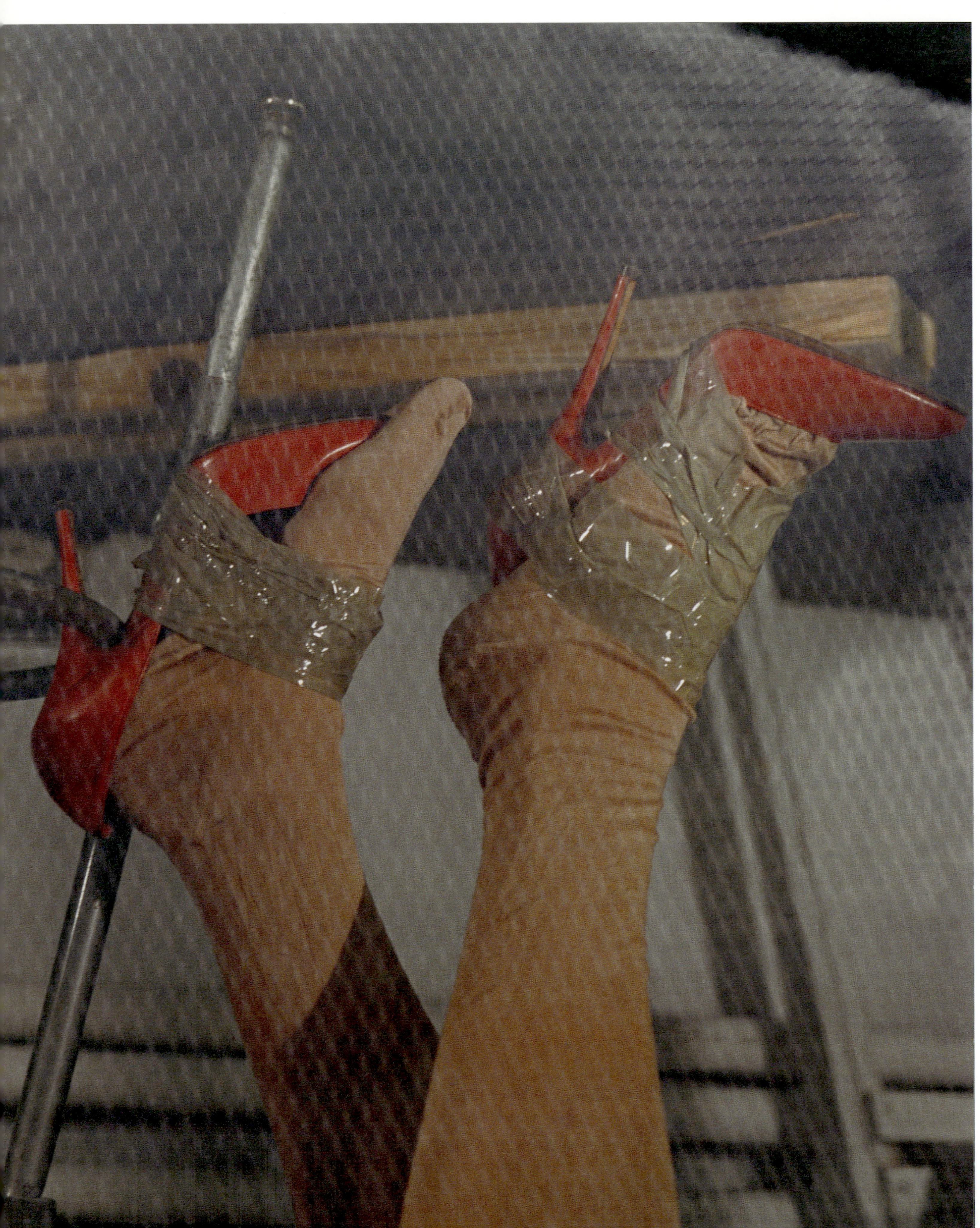

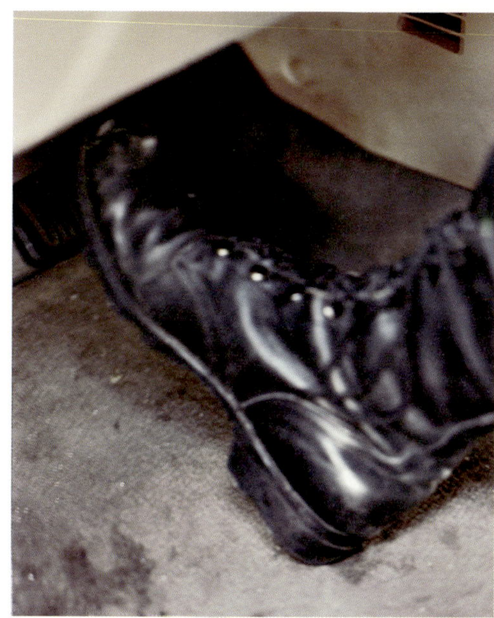

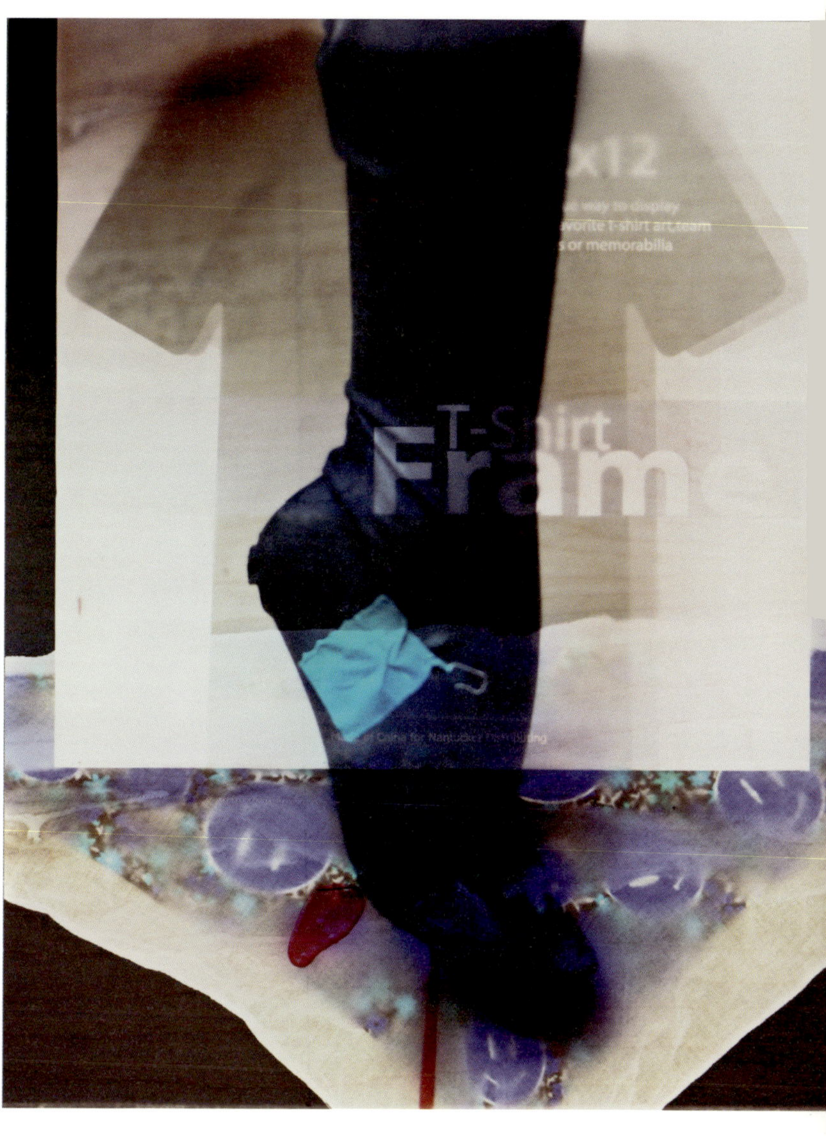

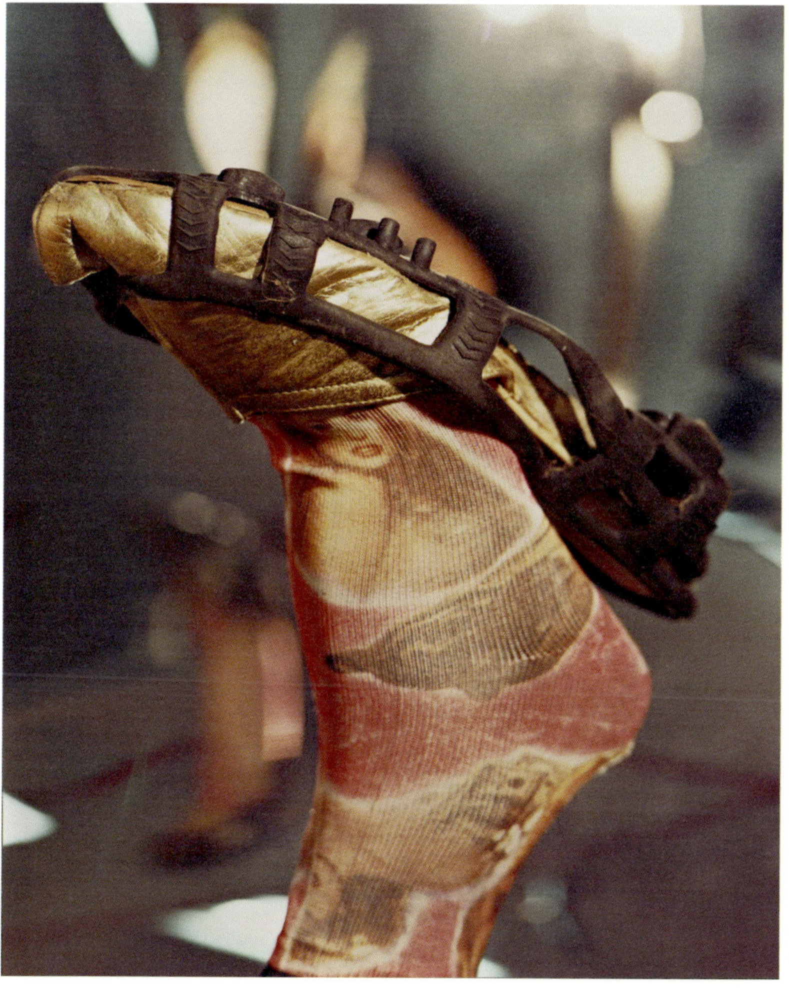

Page 51 The Path 7, 2012. *Page 52* The Path 2, 2012. *Page 53* The Path 9, 2012. *Left* The Path 1, 2012. *On this page, clockwise* The Path 8, 2012, The Path 10, 2012, The Path 5, 2012. *Page 56* The Path 4, 2012. *Page 57* Mr. President, 2012. *Page 58* The Path 3, 2012. *All images cm 40 x 50, photographic C-print with photogram, © the artist, courtesy Reena Spaulings Fine Art, New York*

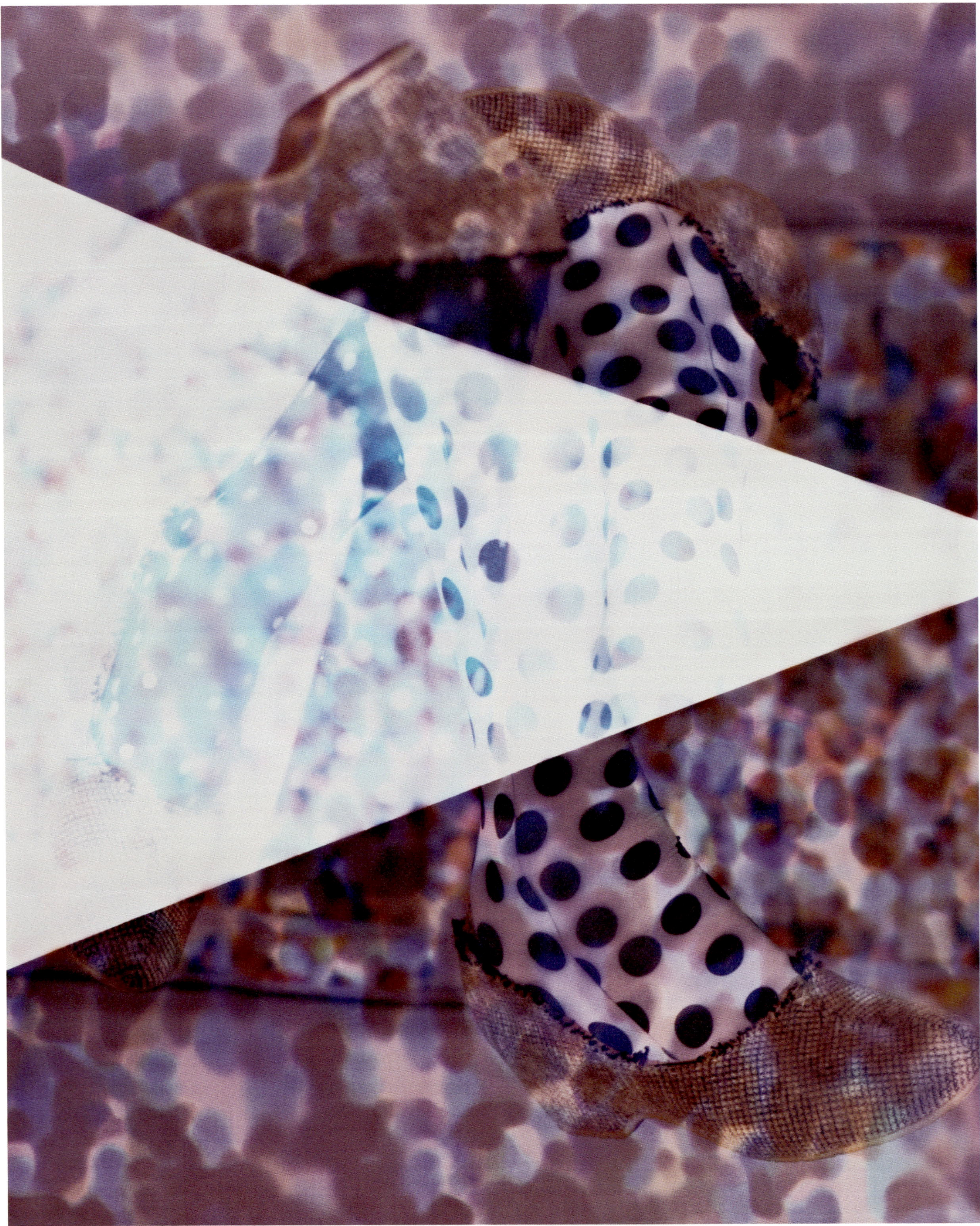

respects, the images conform even less to the conventions of the fashion still than Hardy's previous forays into fashion: blurry and grainy, drained of all but one color, and overlaid with abstract swirls and ghost images of other footwear (in one image, the silhouette of a single sock mimics the angular bend of a sensible looking red pump with black music notes printed on them,) the photographs appear to be almost coincidentally about the shoes they depict, and engage in a more serious debate about all the different effects at a photographer's (manual) disposal to create texture, abstraction, and delirium in a single frame (albeit with multiple exposures.) And in no uncertain her way footwear conforms in its action to the gestalt or projection of the shoe it displays: the platform's promise of elevation is mirrored in the elastic jump of the wearer, the ballerina is modeled in classical ballet's *en pointe*, the Army boot's aggressive agility is underscored by its stepping full force on a gas pedal, and so on. If anything, we must acknowledge Hardy's urgent desire to be true to the basic tenets of an advertisement campaign: to exaggerate the desire promised by the fetish object by means of visual seduction and radical commitment to what a design allows. The series demonstrates that the footwear is employed like the very photography which renders it: to its material limits when in the hand (or foot) of an artist who want to get the most of her material.

Hardy is reluctant to be drawn into over-analysis of the work at the Whitney. She is clear that for her, despite the images featuring very real and recognizable objects, that the work should be seen as abstraction. She comments, "The images are useless in a way in terms of buying something although they are pieces of art. At the same time they do have their own aesthetics and they can be enjoyable in that." Interestingly she admits to being somewhat frustrated by the categorization of her work as low-fi. "Because my resources are limited and they are not glossy digital high resolution photos there is a vintage feel to it but that is because that is what I had to make the work and that is what I will do. People often think that my DIY aesthetic is the thing I like but I am actually not attached to it. All I have been able to do is hand held natural light. I work with the production means that I have. Sometimes I get a little frustrated you know, I am not trying to be DIY or marginal. I am not going to stop making work that's ambitious. Sometimes I exploit the low-fi aesthetic that does come out of fashion because I can. I will do something extra grainy and low-fi because those are the tools I have to hand. At the same time I like to make things fairly fast and not too belabored and improvisational."

During the process of installing the work at the Whitney she noticed a blank area of wall under a stacked group of signage directing visitors to toilets and a fire exit. She decided that this was the perfect spot for an additional unexpected piece of collage work not realizing that this would send alarms bells ringing and upset the protocol of the Whitney cataloguing process. The work was not removed.

She hopes that her photographic installation is somewhat reminiscent of a shoe store, although she also confesses that she rarely goes to shoe stores because the majority of her clothes are found while thrifting.

K8 Hardy has been commissioned to stage a fashion show during the Whitney Biennial. The performance will take place on a modular reconfiguration of an architectural pavilion structure conceived by the artist Oscar Tuazon to be transformed into a stage for Hardy's

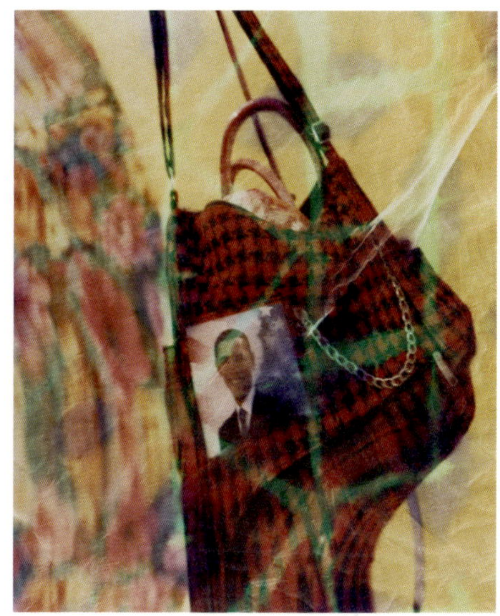

catwalk presentation. It will migrate from its initial context on the first floor of the Whitney to be reconstructed on the fourth floor. The catwalk show will mimic the form of a conventional presentation and even fashion bloggers will be invited. Hardy is taking the preparation very seriously. It will however be open to the public and she is adamant that there will be no front row. One thing remains for her to decide, whether or not to appear from behind the scenes at the end of the show. If she does appear, the audience present will no doubt be treated to the vision of Hardy's unique sartorial sensibility.

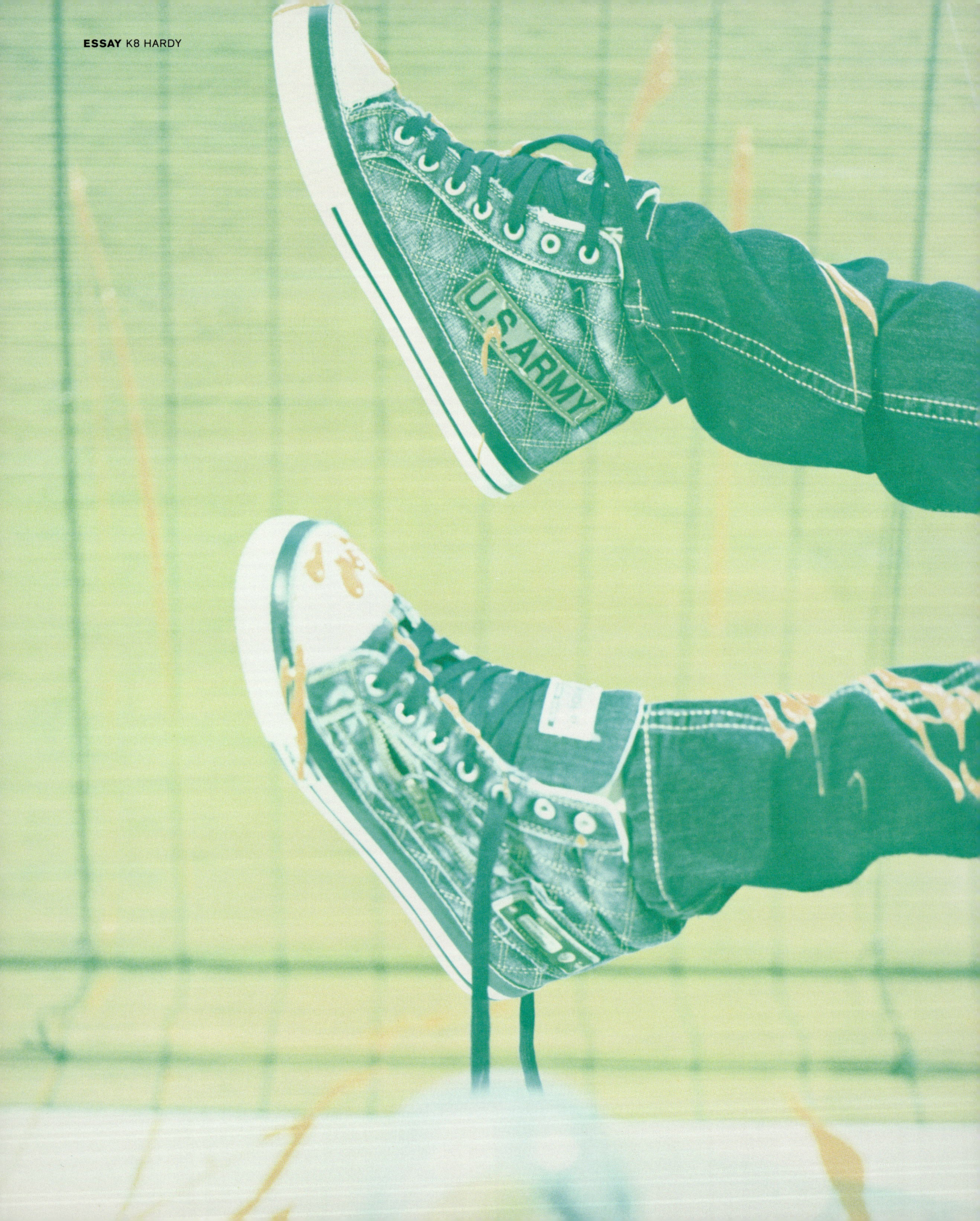

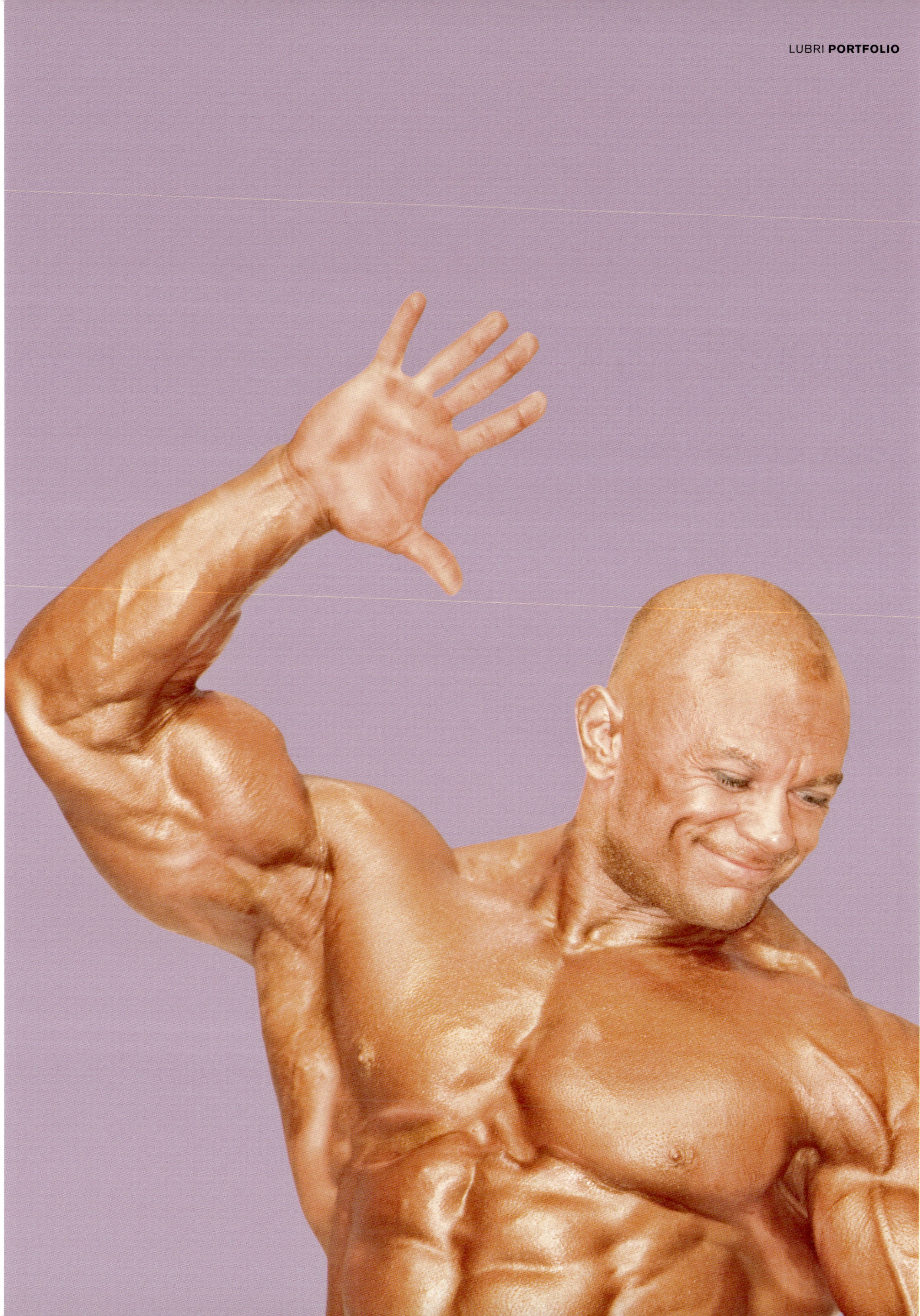

LUBRI Hard Candy Everywhere Lubri goes, he is armed with a semi-amateur film camera, sometimes two. His lens catches almost invariably everything around him, but what attracts him most are the human reactions, the expression, the state of how things are. His snapshots constitute above all a supply of still moments of distilled emotion, caught in milliseconds. Lubri is never overshadowed by distances, emotional or physical, and is always at least a small step into the personal frame of the people he photographs. The lens absorbs images with a voyeuristic passion and an instinctive accuracy of the right moment, even when things lose their clear outline and grace, when the gaze is dazzled by the morning hangover, and madness shines in the eyes of midnight revelers, losers, lovers. In Lubri's shots, everyone is a performer. The *Hard Candy* series is a brief study of facial expressions. The figures are removed from reality in order to outline the bodies of bodybuilders in their sculpture and relief, while the faces are statically grotesque. They are somehow expressive and ecstatic in a baroque way, with expressions that actually do not express anything. Ultimately, this is a choreography of muscle contractions performed in the name of the show, something spectacular on display. What these people are behind their masks of perpetual efforts remains a mystery to us, touching upon the eternal duality of image/identity. An essence which has remained elusive for the visible as ever, leaving fresh marks on the celluloid film. - Lubri is born in Sofia in 1977. His first solo exhibition *Boys Don't Cry* was presented at the Pistolet Gallery in Sofia, 2007. He has also taken part in *Photonic moments*, Ljubljana, Slovenia, 2007; *The Month of Photography* in Vienna and *Persona*, the Institute of Contemporary Art, Sofia, 2010. He was presented by Sariev Gallery in "Background: Young Artists 2011." His photographs have appeared in *Future Images,* by M. Cresci and R. Stern; in *One Magazine's* Selected Works and Events 02-09. *(Vera Mlechevska)*

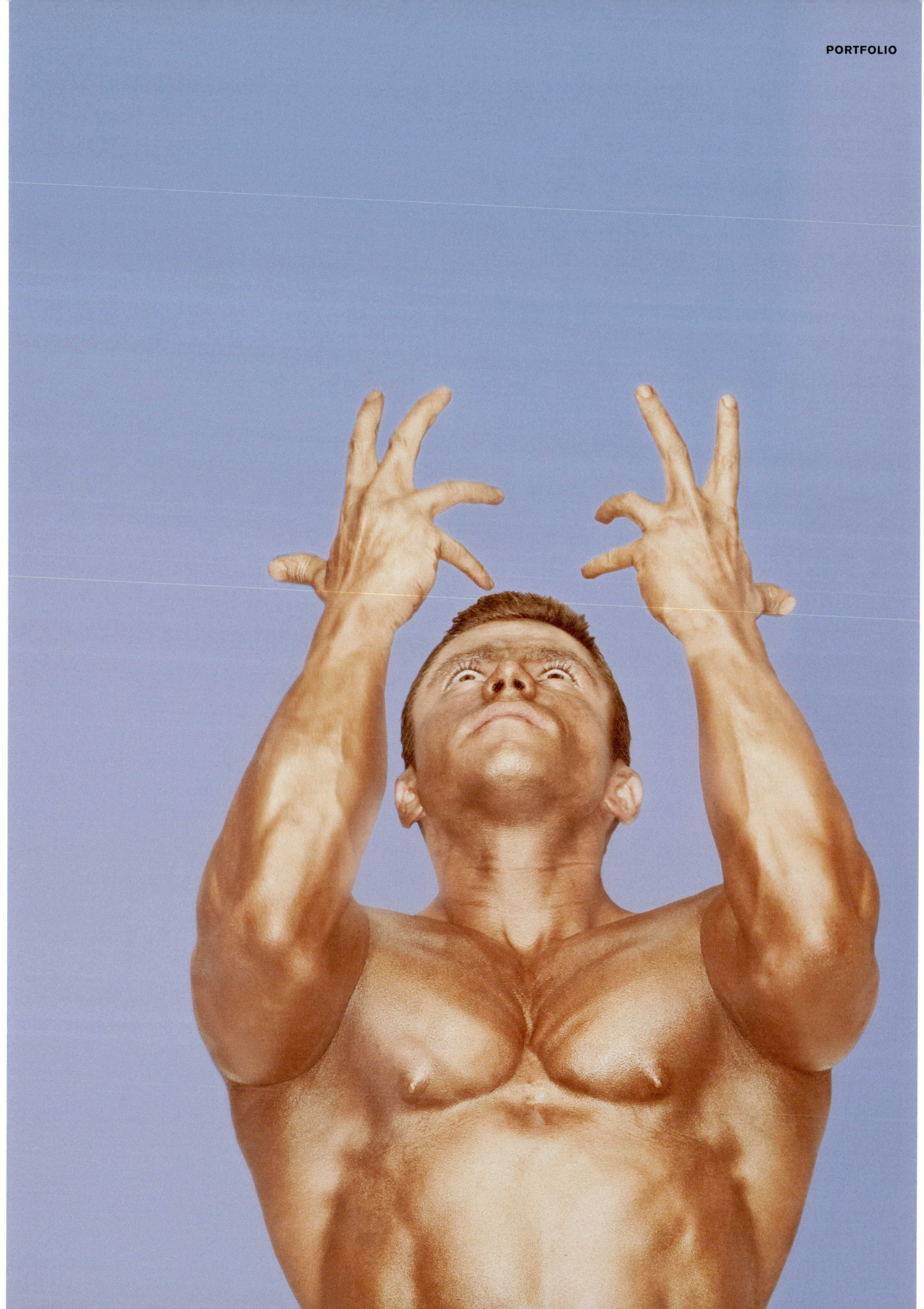

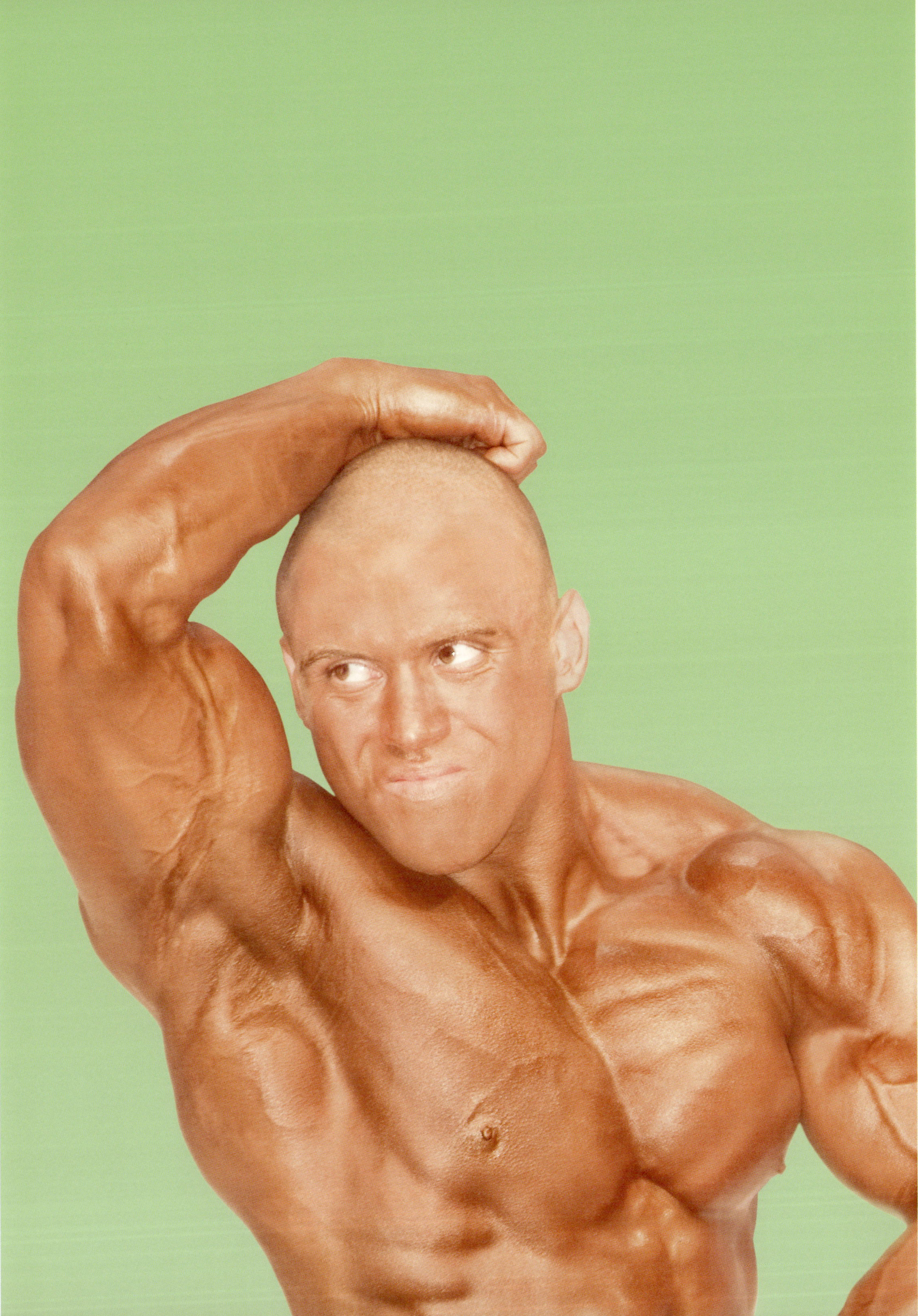

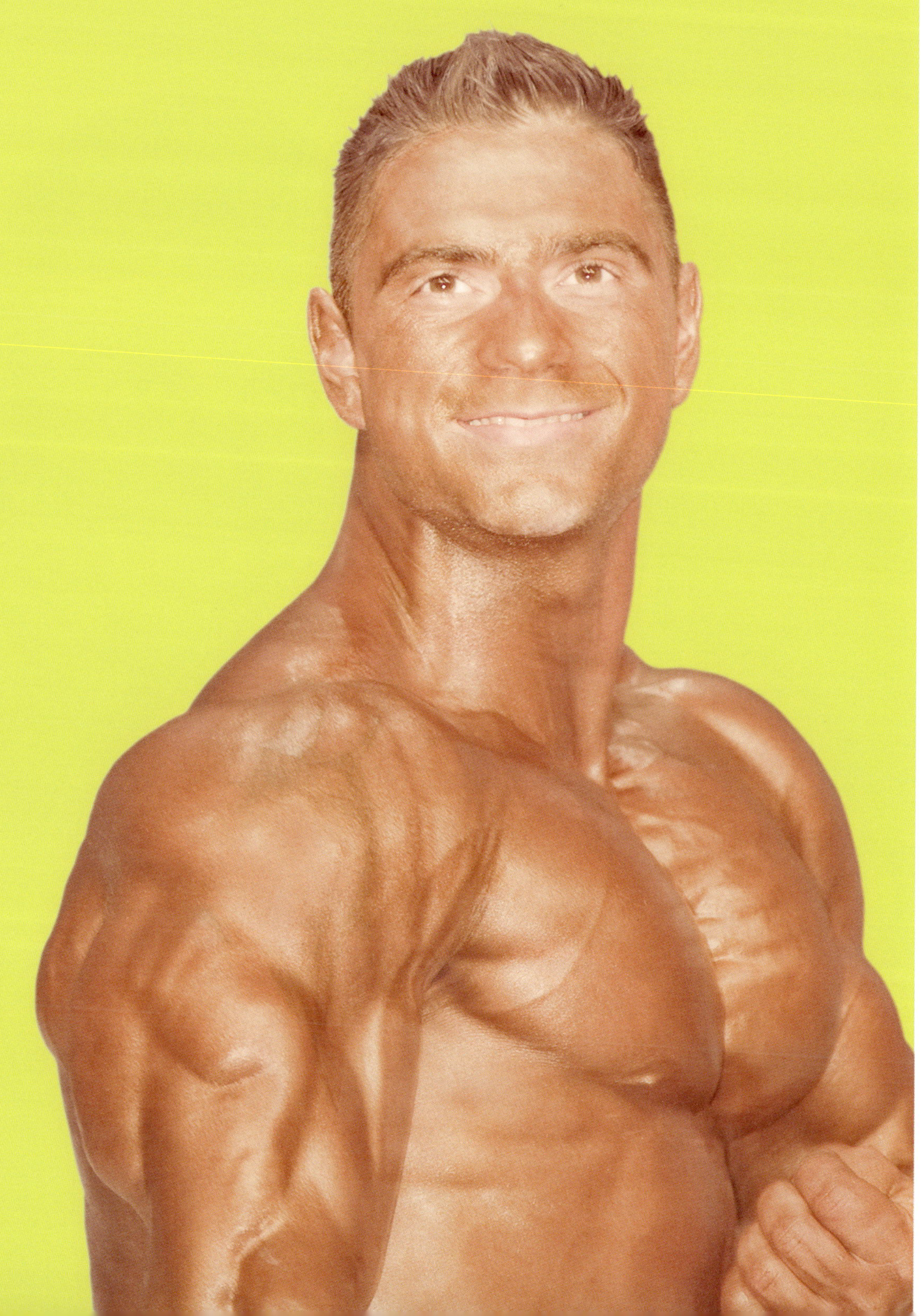

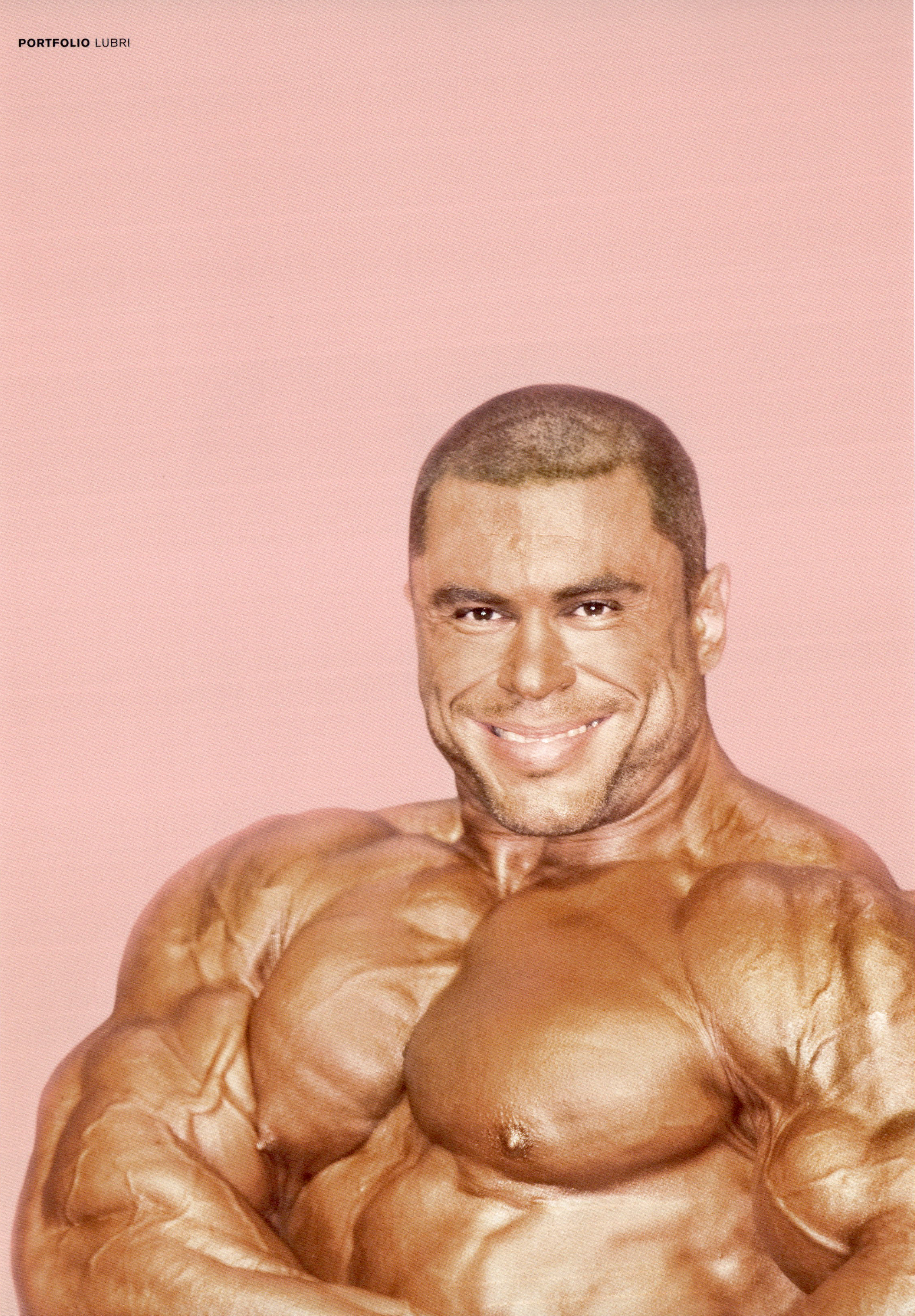

FRANCESCO ZANOT
VISITS THE COLLECTION OF
ERIK KESSELS

Erik Kessels is an art director, graphic designer, curator and publisher based in Amsterdam. He's also a founding partner of communications agency KesselsKramer *(kesselskramer.com.)* As well as its Dutch headquarters, KesselsKramer runs KK Outlet in London. This combined shop, agency and exhibition space opened in January of 2008, and is located in Hoxton Square *(kkoutlet.com.)*

Kessels started collecting amateur photographs around 10 years ago, around the time he edited the first issue of the 'In Almost Every Picture' series for KesselsKramer Publishing *(kesselskramerpublishing.com.)* The agency's in-house publisher now features a catalogue including numerous photobooks and the celebrated magazine *Useful Photography.*

"A photography collection in itself doesn't mean anything to me," Kessels says. "I see the pictures I gather as working material. I use them for publications and exhibitions." He's not searching for flawless pieces of art, but instead finds naivety inspiring, and mistakes worthy of celebration.

"Usually, family pictures are a form of propaganda," Kessels continues. "They try to 'sell' families by making them look as good as possible. I look for errors that tell the truth and make a picture interesting."

A selection from Kessels' collection is exhibited at Foam, Amsterdam, under the title *Album Beauty,* from June 29th to October 14th.

1. FINGER · MANUAL ABILITY Thanks to a simple system consisting of a mirror and a pentaprism, reflex cameras allow their users to see their subjects through the lens instead using a separate viewfinder. The advantage is clear: the end shot is exactly what the photographer saw when he pressed the shutter. It also minimises the risk of running into that peculiar and involuntary form of self-portrait that results from placing a finger on the lens. Henri Cartier Bresson's famously noted that, metaphorically speaking, "To take a photograph is to align the head, the eye and the heart." These pictures show that, actually, photographs are taken with hands.

2. FIVE WOMEN · THE ENEMY One of the most obvious merits of photography is its capacity to record an abundance of details without the photographer being consciously aware of them. Sometimes this can also turn out to be a flaw, as subjects one might have preferred to exclude may live on in the photograph. From a political perspective photography is thus not merely characterized by this form of democracy but also by its inevitable neutrality. A camera is unable to distinguish friends from enemies. There are those, for example, who might imagine that the figure cut from this group portrait of five women is precisely that of a man.

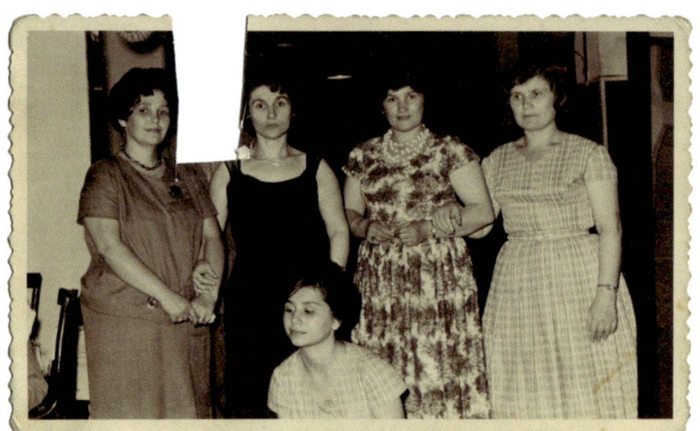

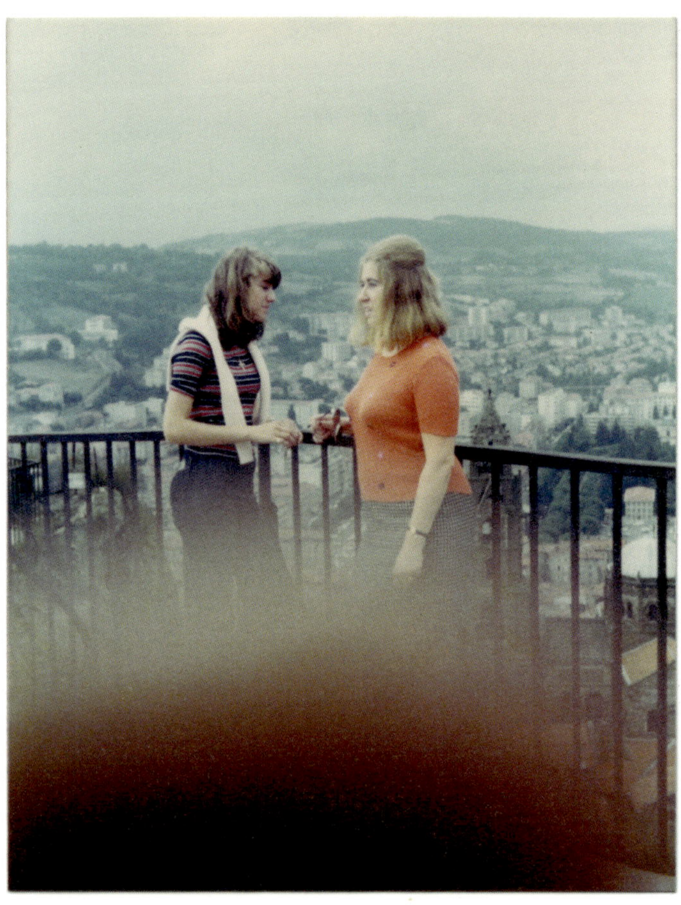

3. PORTRAIT OF A WOMAN · CALLIGRAPHY Every photograph invites the viewer to penetrate it. We must forget that it is a two-dimensional image and advance into the depths of the space it describes. However, all it takes is a stain on its surface to unexpectedly flatten its world and return to the point of departure: the photograph is, first and foremost, an extraordinary exercise in calligraphy.

4. GOOSE · PHOTOMONTAGE If a photograph is a radical reinterpretation of reality, then two are enough to transform reality into science fiction, with women morphing into men, four-footed geese and trees planted in water.

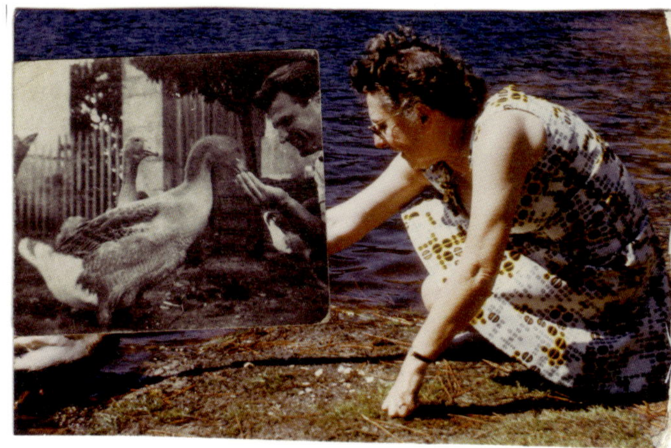

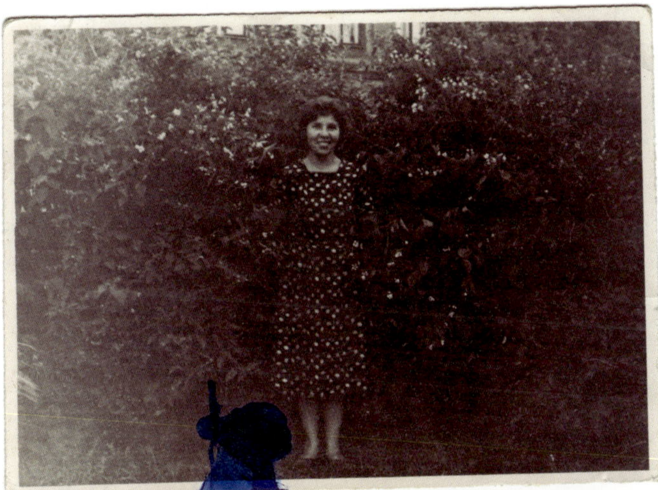

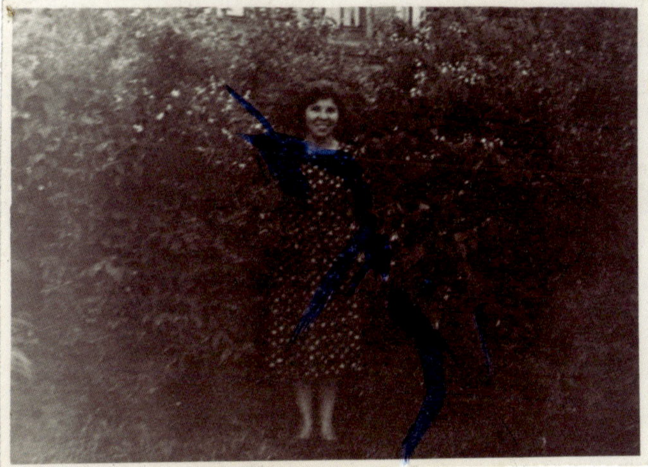

5. THREE MEN - MOVEMENT The fundamental assumption of snapshots is simple: no two can be identical. This is why the superimposition of two or more snapshots inevitably produces dynamism. It is that phenomenon which, in painting terms, forms the basis of Marcel Duchamp's *Nu descendant un escalier*, as well as numerous Futurist works. This is why, if we observe the first man on the left of the three individuals portrayed in this photograph, we see him opening and closing his mouth or vice versa.

6. STAPLES - TORTURE The photograph is a subtle form of torture. It forces us to look at the past, triggering an inevitable comparison with the present. It is a process it shares with any other memory-preserving apparatus, from museums to diaries. At the root of our suffering lies our absolute certainty that, in the very second we observe the image, anybody or anything that is shown there has either aged or no longer exists.

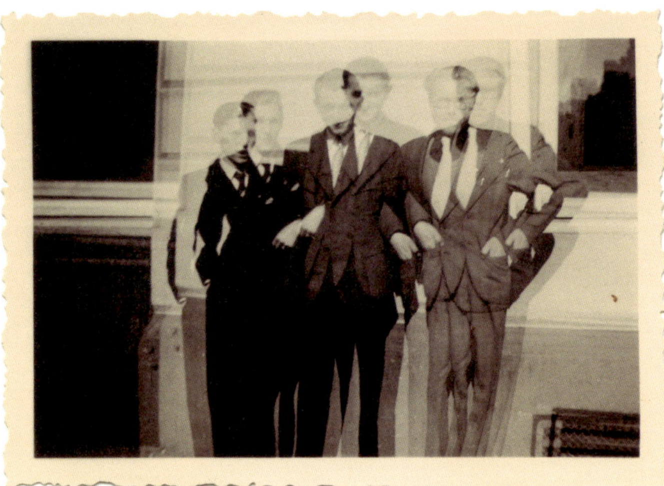

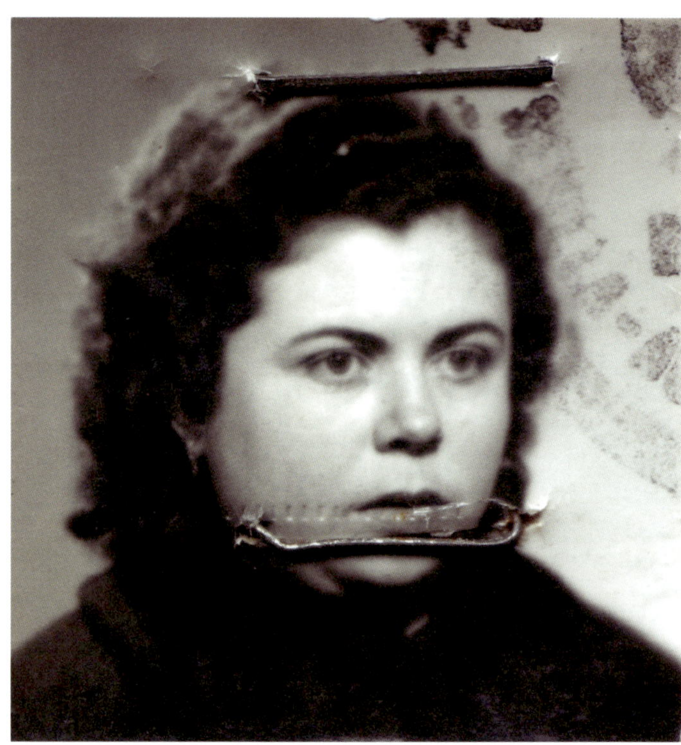

7. FAMILY - THE SMILE The smile is the most damning of the curses of family photography. It means our albums lack the broad range of feelings and appetites that friends and relatives are able to communicate. The result is scores of private records that show vast swaths of humanity all forcing themselves to look happy. This is true to the point that the appearance of some menacing dark patches around the only unsmiling individual in this photograph does not seem wholly accidental. It is as though the child in question, having felt some strange premonition, had tightened his lips and crossed his legs.

8. PINEAPPLE - DISTRACTION A powerful device for focusing the attention of the observer on a specific subject, the photograph can work just as efficiently in order to distract him. The intense expression in the eyes of the woman leaning to the left edge of the frame, the geometrical silhouette of the sweater she wears, and the pineapple in the centre seem to have been placed there on purpose so that we center our eyes from the elongated form of the ear of the girl who is holding in her hand the most common of tropical fruits.

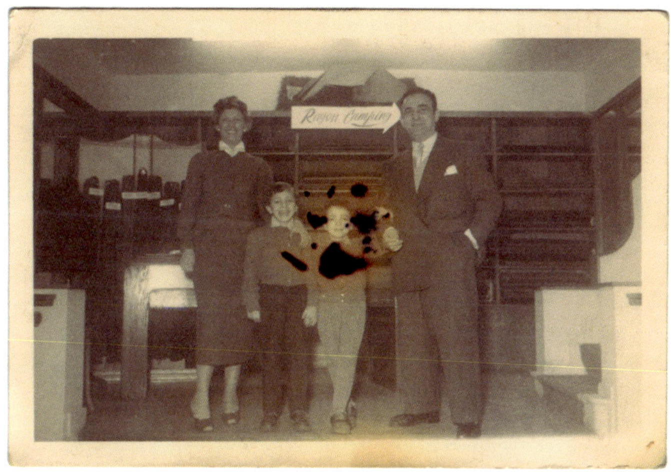

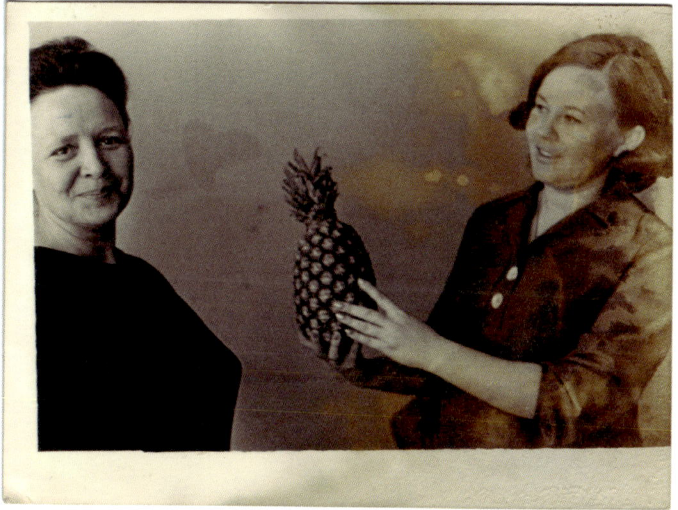

9. IN THE GARDEN - LIGHT Every photograph is, first and foremost, the result of a specific metering of light. The action of light causes an image to emerge on sensitive film and yet, at the same time, it can bleach it to the point of making it dissolve altogether should its intensity or duration be increased. Light is the supreme deity of photography: it is the only factor that, by itself alone, can both generate and destroy it.

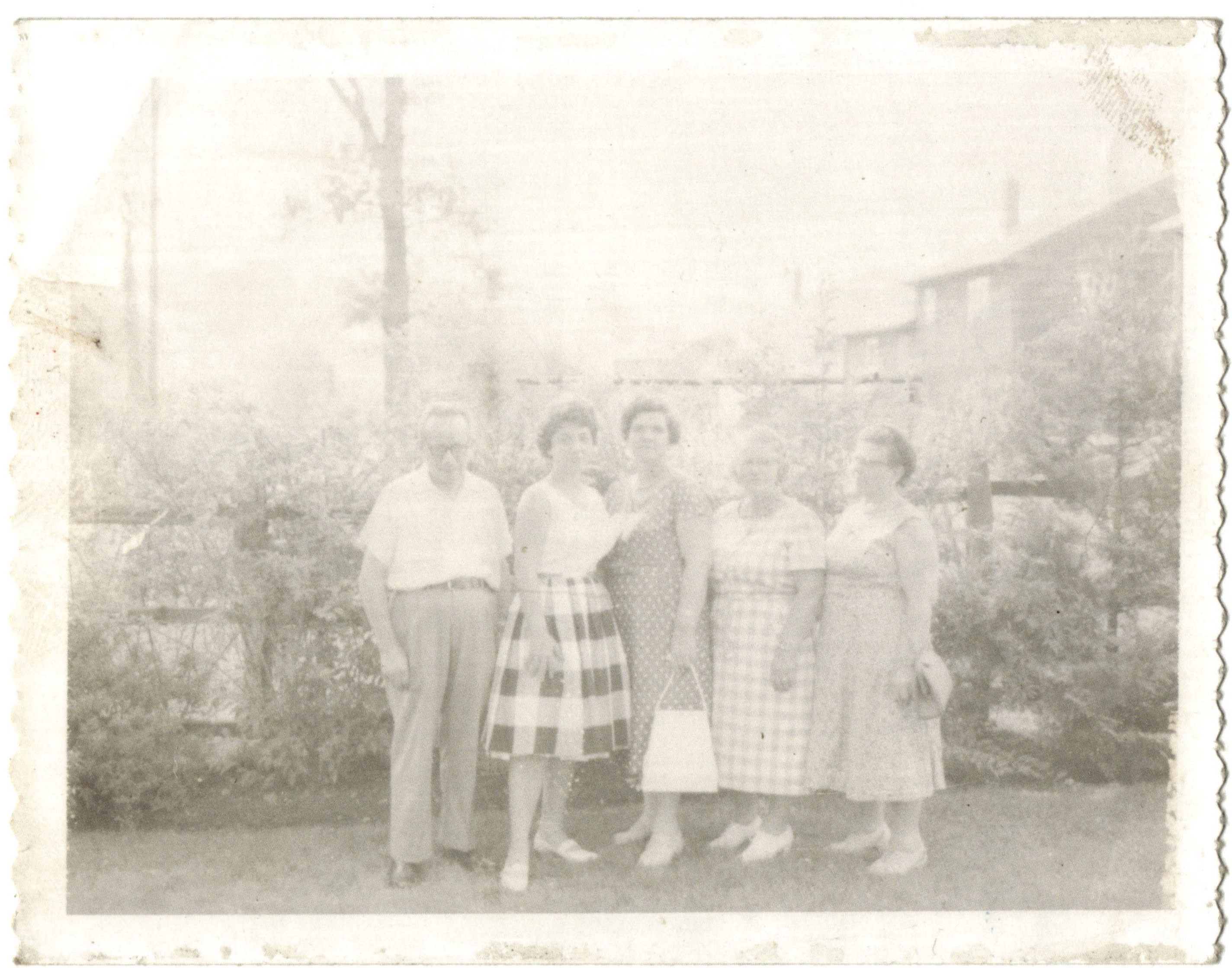

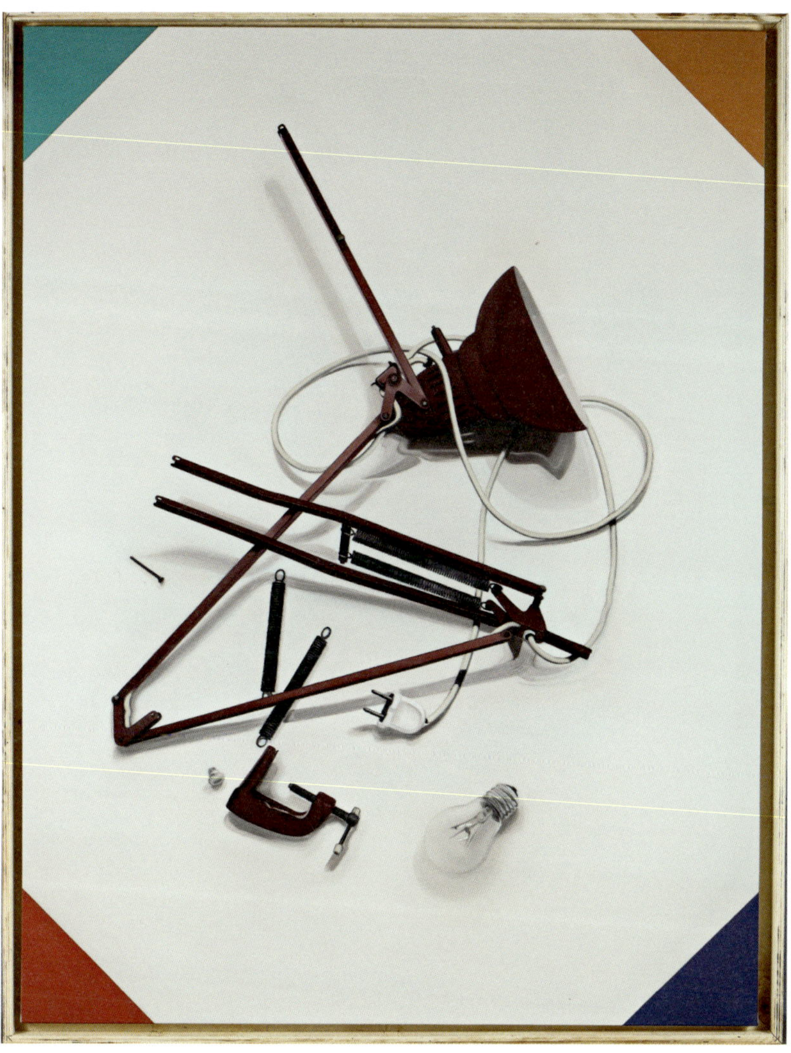

LEYLA GEDIZ

The representation of images in the world of Leyla Gediz is constructed in a way that simultaneously commemorates and confuses personal and collective memory.

The paintings are conceptually based, with a critical eye that personalizes as if to create a 'diary' of occurrences, of ephemera, of relationships, the underflow of currents and the means in which these all connect to the artist herself. She invites us into her world, a world most often materialized with oil and acrylic paints, though she also works with installation.

Her experiments hint at a psychological distance that is oft-times fragmentary. Isolation and intimacy meet in close proximity, as if to dialogue from disparate but contingent vantage points. As such we find the source images decontextualized from its physical reality to bridge pathways to a more psychological realm.

Gediz was born in 1974 in Istanbul, where she is currently based. She studied at Slade School of Fine Arts, and received her MA in Visual Arts from Goldsmiths College, University of London. Her work has been exhibited internationally, including Rampa Gallery, Istanbul; HIAP's Cable Gallery, Helsinki, Fabian Claude Walter Galerie, Zürich; Roberts & Tilton, Culver City, California' and the National Museum of Women in the Arts, Washington, DC. She also works as an independent curator.

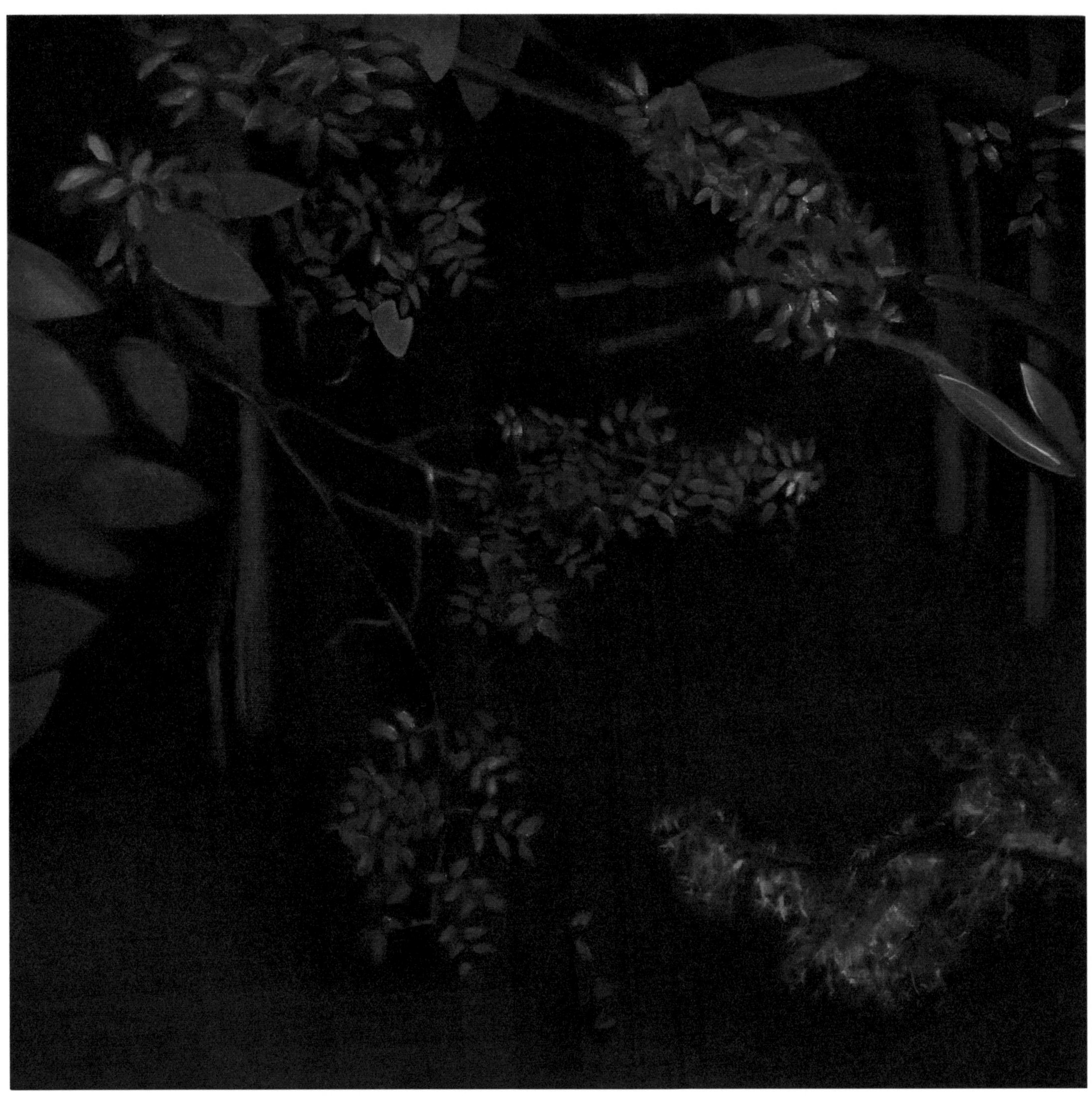

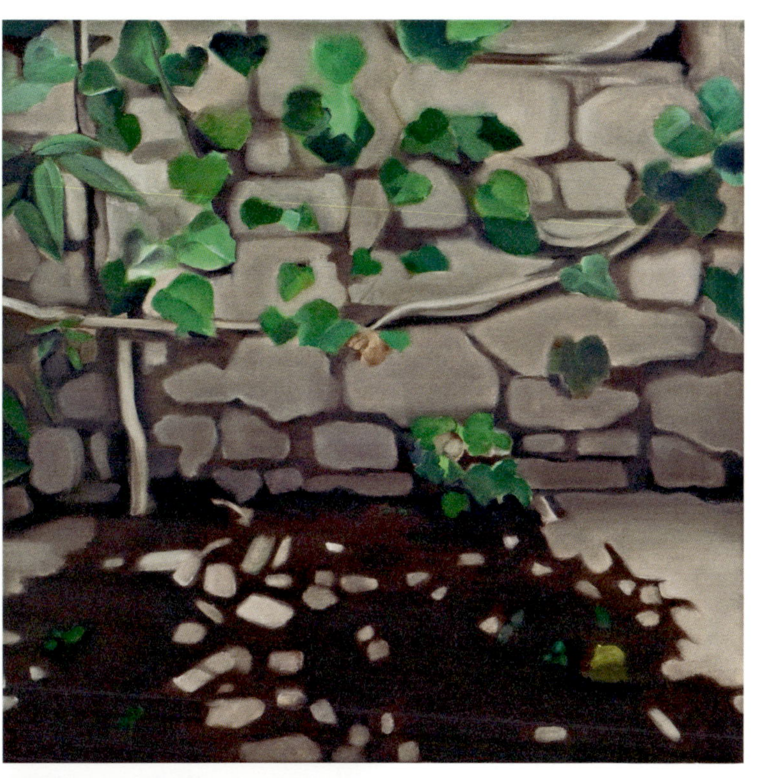

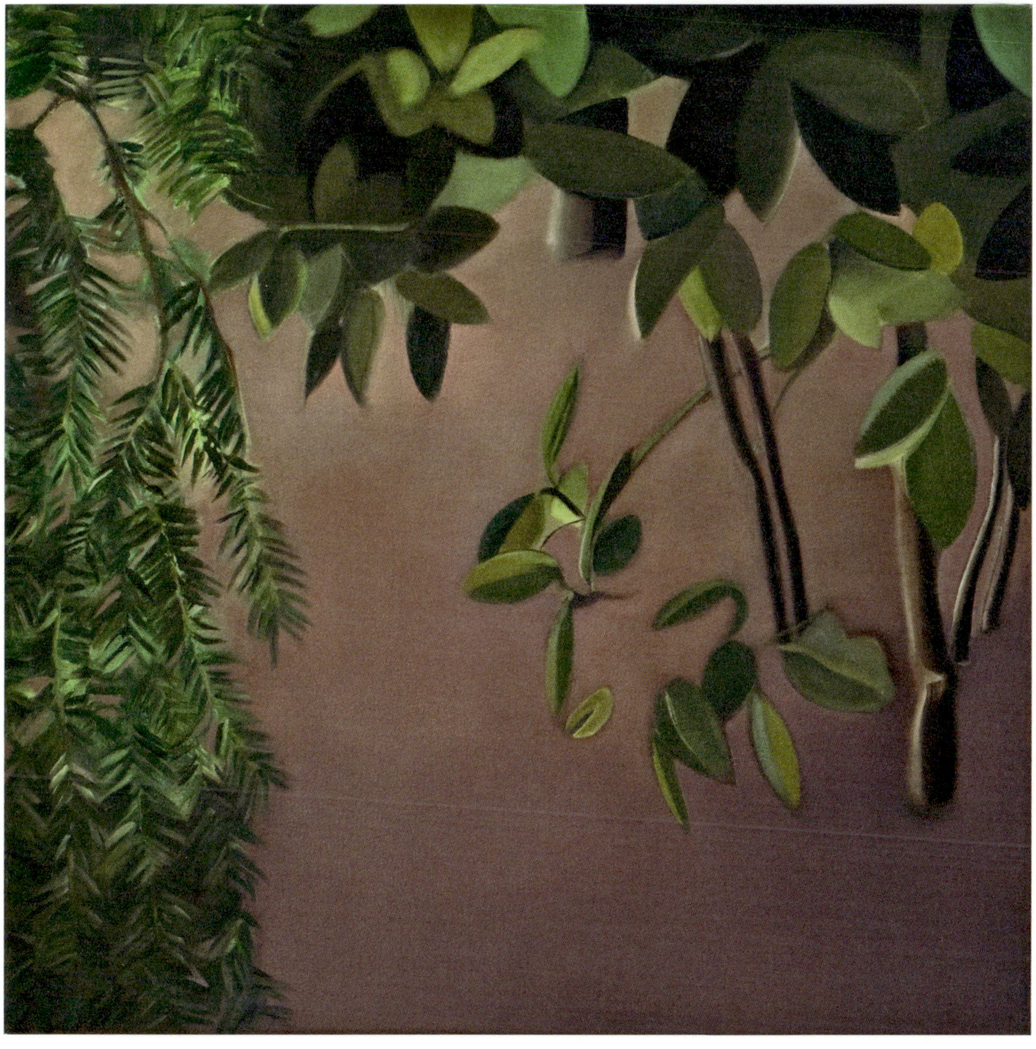

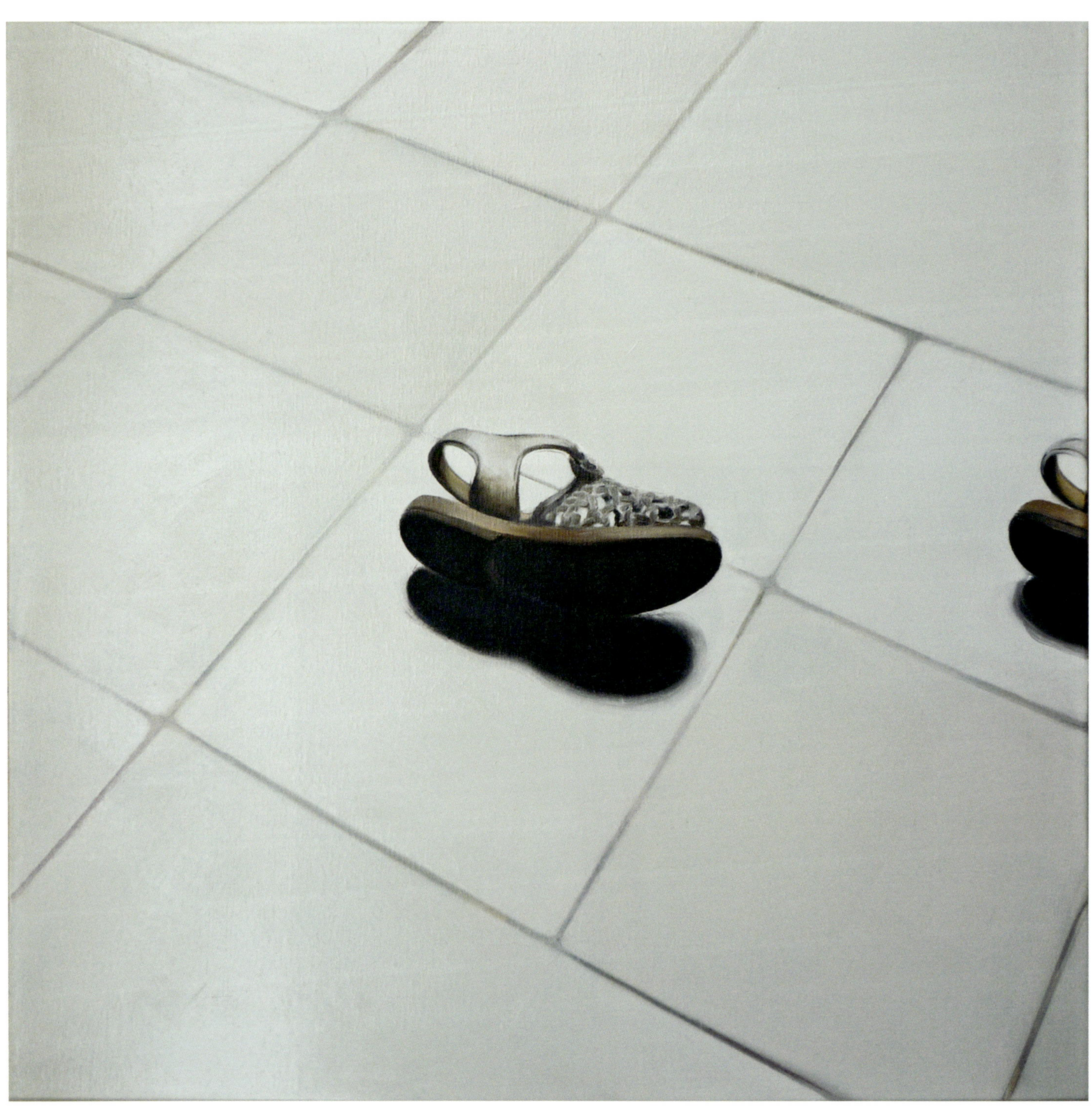

Page 71 Death of an Acrobat, 2009, *cm 170 x 126, oil on canvas. Page 72* A Darkling Garden (22.08.2011), 2011, *cm 50 x 50, oil on canvas. Page 73 above* A Darkling Garden (15.08.2011), 2011, *cm 50 x 50, oil on canvas, below* A Darkling Garden (7.08.2011), 2011, *cm 50 x 50, oil on canvas. Above* Echo, 2010, *cm 50 x 50, oil on canvas. Right* No me mientas, 2011, *cm 130 ø, oil on canvas. Page 76* Your Ghost, 2011, *cm 240 x 165, oil on canvas. Page 77* Paraphernalia, 2011, *cm 120 x 120, oil on canvas. All images © the artist, courtesy the artist and Rampa Gallery, Instanbul*

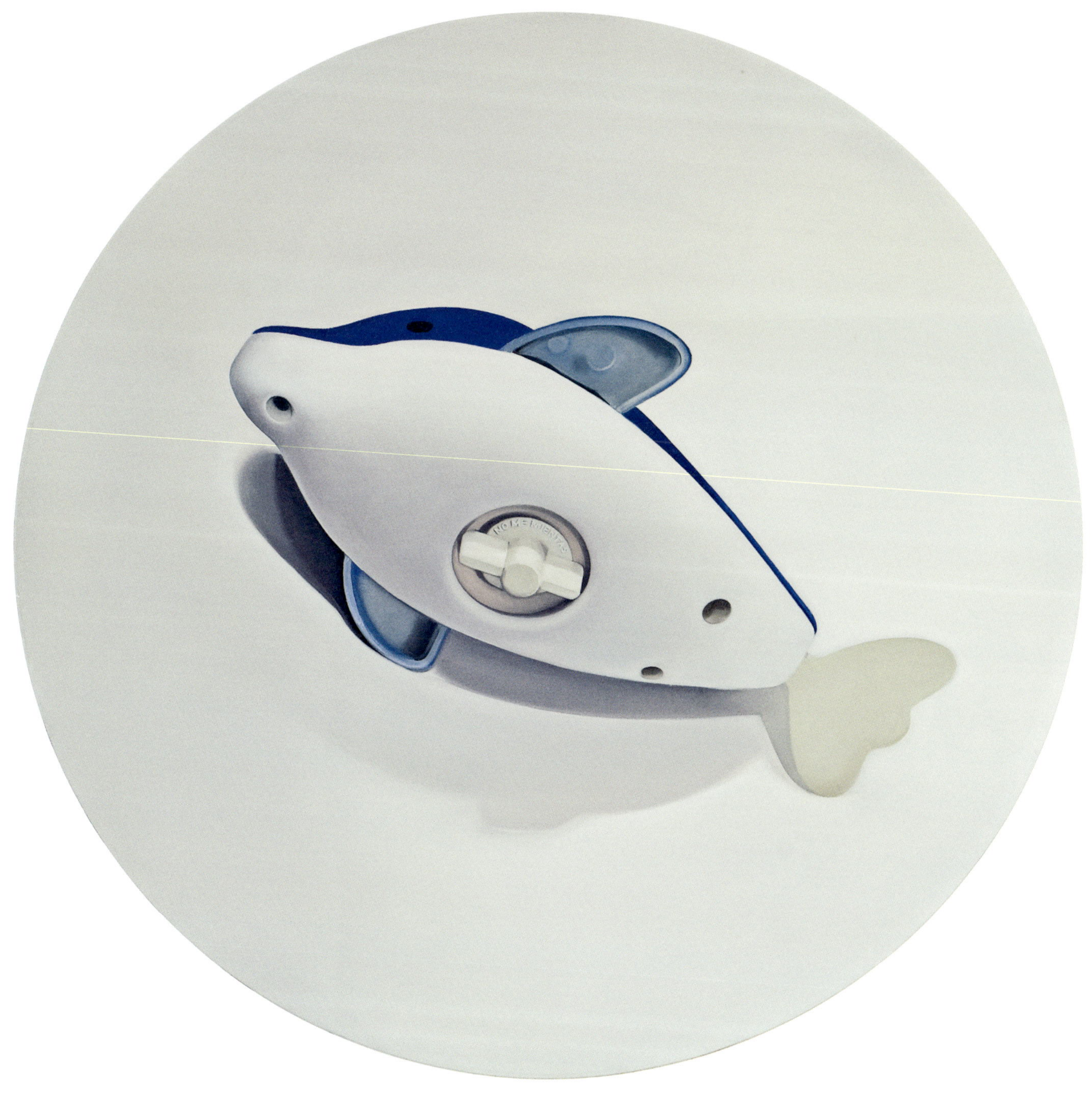

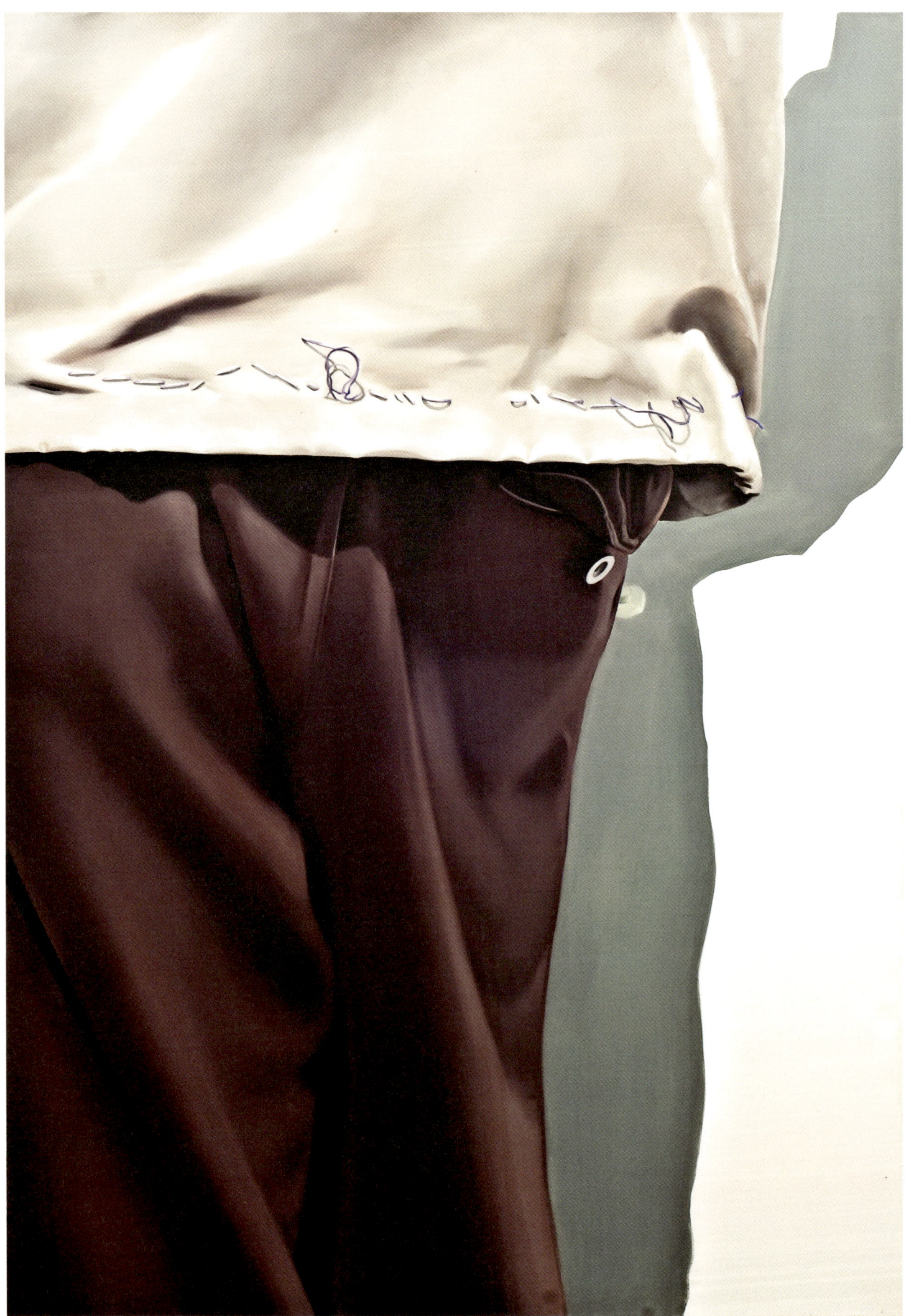

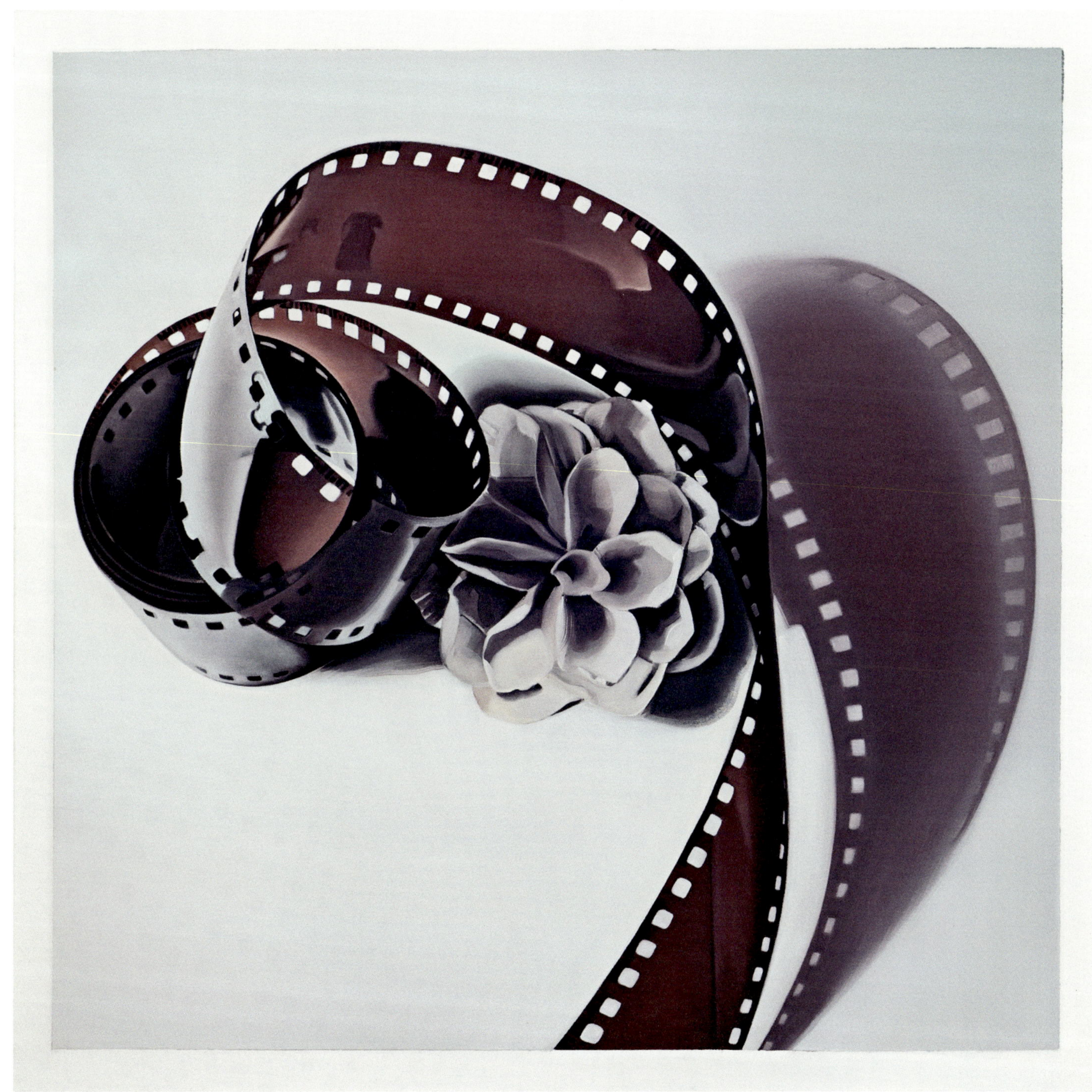

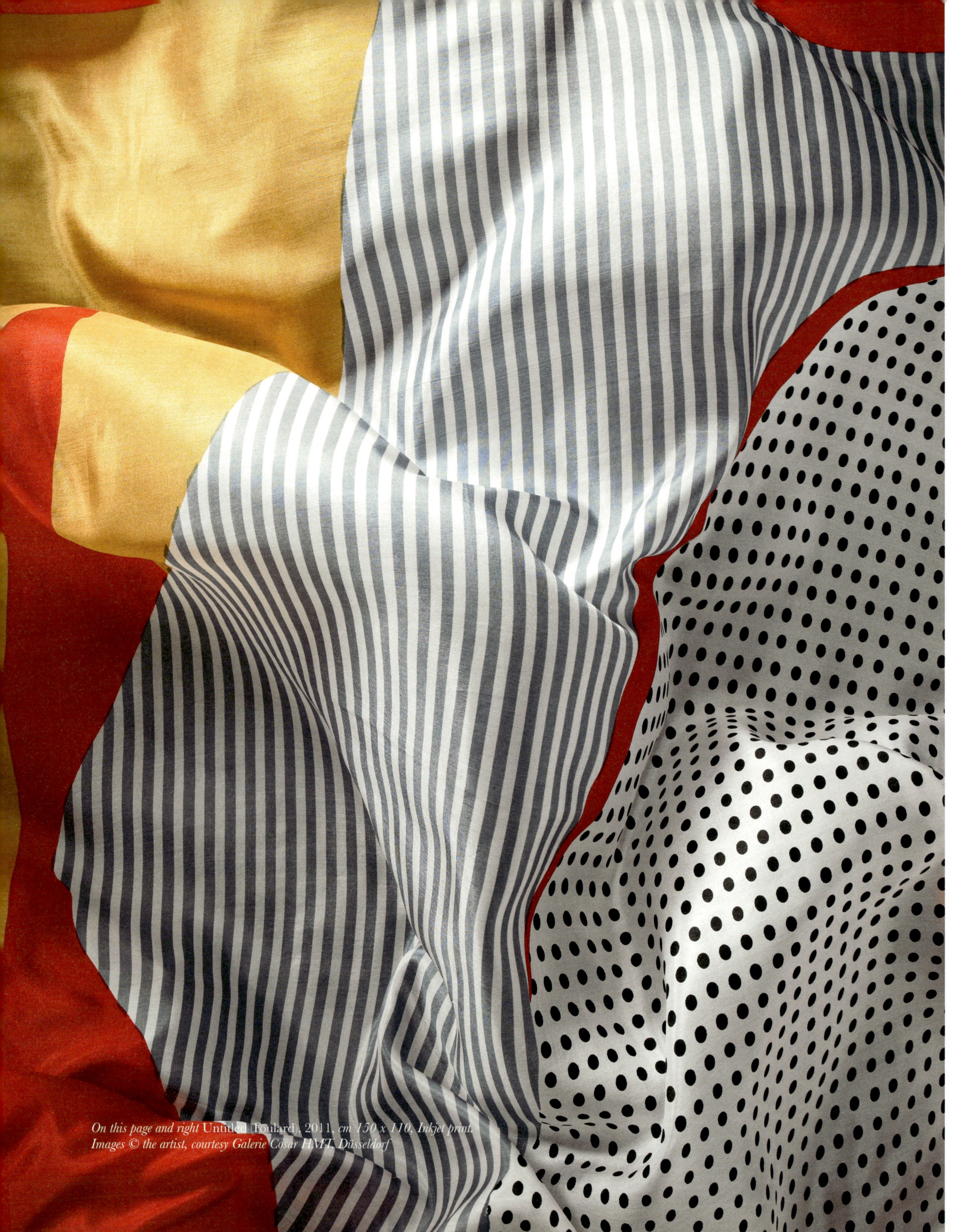

On this page and right *Untitled (Foulard), 2011, cm 150 x 110, Inkjet print.*
Images © the artist, courtesy Galerie Cosar HMT, Düsseldorf.

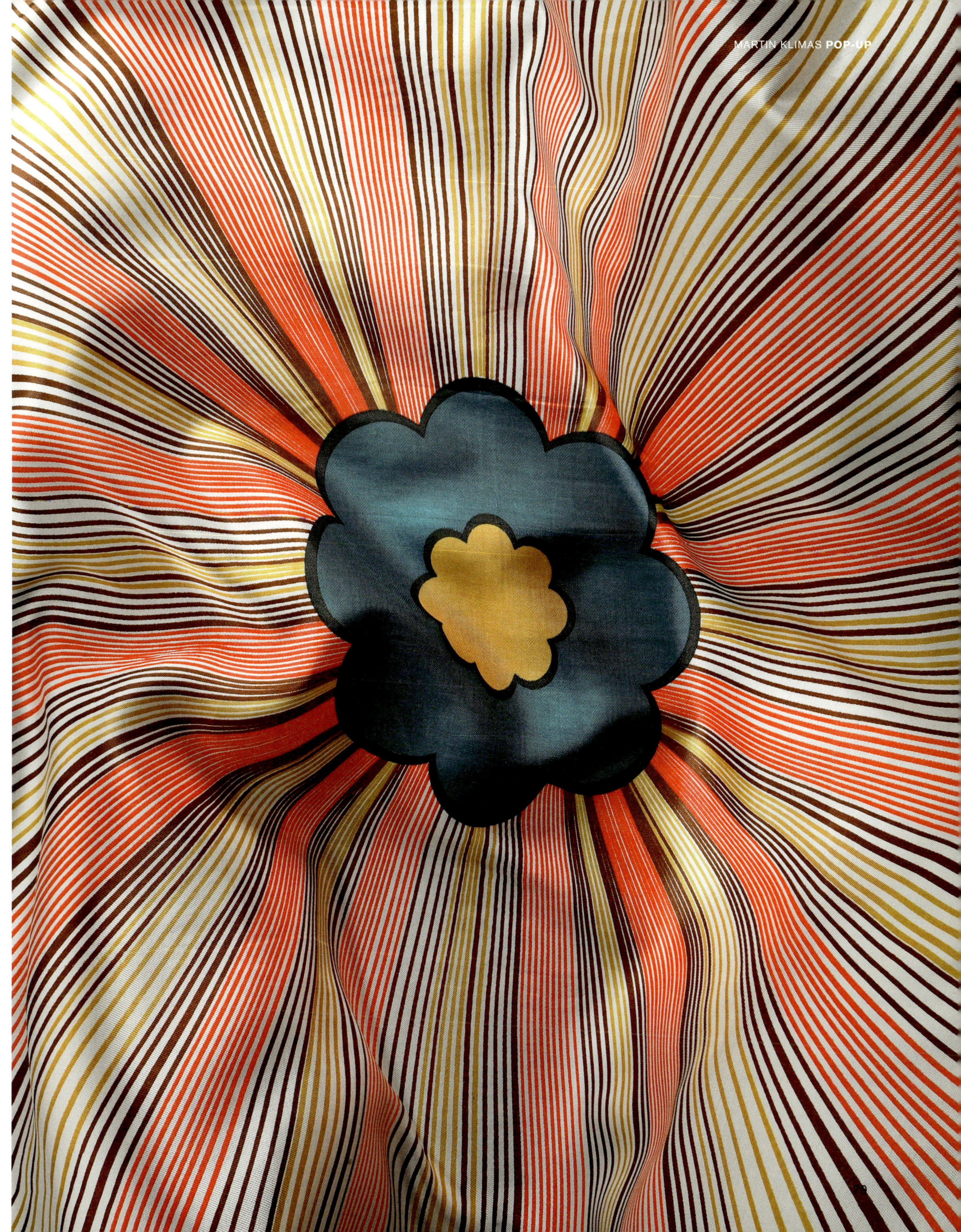

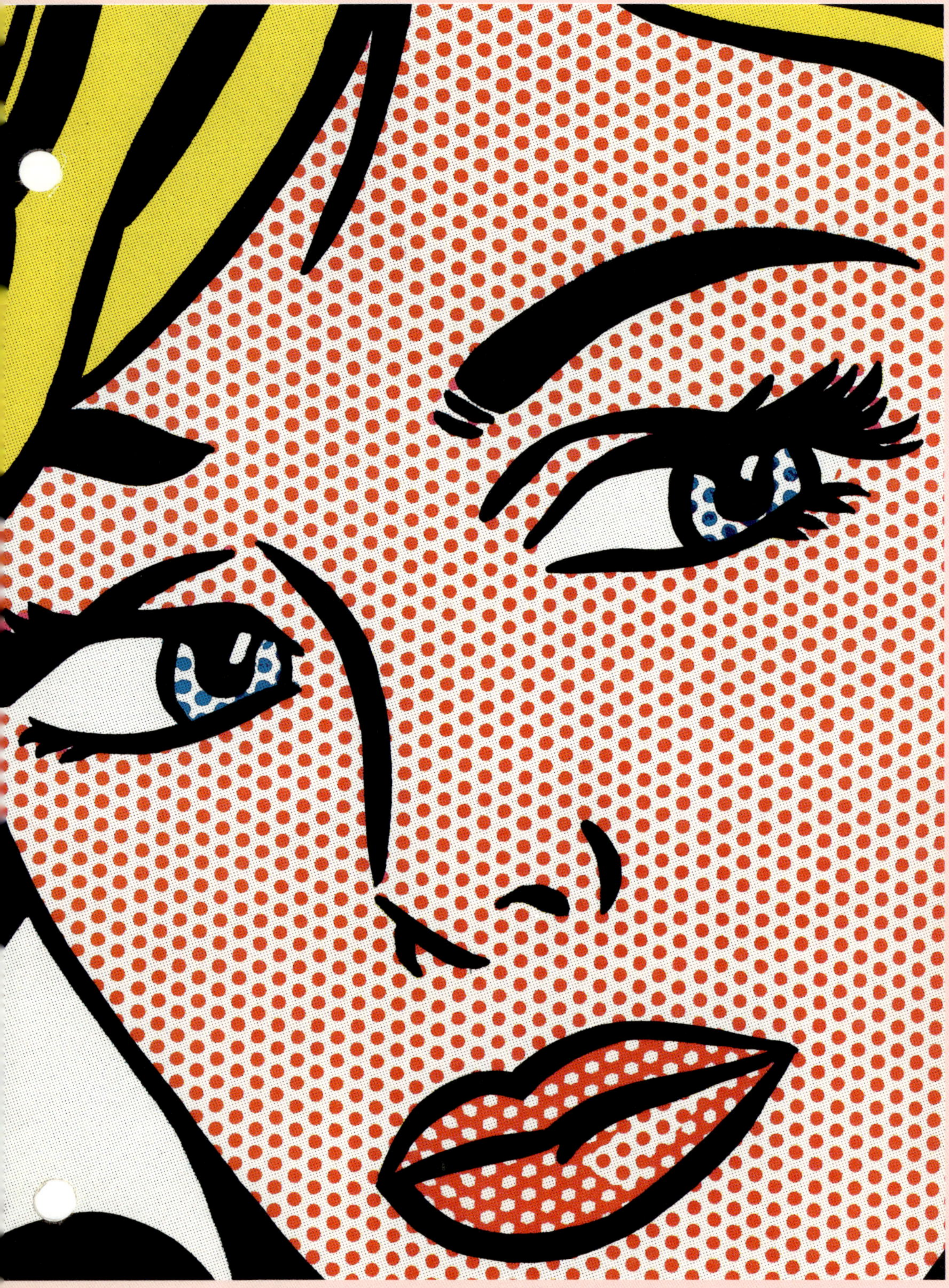

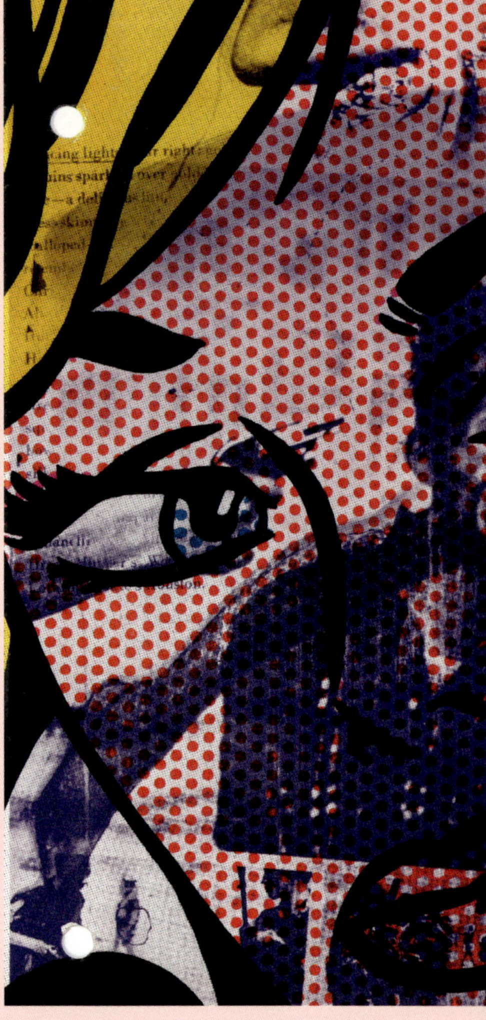

The unfolding changing cover of Art of the Sixties, *detail from* M Maybe (A Girl's Picture), *Roy Lichtenstein 1965*

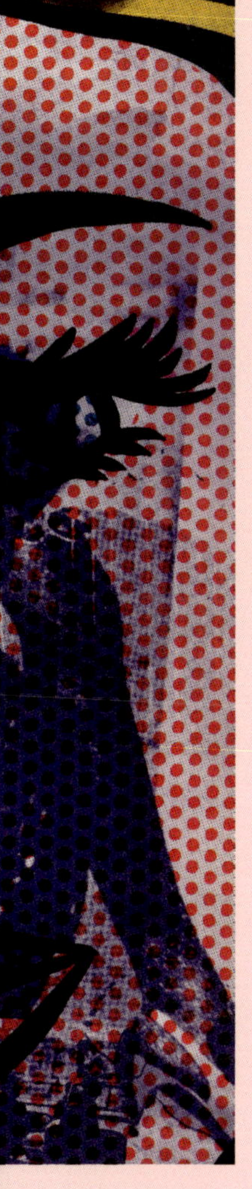

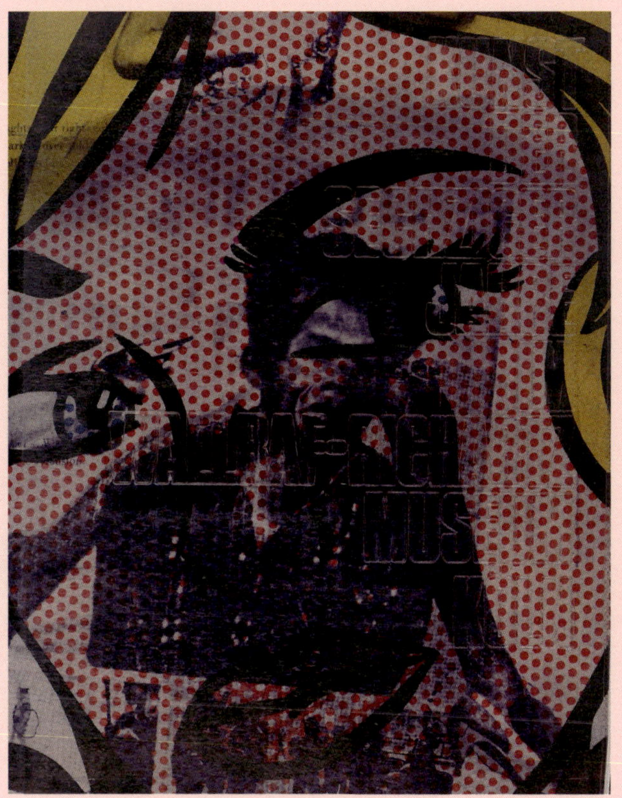

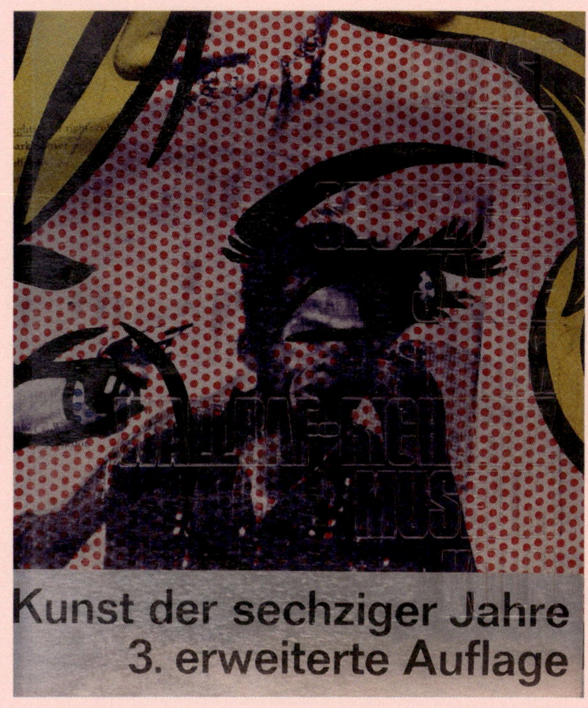

SAMLUNG LUDWIG:
ART OF THE SIXTIES
sampled by Ginevra Elkann

I ran into this beautiful book at the Karma bookstore in New York, run by very talented graphic designer Brendan Dugan. I fell in love. I had never seen a catalogue like this. Testimonial of late 1960's graphic design at its absolute best. The first publication was created by artist Wolf Vostell to document the collection of Peter and Irene Ludwig (of the eponymous museum in Cologne.) Produced in five expanding editions between January 1969 and November 1971, the catalogue is a true design object. It is wrapped in vinyl covers with a Plexiglas spine and stainless steel screw binding. Inside it has transparent pages with black and white artist portraits and an encyclopedic content of art of the Sixties as collected by the Ludwigs. All photographs of the paintings are glued on kraft paper, representing more than 200 works. This volume is rare, it has many dimensions and reads in so many ways, more like an installation than a book.

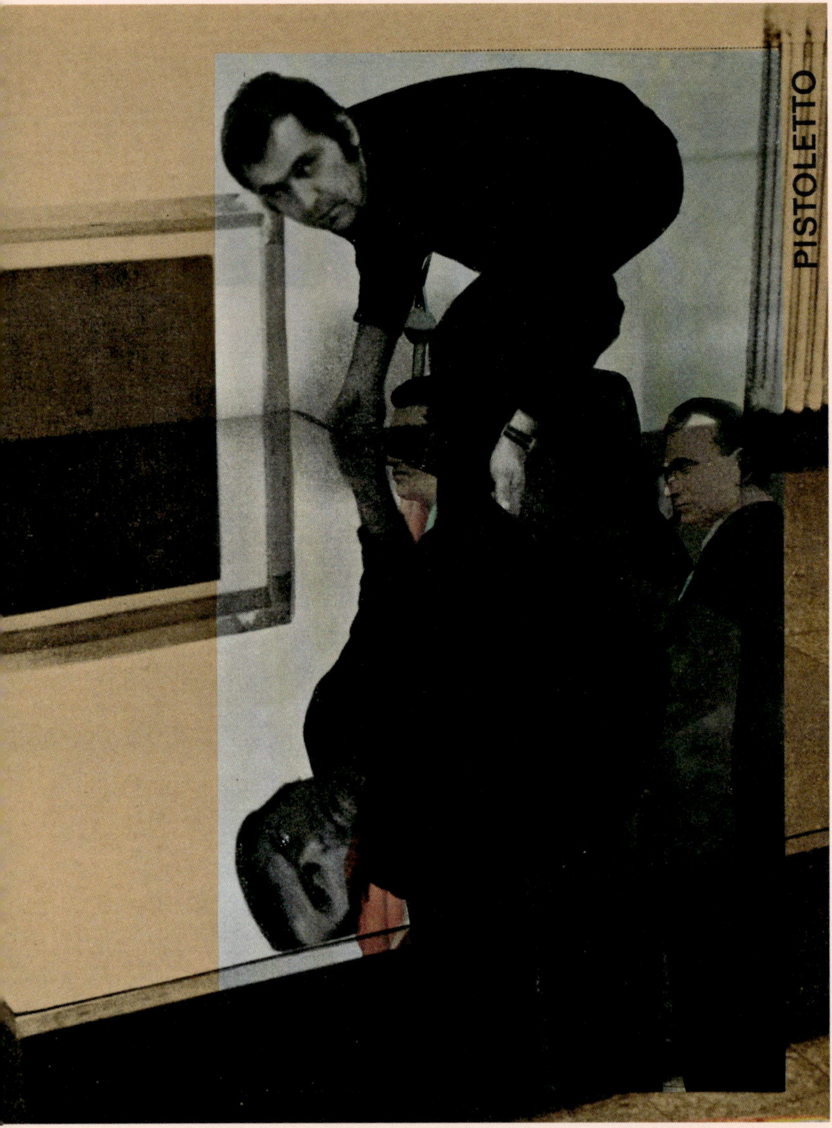

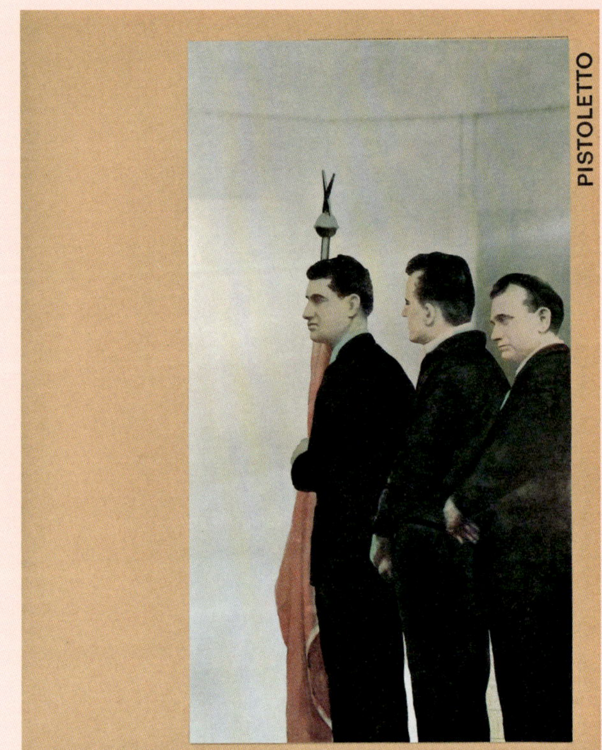

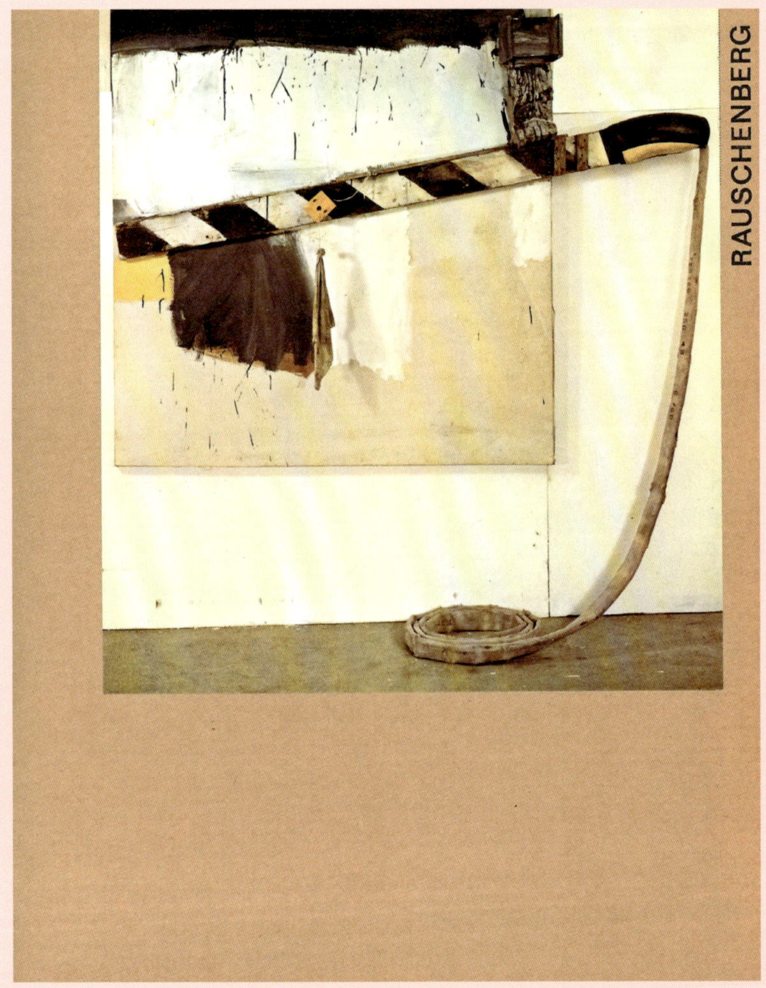

Above and top right Michelangelo Pistoletto, Comizio n 2, 1965, *cm 215 x 120, collage. Right and next page,* Roy Rauschenberg, Wall Street 1961, *cm 182 x 226, combine painting.*

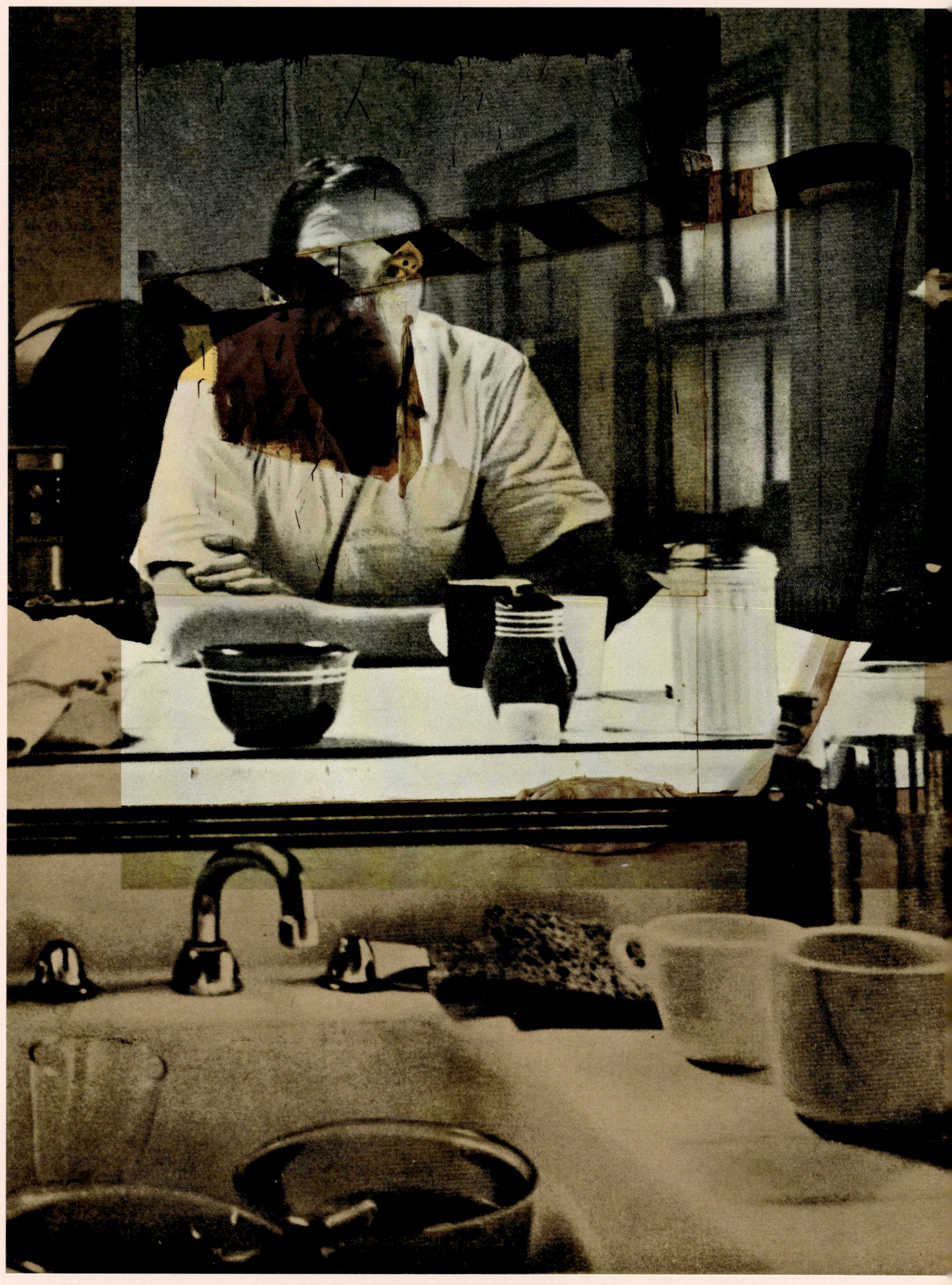

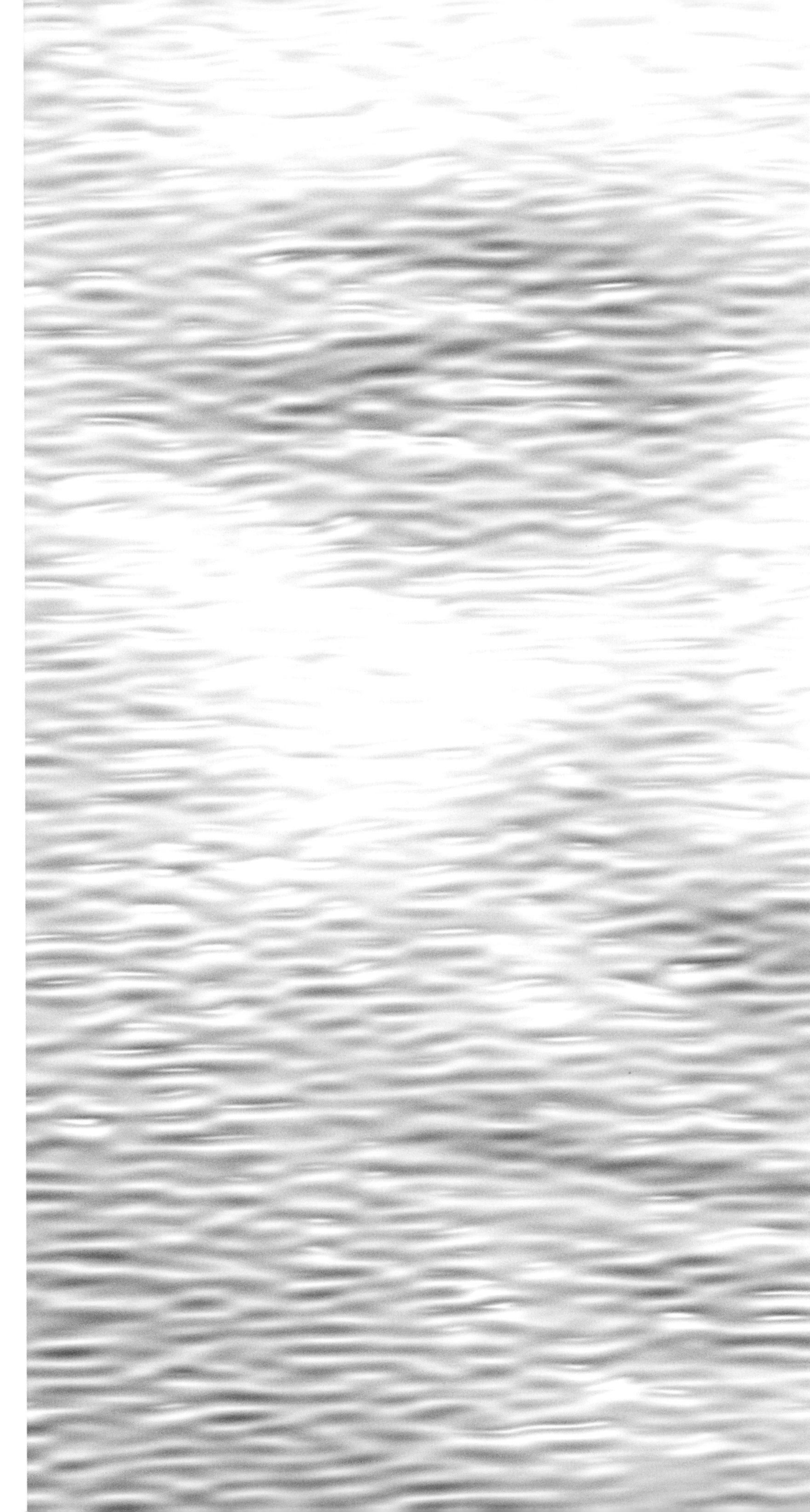

PAUL THOREL These hazy, ambiguous images call to mind the scrambled transmissions of a pre-digital television era; and appropriately so, as their 'shifting' nature are a recurring aesthetic and conventional code that informs the artist's larger practice. These digital and often large-scale works pose more questions to the viewer than they offer conclusive answers, forcing one to read between the obscured details, seeking hints or allusions to original subject matter, which may range from portraiture and group scenes, landscape, and also still lifes. Thorel works in a way that is entirely transgressive to traditional, representational photography. In the series Un - Vrai - Semblables his method is particular: using the original image as a launching point, it is then superimposed and displaced by other pictures, each layer transposing the next. What results is a distortion made from hundreds of various overlays, creating a ruptured version of an original entity. As such, the viewer is led to re-evaluate their methods of 'seeing' and 'reading' pictures, and even furthermore led to question their methods of evaluation, launching the photographs then into a psycho-emotional realm. - Born in London, 1956, Thorel embarked as a painter and began experimenting with computer imaging technology in 1980, becoming one of the first artists to focus exclusively on photography and new media. Thorel has had solo exhibitions in Naples' National Archaeological Museum; the French Institute in Florence; and the Turin International Biennial for Photography, among others and in group exhibitions including Photo Espana; The Aperture Foundation; the Philadelphia Museum of Art; and the Tampa Museum of Art. He lives and works in both Naples and Paris.

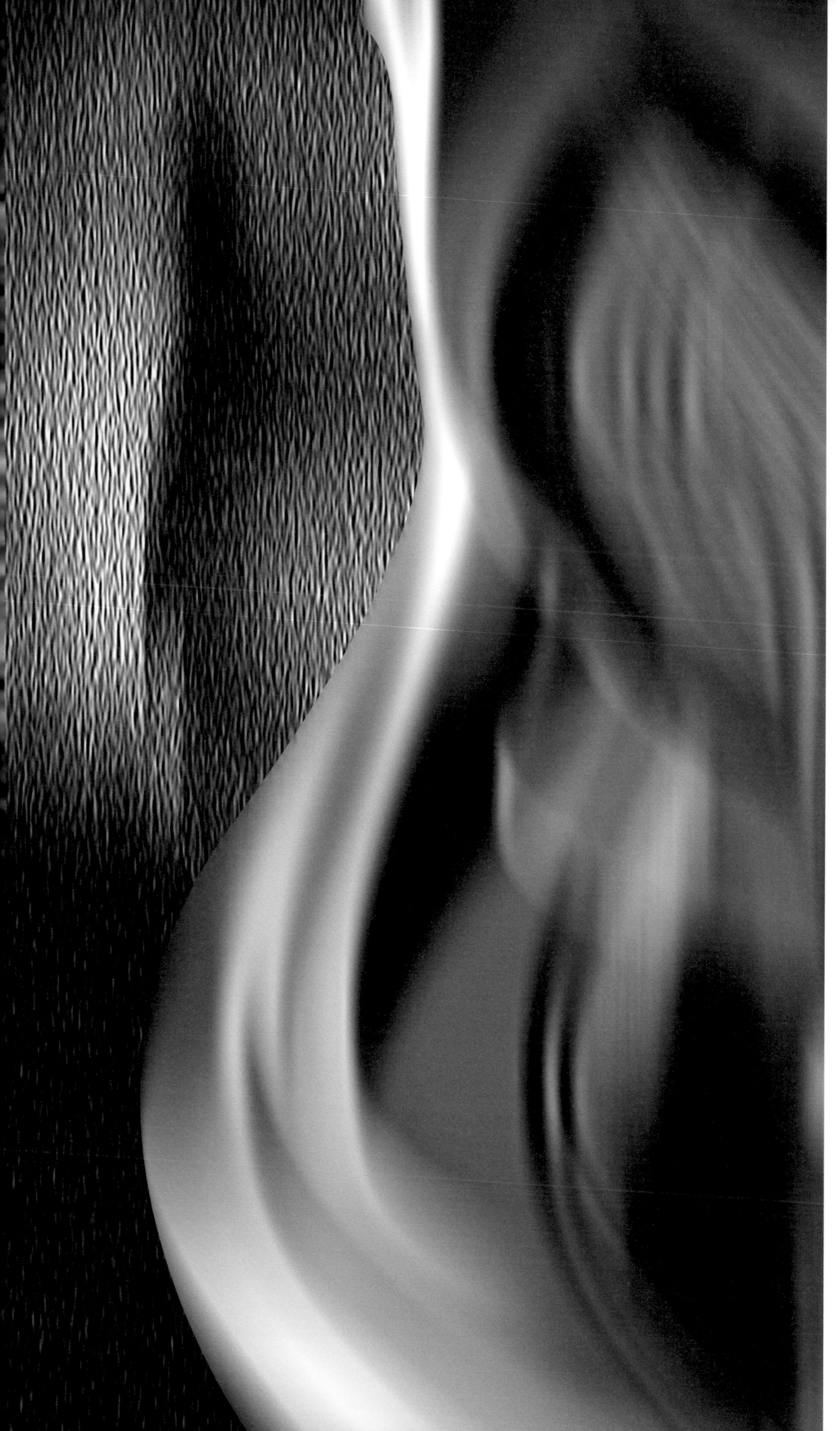

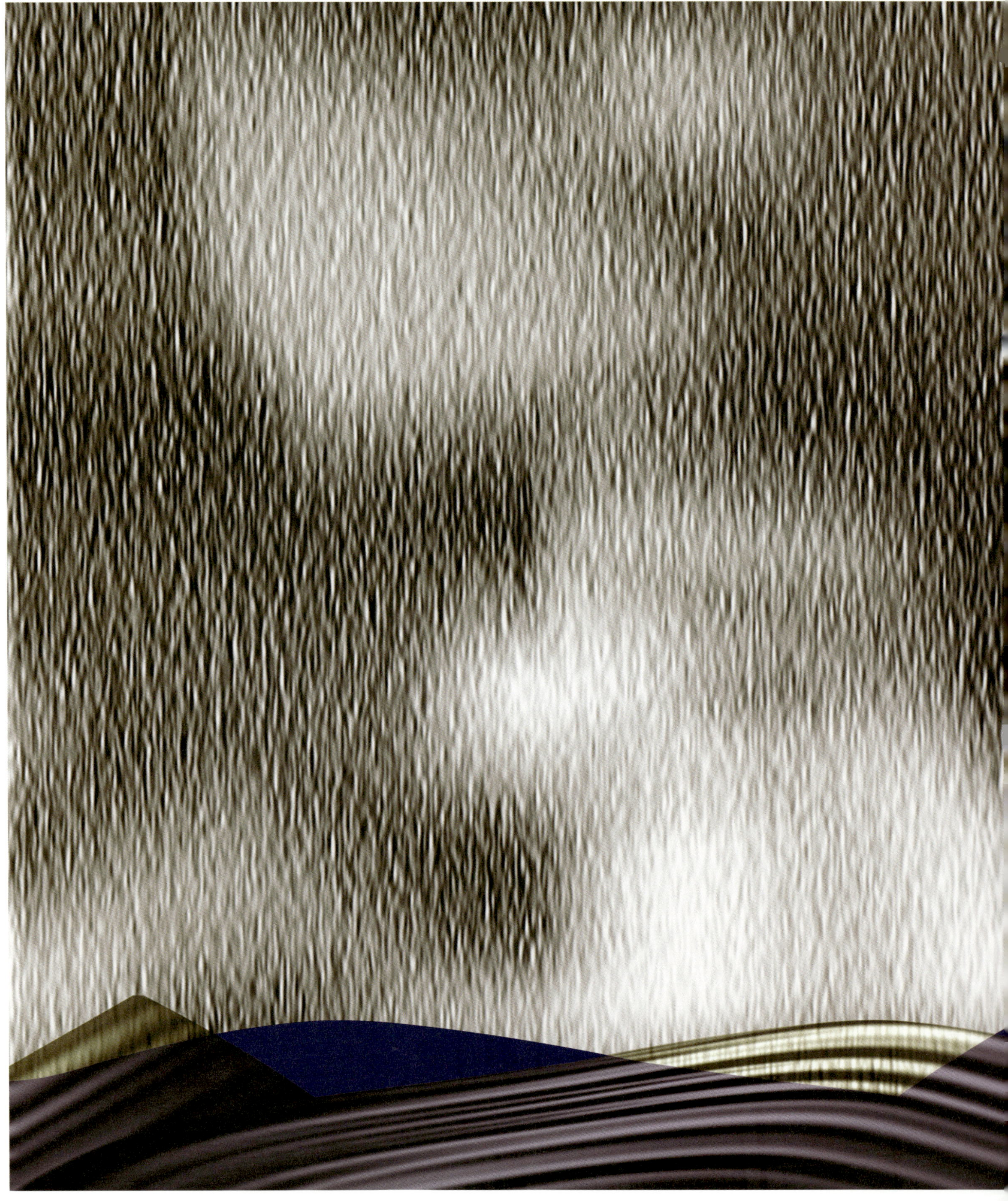

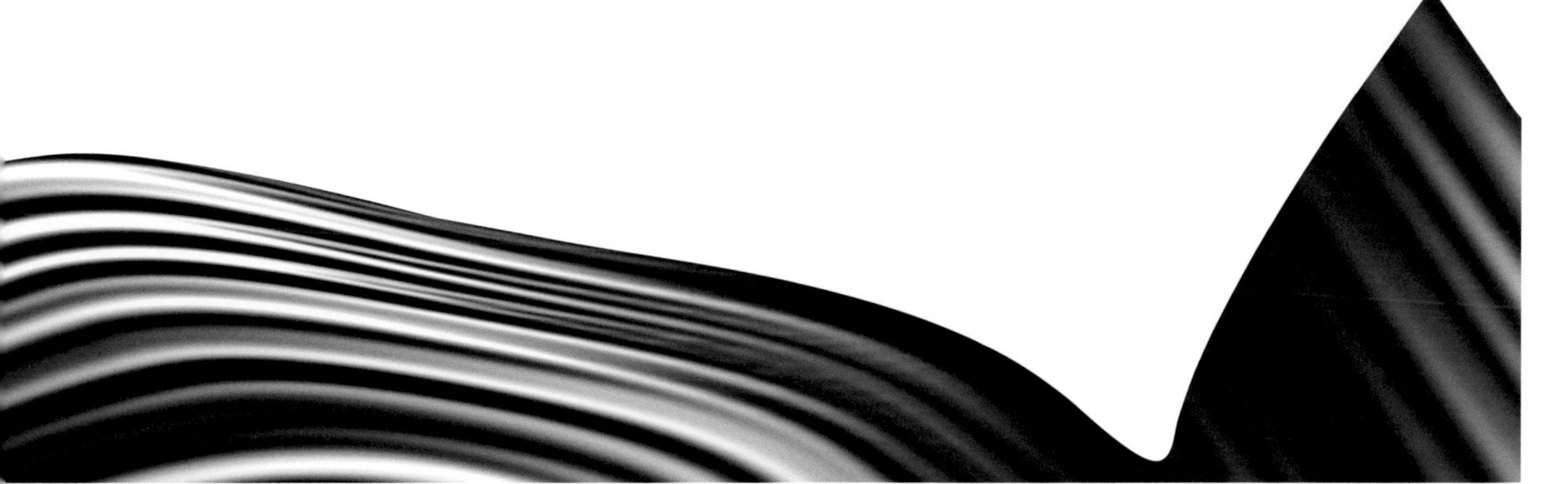

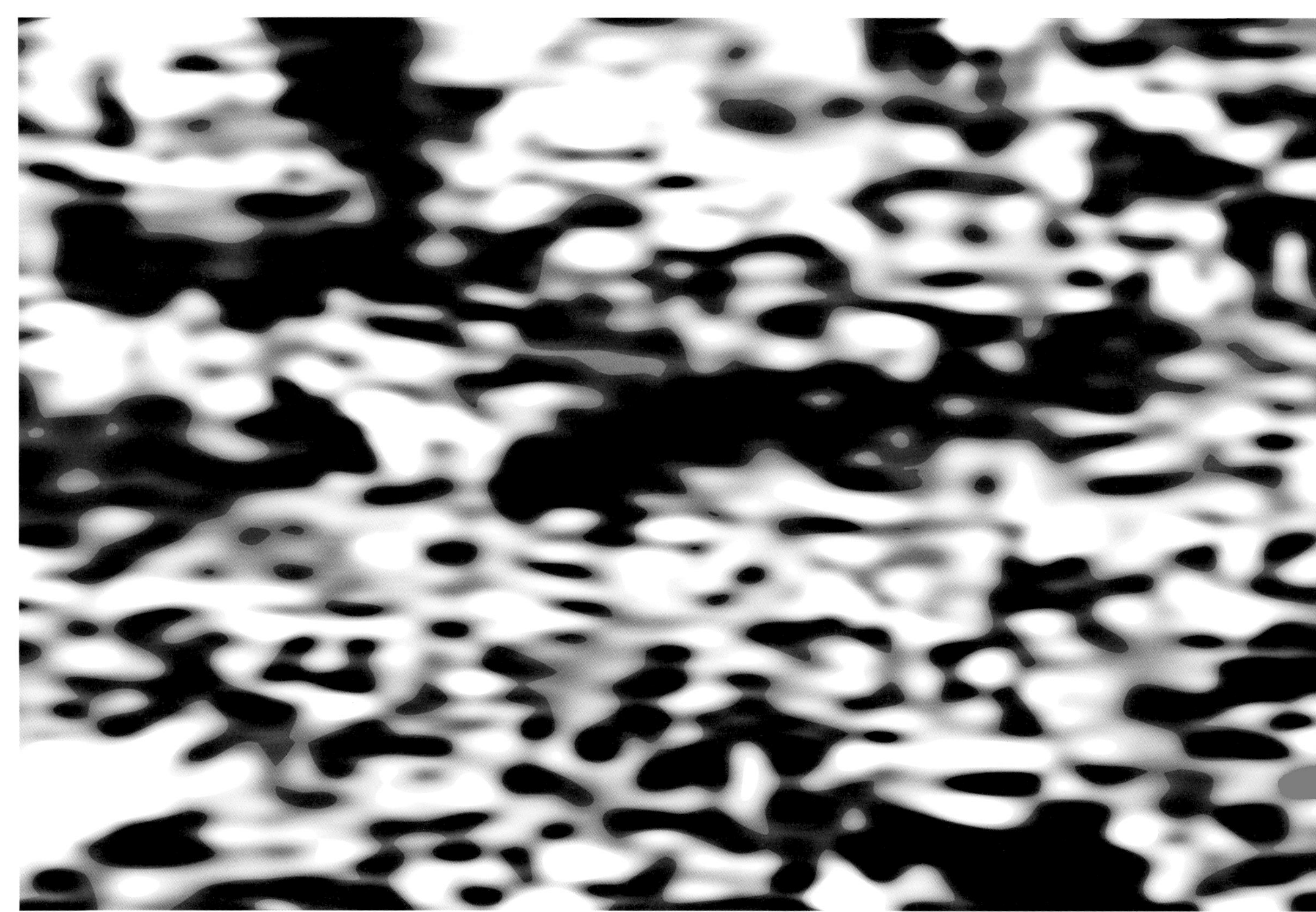

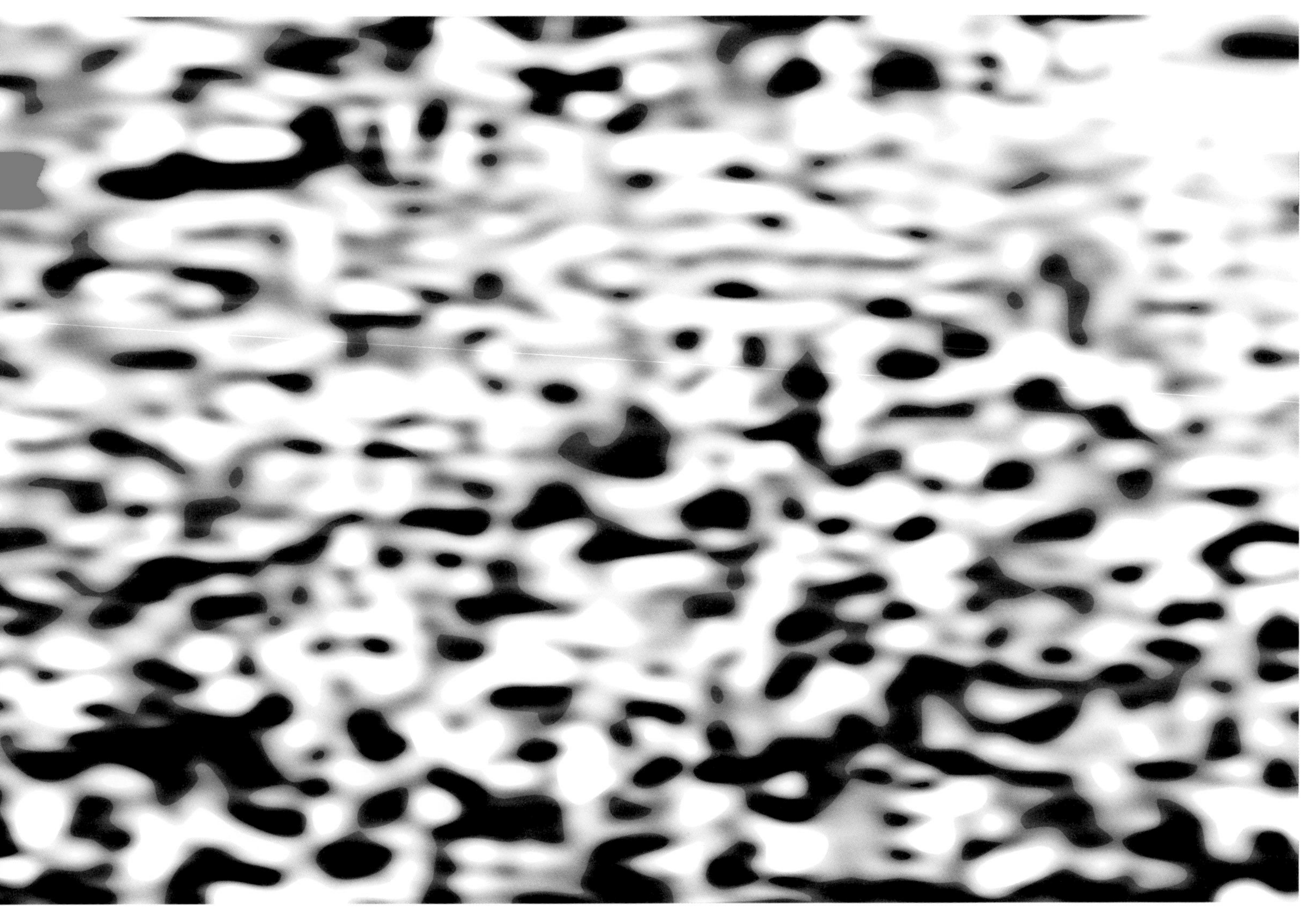

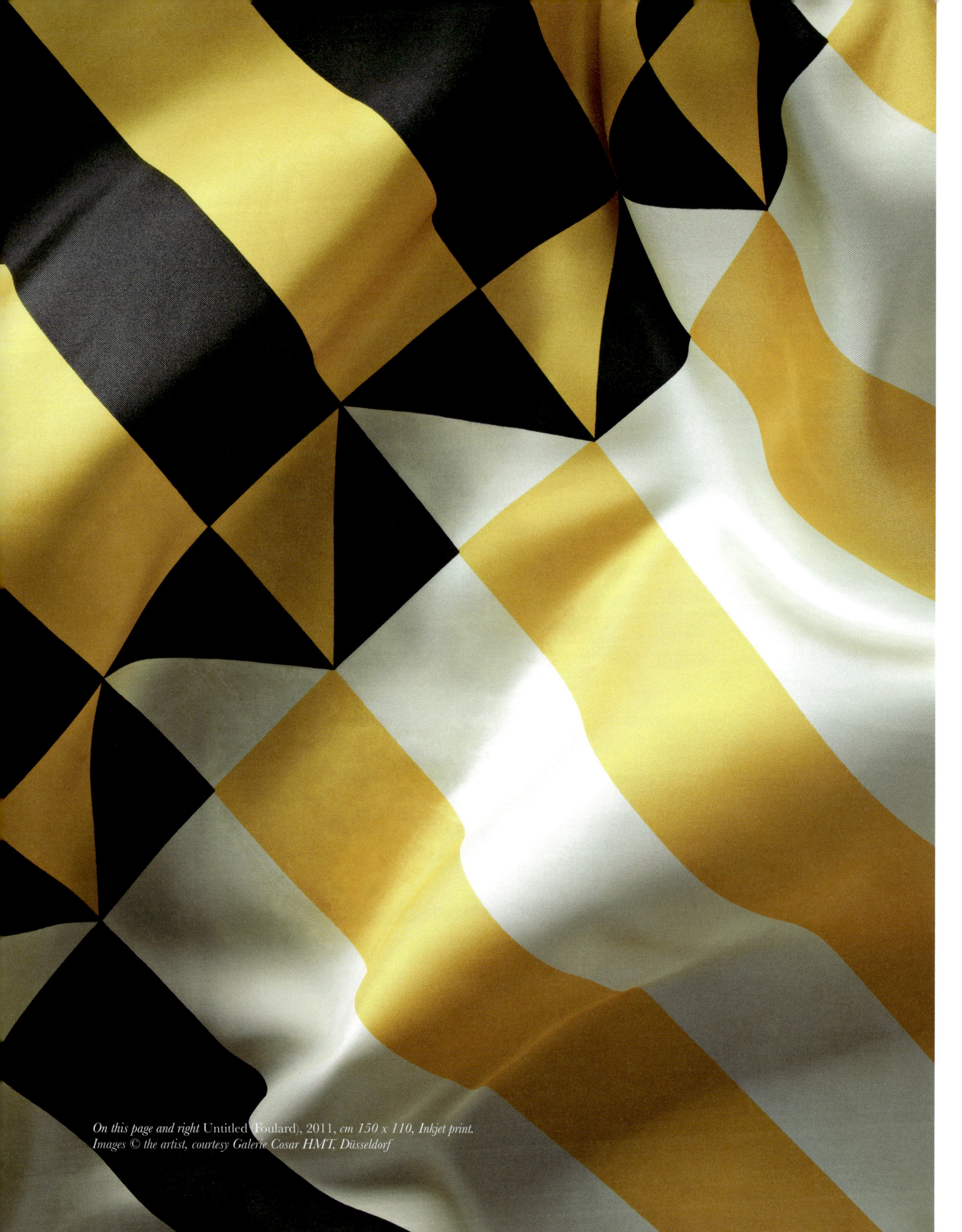

On this page and right Untitled (Foulard), 2011, *cm 150 x 110, Inkjet print.*
Images © the artist, courtesy Galerie Cosar HMT, Düsseldorf

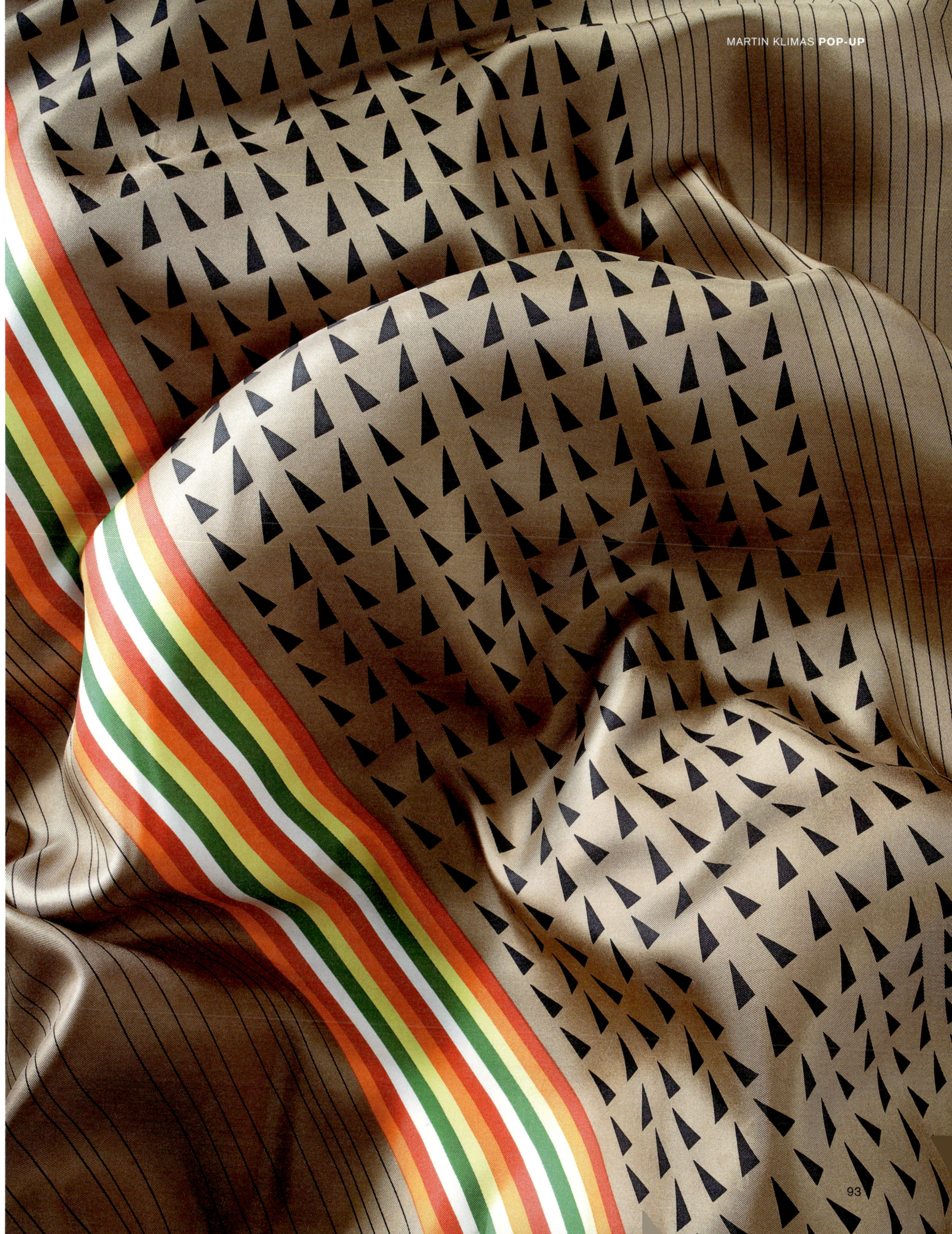

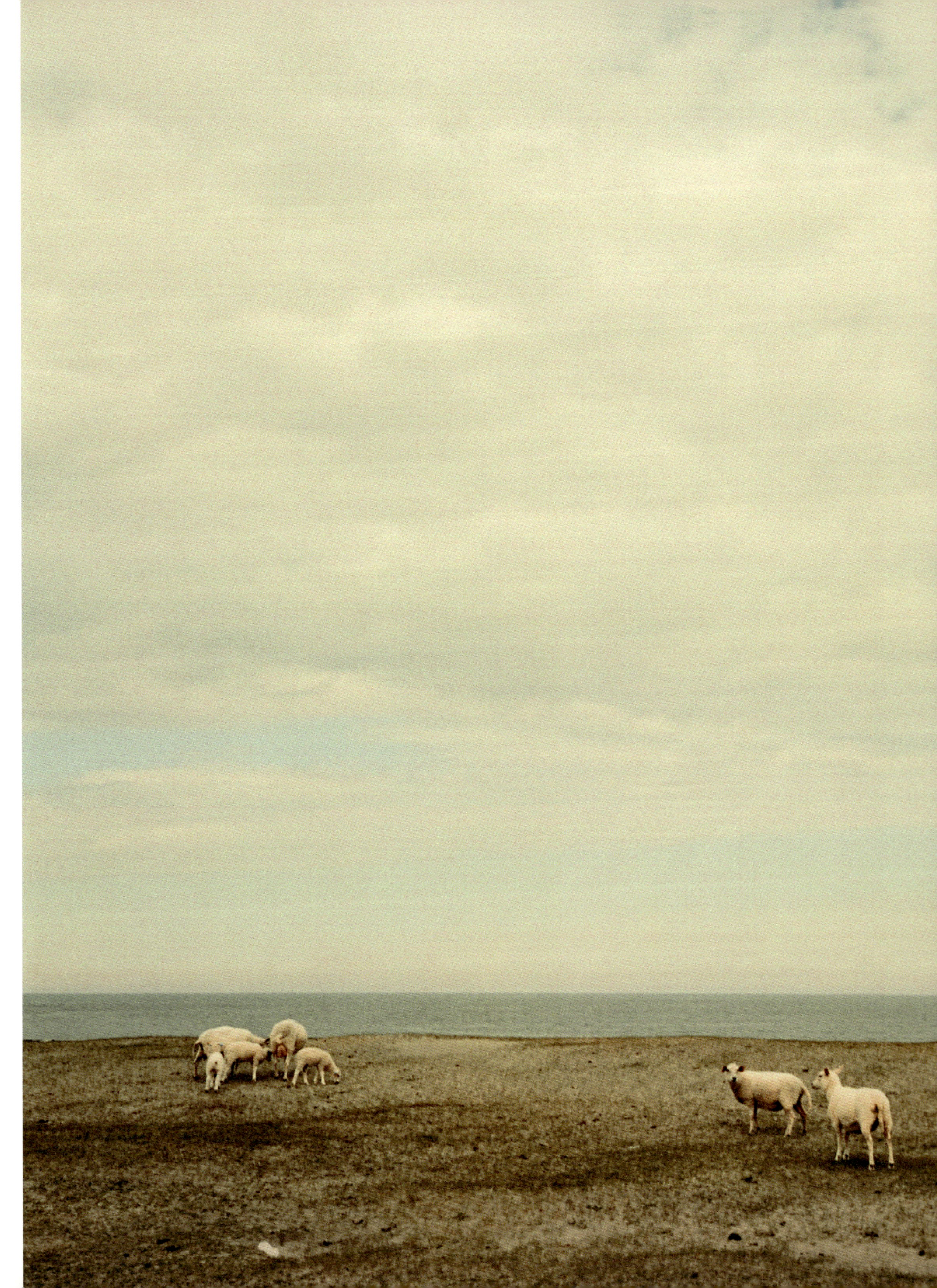

KARINE LAVAL
THE ROAD AT THE EDGE
by Elisabeth Biondi

Imagine yourself driving at the northern tip of Norway listening to Nick Cave and the Bad Seeds on the longest day of the year. What would that be like? Karine Laval spent one summer in the tiny fishing village of Vadsø roaming the seaside with her camera.

The days were long and the northern light sublime, so different from light in France where she grew up. The arctic landscape shimmered in subtle greens, and the sky merged blue with the sea. She had been there two years earlier during fall when the days were shorter and the seashore more gloomy. Both times she followed a narrow road at the edge of the fjord on the fringe of Europe. Hence the chosen title: *The Road at the Edge.* Before going to Norway, Laval had been developing her on-going series, *Poolscapes*, wherein water takes the place of landscape as a fluid surrounding for her abstracted representational subjects. Inspired by the unfamiliar surroundings, Laval has created a series of pictures that go far beyond traditional landscape photography. Her particular fusion of color, light, form, and texture imbue these remote scenes with a sentiment that lingers somewhere between the real and the surreal, the natural and the man made: looking, re-looking, exploring, discarding, and abstracting until what gets translated into a photograph fully incorporates her experience.

Just as landscape dominates the figure in Caspar David Friedrich's exquisite moody paintings, in Laval's photographs the geographic and abstract coexist in her portrayal of a remote island with the Old Norse name that translates iconically as "island with water."

Born in Paris, Laval currently lives and works in New York. Educated at the University of La Sorbonne and the University of ASSAS in Paris, where she majored in communications and journalism, she completed her education with photography and design courses at Cooper Union, SVA and the New School of New York. She has alternated magazine commissions and publications with artistic practice, wherein she combines portraiture with images of geographical locations and visual narratives. Among her solo shows are French Cultural Center, Oslo and Nattgalleriet (The Night Gallery;) Sorlandet Art Museum, Kristiansand, Norway; Bonni Benrubi Gallery, New York City; Yancey Richardson Gallery, New York City; and M+B Gallery, Los Angeles. Laval has also exhibited at festivals and institutions such as the Palais de Tokyo, Paris; Lodz Festival, Poland; Rhubarb-Rhubarb, Birmingham; and Les Rencontres d'Arles in France, to name a few.

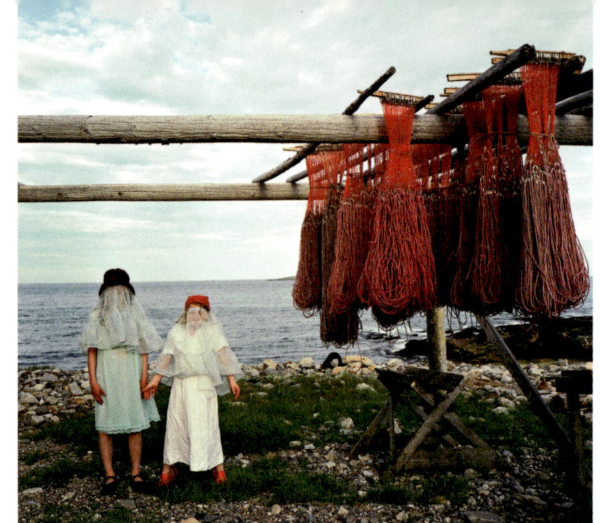

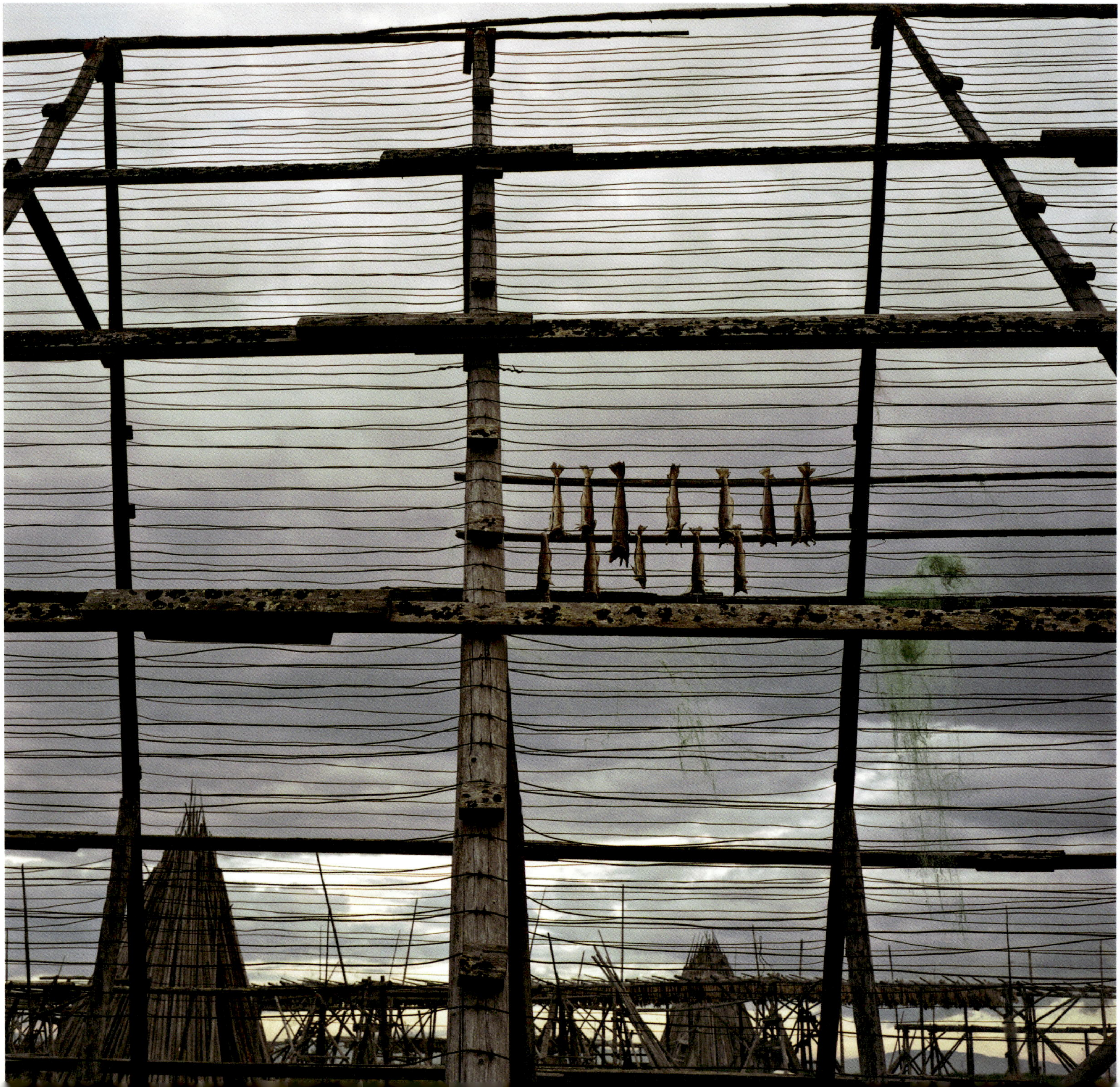

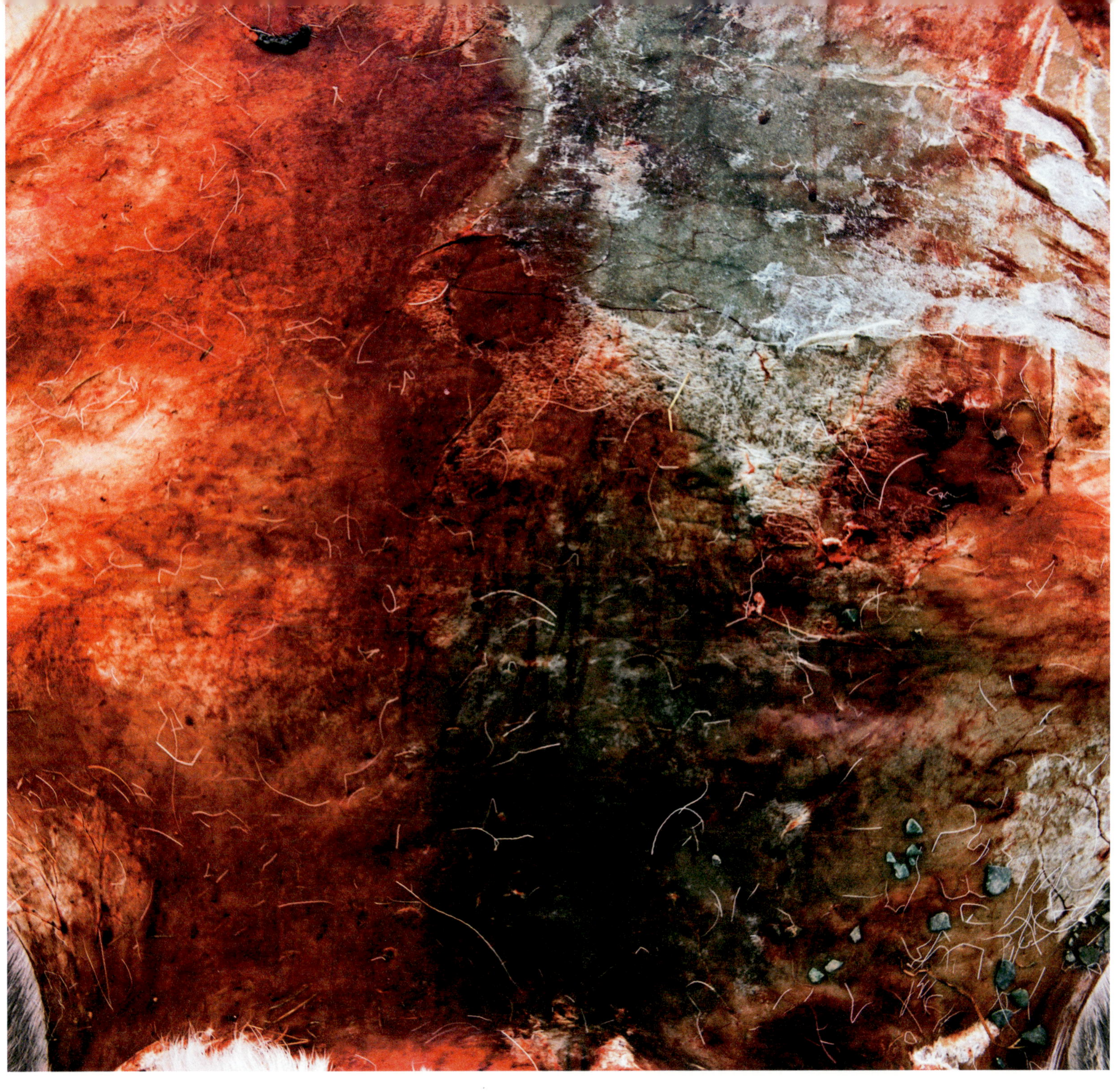

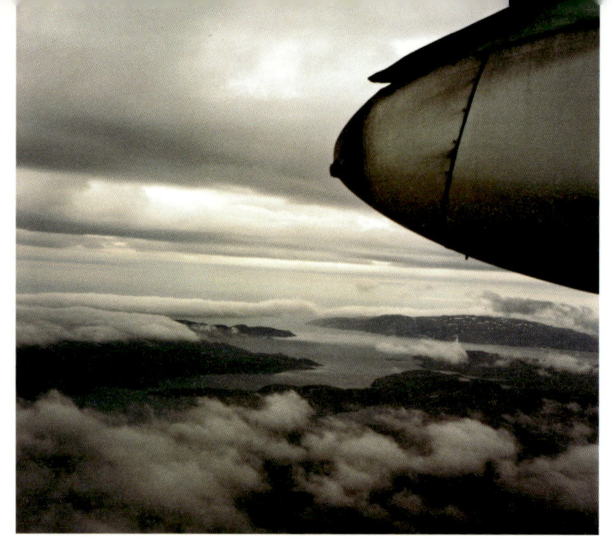

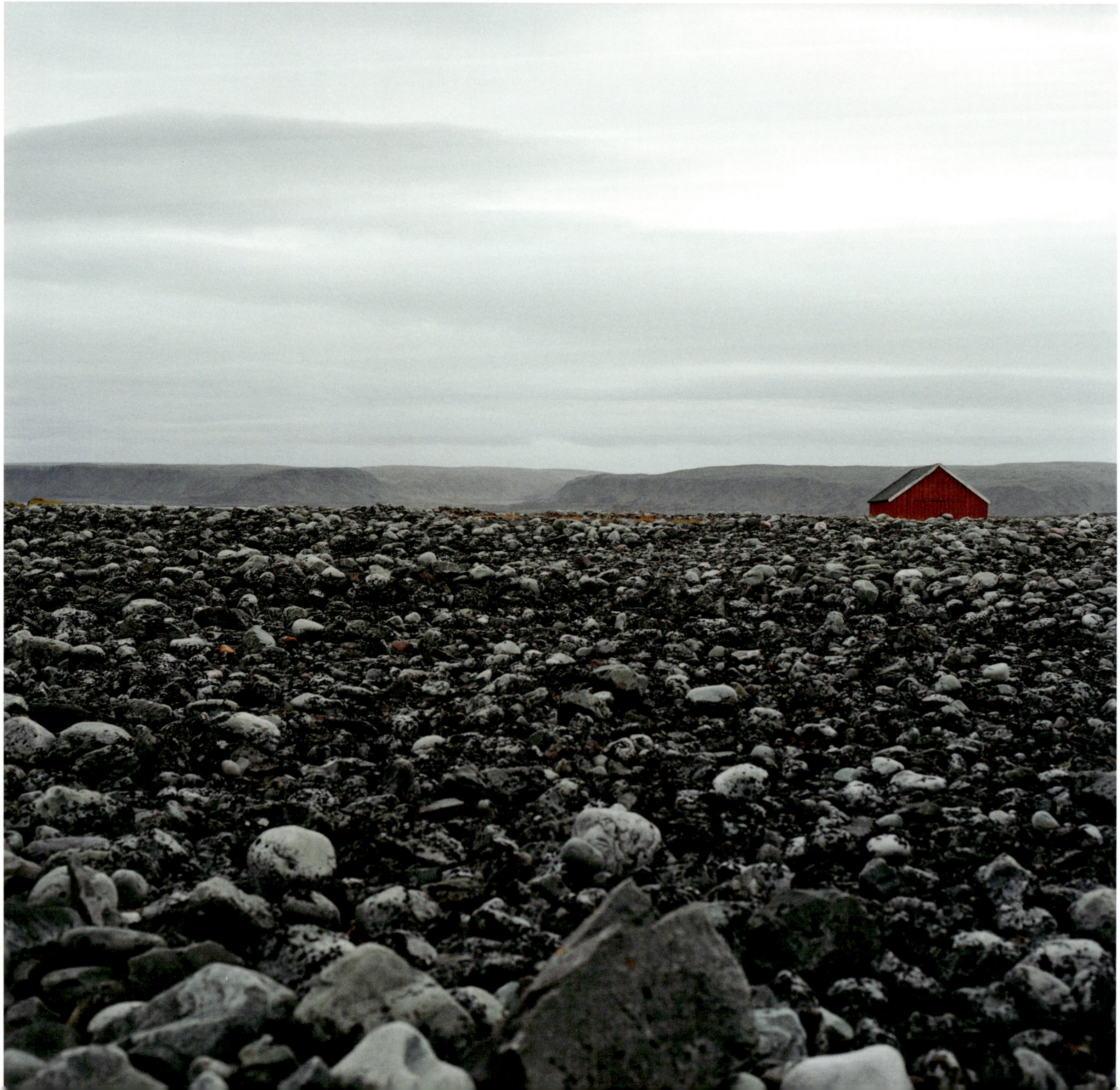

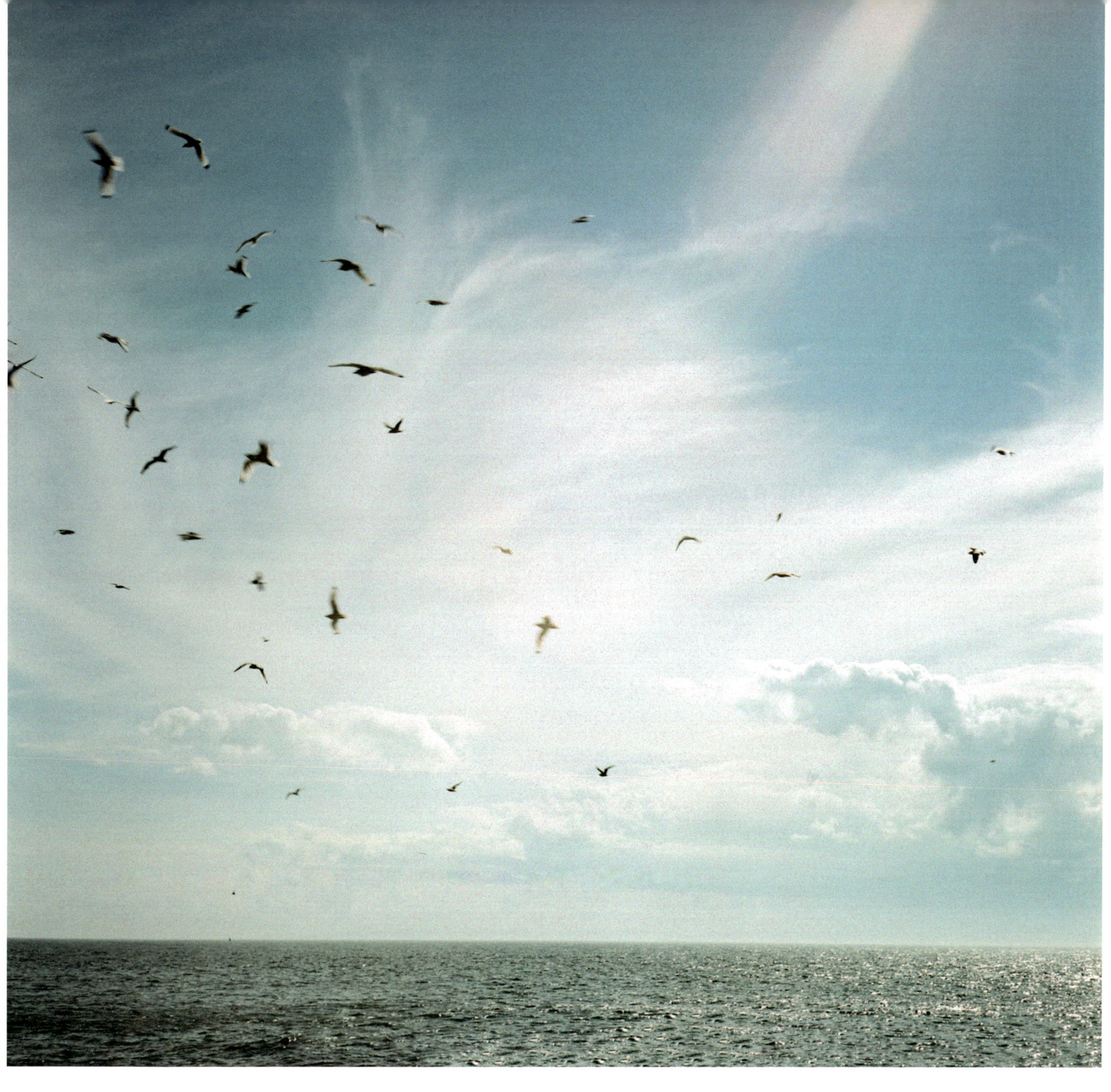

Page 94 Untitled #25, 2008. *Page 96 above* Untitled #38, 2008, *below* Untitled #2, 2008. *Page 97* Untitled #28, 2006. *Page 98 above* Untitled #1, 2008, *below* Untitled #8, 2006. *Page 99* Untitled #21, 2008. *Right* Untitled #47, 2006. *All images from the series* The Road At The Edge, © *the artist, courtesy the artist and Bonni Benrubi Gallery, New York*

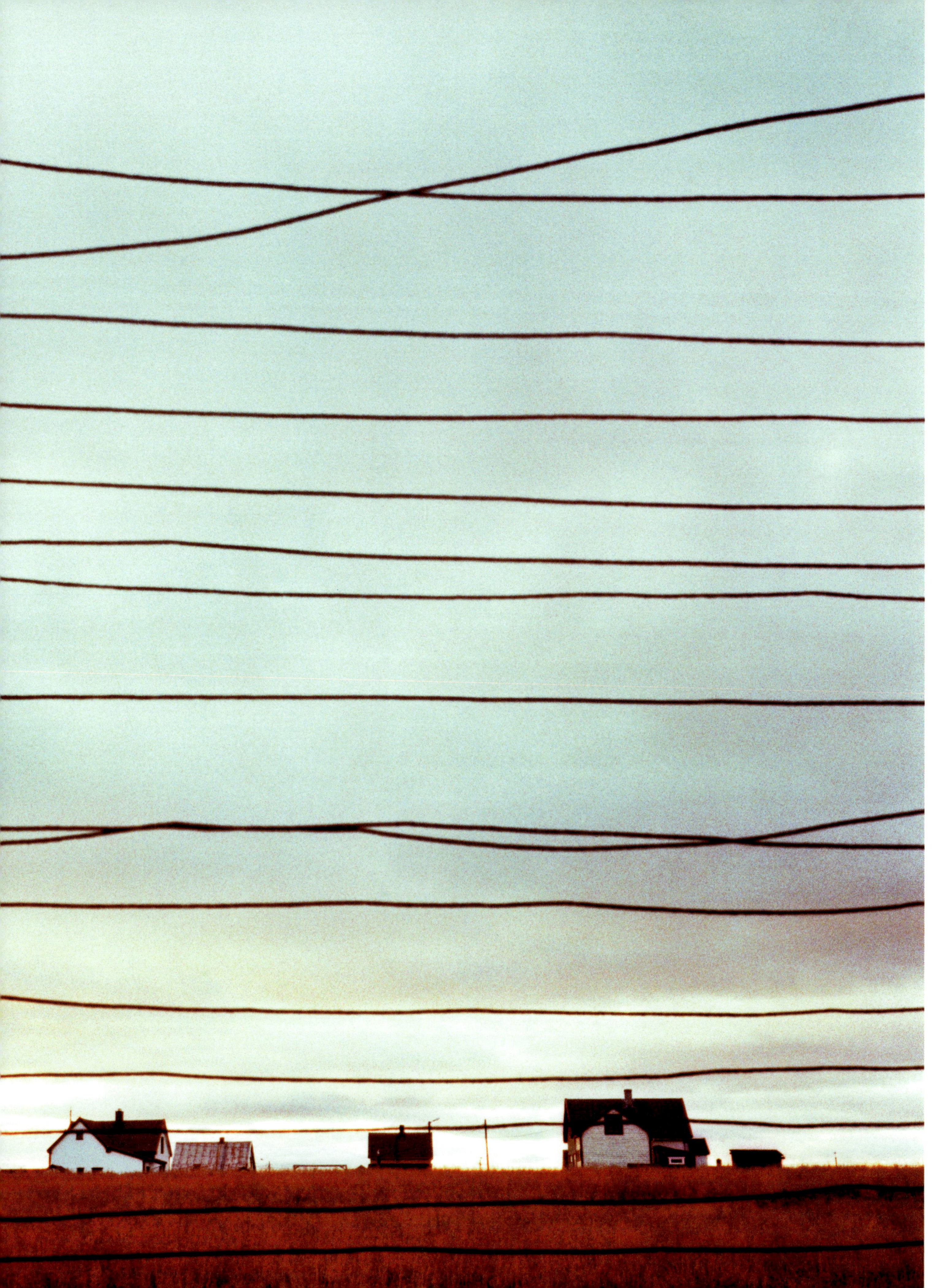

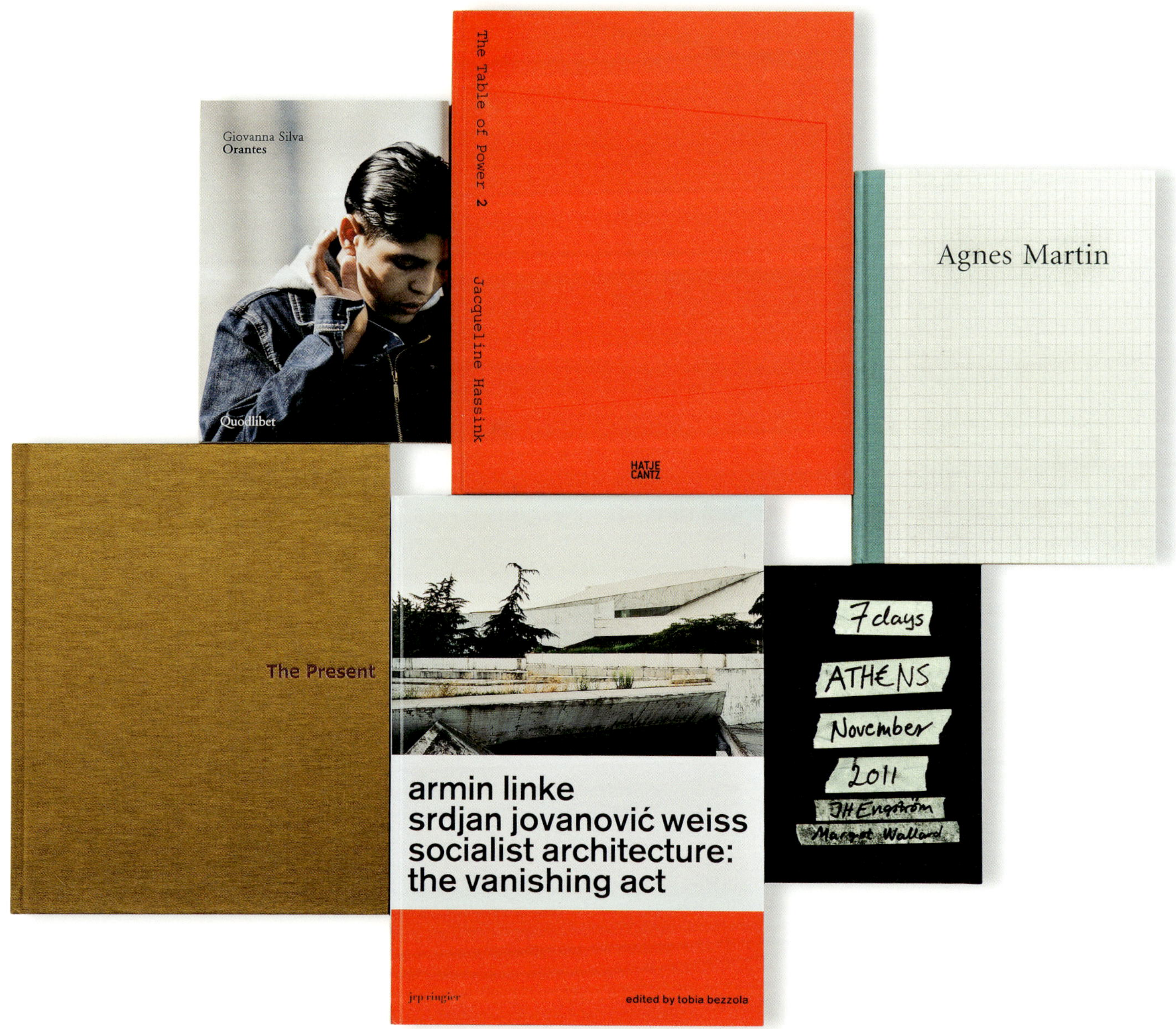

ON OUR SHELVES

Top row, from left:

Orantes, Giovanna Silva, 120 pp., Quodlibet, *quodlibet.it*

The Table of Power 2, Jacqueline Hassink, 224 pp., Hatje Cantz, *hatjecantz.de*

Agnes Martin, edited by Lynne Cooke and Karen Kelly; 268 pp., Yale Press, *yalepress.yale.edu*

Bottom row, from left:

The Present, Paul Graham, 114 pp., MACK, *mackbooks.co.uk*

Socialist Architecture: The Vanishing Act, Armin Linke & Srdjan Jovanovic Weiss, 132 pp., JRP|Ringier, *jrp-ringier.com*

7 days ATHENS November 2011, JH Engström and Margot Wallard, 56 pp., Super Labo, *superlabo.com*

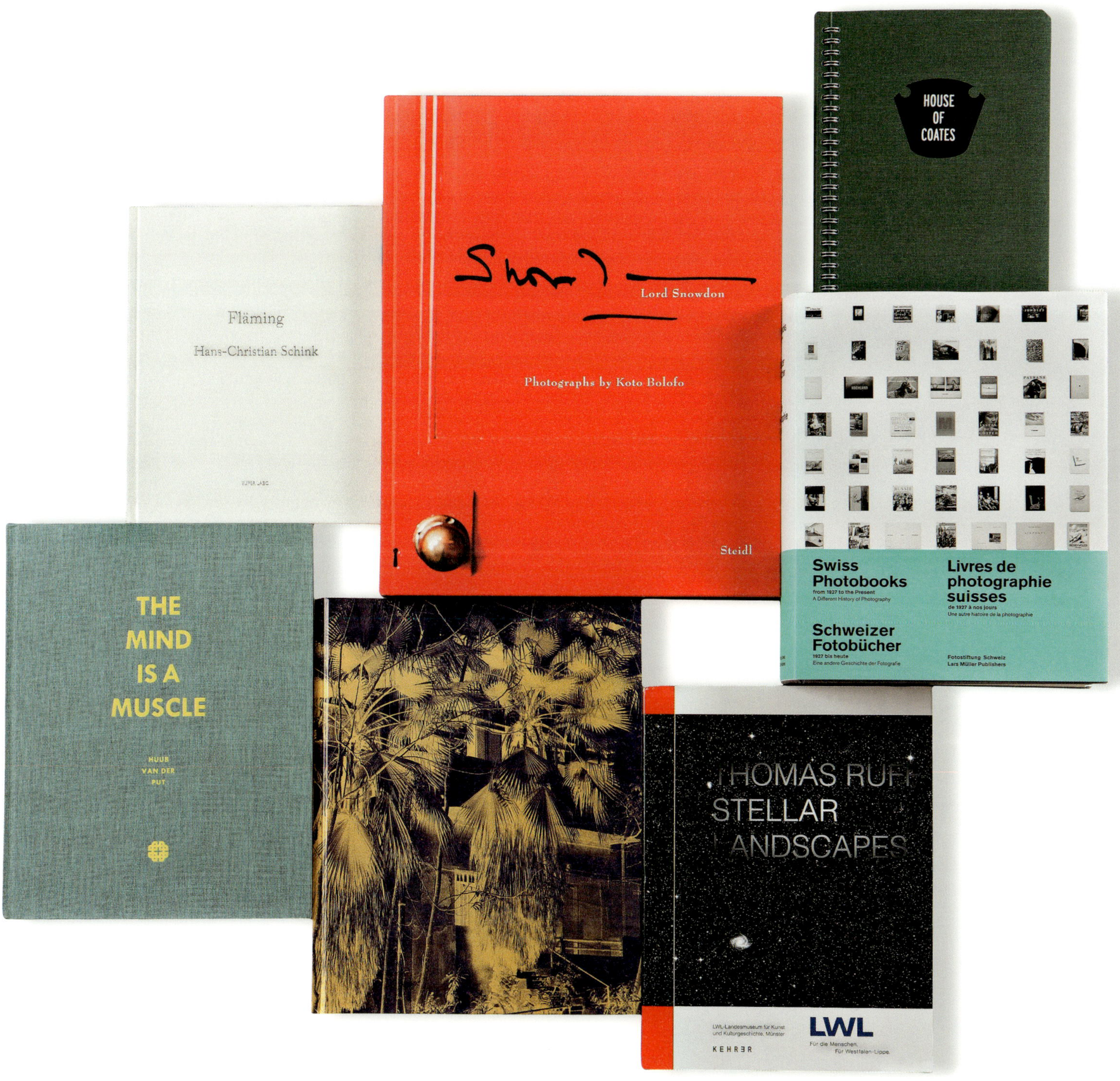

Top row, from left:

Fläming, by Hans-Christian Schink, 44 pp., Super Labo, *superlabo.com*

Lord Snowdon, Koto Bolofo, 208 pp., Steidl, *steidlville.com*

House of Coates, Brad Zellar with photos by Lester B. Morrison, designed by Hans Seeger, 118 pp., Little Brown Mushroom, *littlebrownmushroom.com*

Swiss Photobooks from 1927 to the Present / A different History of Photography, edited by Peter Pfrunder, Fotostiftung Schweiz in cooperation with Martin Gasser and Sabine Münzenmaier, 704 pp., Lars Müller Publishers, *lars-mueller-publishers.com*

Bottom row, from left:

The Mind is a Muscle, Huub van der Put, designed by Erik Kessels, 152 pp., Epos | House Home of Art Books, *homeofartbooks.nl*

Things here and things still to come, José Pedro Cortes, 116 pp., Pierre von Kleist Editions, *pierrevonkleist.com*

Stellar Landscapes, Thomas Ruff, 114 pp., Kehrer Verlag, *kehrerverlag.com*

Photos by Matteo Weber

MARTIN KLIMAS 'Foulard' is a French word for a lightweight, multi-colored, silk fabric. In this edition of Pop-Up, Martin Klimas takes an unconventional approach to the representations of textiles, abstracting the recognizable motifs of high fashion brands from their physicality and tactility. Referencing Abstract Expressionism and Pop Art, Klimas chooses to scale the images to overtake the frame, capturing in the moment the flutter of a fabric that seems to breathe. What results is the exploration of a polemical dilemma so intrinsic to photography. As Klimas states, he is "oddly undecided whether they are two- or three-dimensional, whether they are pictures or objects, these scarves are an identity crisis in its visible, physical form. Their styles reference the artistic movements of their times." Martin Klimas is a German artist born in Singen in 1971. He studied Visual Communications and Photography, at the Fachhochschule in Düsseldorf, where he continues to live and work. He has exhibited at Cosar HMT, Germany, Foley Gallery, New York, Andy Warhol Museum, Pittsburgh, and Galleria Suzy Shammah, Milan. *martin-klimas.de*

ELISABETH BIONDI joined The *New Yorker* in 1996 as Visuals Editor. In this newly created position, she established photography in the publication and left in 2011 to work as an Independent Curator. Ms. Biondi has also worked as Director of Photography with *Stern*, the German newsweekly, *Vanity Fair*, and *GEO*. Recent curatorial projects include Photography Now: engaged, personal, & vital, NYPHOTO 2011; New Yorker Fiction/Real Photography, Steven Kasher Gallery; Beyond Words: Photography in The New Yorker, Howard Greenberg Gallery; and Widely Different: Panoramic Photography by Jeff Liao and Sylvia Plachy, Seaport Museum New York.

ALEX GARTENFELD is an art critic and Online Editor for Interview Magazine and Art in America. He is the co-founder of West Street Gallery, a project space in New York. *weststreet.info*

ADRIAN GAUT originally studied painting and soon adopted photography, finding inspiration in Minimalism of early 20th century painting. Though his oeuvre encompasses a wide spectrum of themes and subjects, architecture and minimalism inform the essence of his practice. Gaut has worked with a diverse range of clients, including HSBC, Stella Artois, Starbucks, and publications including *The New York Times, Wallpaper*, Abitare, Wired, Japanese Vogue, GQ China, Newsweek,* and *Monocle,* to name a few. He is also the first photographer to shoot the Virgin Galactic commercial space program in Mojave, California, has photographed the art collection at the Inhotim Institute in rural Brazil, as well the rugged north shore of Kauai. Born in Portland, Oregon, Gaut is now based in New York City.

GINEVRA ELKANN was born in London, 1979, and is currently based in Italy. She holds a BA from American University of Paris and a Masters in Film Directing from the London Film School. She is the co-founder of several film production and distributions houses including Caspian Films, the CEO of Asmara Film, and the co-founding president of Good Films. Elkann is also the president of the Pinacoteca Giovanni e Marella Agnelli, Turin, and on the advisory board at Christie's. She is a member of the acquisitions and executive committees at the Fondation Cartier, Paris, since June 2008. She also works as the editor at large of *TAR* and collaborates with *Wired. pinacoteca-agnelli.it / fondation.cartier.com / tar-mag.com*

MARCO LORENZI was born in Vicenza, Italy, and is currently based in Shanghai. He has been passionate about astronomy since adolescence, and began shooting astrophotography at age 13. He has been published in several astronomy magazines and is a founding member of his local astronomy club. In 2011 he won the prestigious award Astronomy Photographer of the Year, run by the Maritime Museum and Royal Observatory of Greenwich in London, on both deep-sky and robotic imaging sections. *glitteringlights.com*

VERA MLECHEVSKA is freelance critic and curator based in Sofia, Bulgaria. She graduated Art History at the National Academy of Art, Sofia, and CuratorLab at Konstfack University in Stockholm. She has contributed to a various Bulgarian publications, and works as editor of *Blister Magazine,* a platform for art criticism. Mlechevska is co-founder of the Art Affairs and Documents foundation and is responsible for the residency program. She has been a guest curator for many institutions and organizations in Bulgaria as well as the Unicredit Studio, Milan. *blistermagazine.com / aadfoundation.blogspot.com*

FRANÇOIS SAGE practiced copyright law for 35 years in Paris and then decided to fulfill his dream of opening an art gallery. Since 2004, SAGE Paris has shown a particular interest in Masterworks of photography of the nineteenth and twentieth century that has led him to present museum quality exhibitions. He has also a keen interest in contemporary photography, especially Japanese, and has worked with Daido Moriyama, Miyaco Ishiuchi and Naoya Hatakeyama. *sageparis.com*

FRANCESCO VEZZOLI graduated from Central Saint Martins in 1995 and has since been based in Milan. Embracing multimedia techniques, he draws on a range of disciplines from embroidery to live performance, photography, sculpture and video installation. Obsessed by what he calls 'the media circus,' and fascinated by the iconography of female identity, Vezzoli's work unites pop icons, auteur cinema, art history and politics. His work has been featured in numerous museums, including, The New Museum, New York; Fondazione Prada, Milan; Museu Serralves, Porto; Le Consortium, Dijon; Moderna Museet, Stockholm; Kunsthalle Wien; Garage Center for Contemporary Culture, Moscow; Guggenheim, New York; MOCA, Los Angeles; and biennials such as Venice, Istanbul, Shanghai and the Whitney.

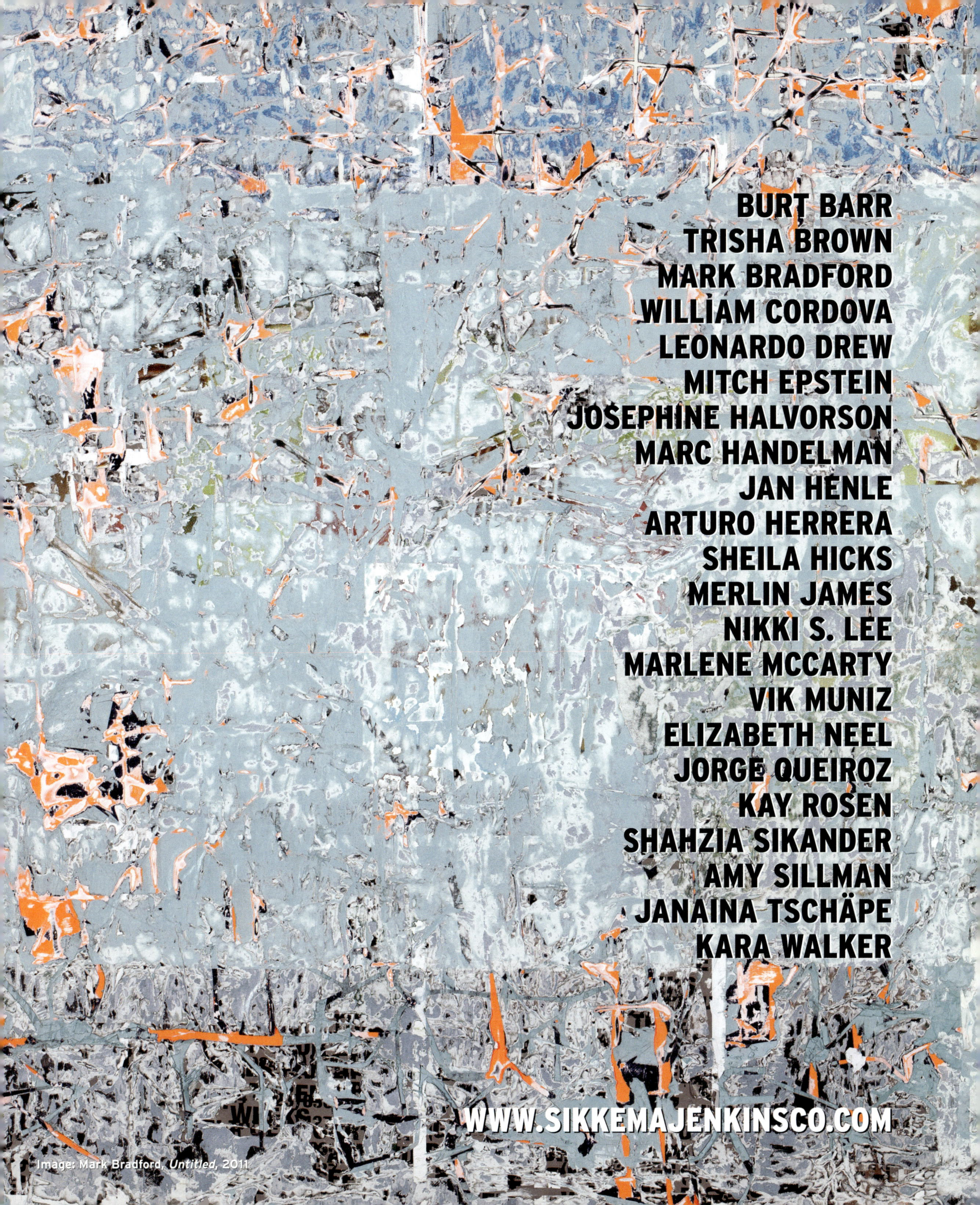

Image: Mark Bradford, *Untitled*, 2011

COLOPHON

EDITORS
Cay Sophie Rabinowitz, Selva Barni
editorial@fantomeditions.com

ASSOCIATE EDITOR
Francesco Zanot
francesco@fantomeditions.com

CONTRIBUTING EDITOR
Emma Reeves
emma@fantomeditions.com

ART DIRECTOR
Fabrizio Radaelli
nuclearlab.it

EDITORIAL OFFICE
Didier Falzone
didier@fantomeditions.com

EDITORIAL ASSISTANT
Arianne Di Nardo

EDITOR-AT-LARGE
Massimo Torrigiani

TRANSLATIONS
Judith Mundell

THANKS TO
Agnese Bossi, Christian Rattemeyer, Davies Costacurta, Luca Cipelletti,
Luca Martinazzoli, Martina Scapinello, Massimo Mezzavilla,
Pasquale Marini, Pino Musi, Pino Pipoli, Roberto Rossi Gandolfi, Skype,
Sofia Sizzi and Iacopo Falai, Stefano Pitigliani,
Vittoria Corbetta Marini, Luciano Cirelli.

WWW.FANTOMEDITIONS.COM

FANTOM OFFICE
Via Lanzone 22, 20123 Milan, Italy

ADVERTISING ENQUIRIES
info@fantomeditions.com

SUBSCRIPTIONS
Bruil & van de Staaij
PO Box 75, 7940 AB Meppel, The Netherlands
T +31 522 261303 - F + 31 522 257827
www.bruil.info

DISTRIBUTION
Italia and International: SO.DI.P. SpA
Via Bettola 18, 20092 Cinisello Balsamo (MI), Italy
T +39 02 66030400 - F +39 02 66030269
sies@siesnet.it - www.siesnet.it

North America: D.A.P./Distributed Art Publishers
155 Sixth Avenue, 2nd Floor, 10013 New York, NY, USA
T +1 212 627 1999 - F +1 212 627 9484
www.artbook.com

PUBLISHED BY
Boiler Corporation Srl
Piazza Castello 19, 20121 Milan, Italy
Numero di Iscrizione al R.O.C. 19.061 del 12/10/2009

PUBLISHERS
Ivan Maria Vele, Massimo Torrigiani, Susanna Cucco

PROJECT MANAGER
Pier Mario Simula
p.simula@boilercorporation.com

ASSISTANT
Simone Castelli
s.castelli@boilercorporation.com

Printed in Italy by Grafiche Antiga, Via delle Industrie 1
31035 Crocetta del Montello (TV)
www.graficheantiga.it

Periodico registrato presso il Tribunale di Milano
N° 436 del 07/10/2009
Direttore Responsabile: Selva Barni

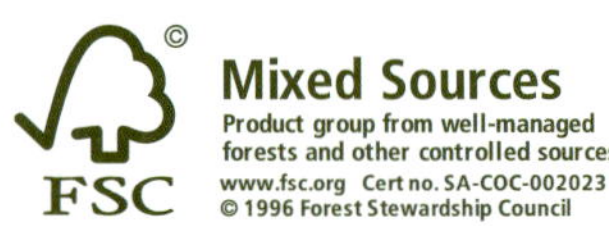

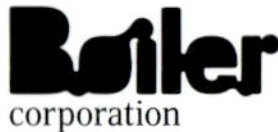

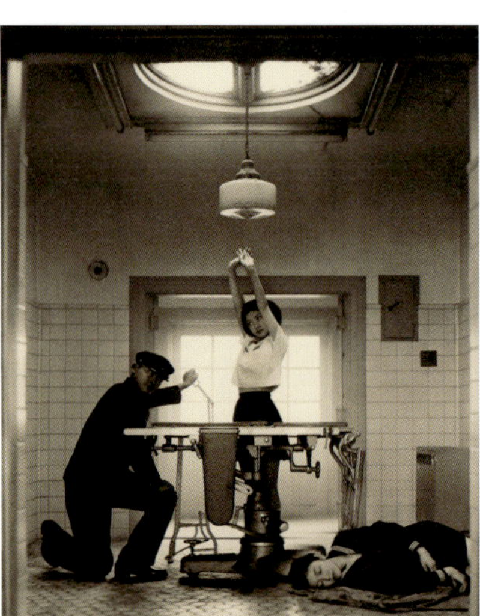

Fantom cover artist Hisaji Hara will be featured in our next issue,
out in Summer 2012. On the cover: A study of The Mountain, 2010,
from the series *A Photographic Portrayal of the Paintings of Balthus.*
Image © the artist, courtesy MEM Gallery, Tokyo

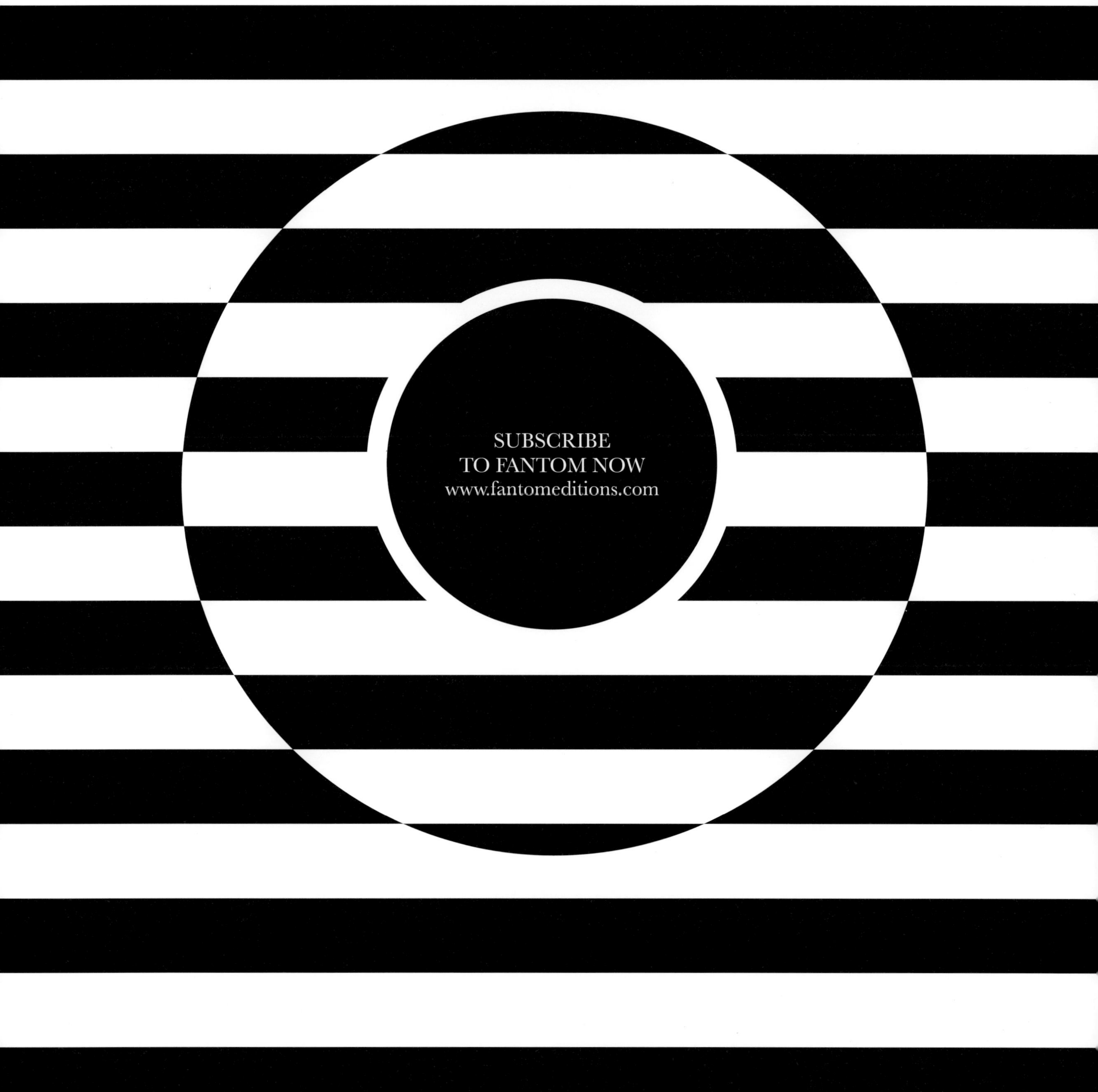
SUBSCRIBE
TO FANTOM NOW
www.fantomeditions.com

FANTOM

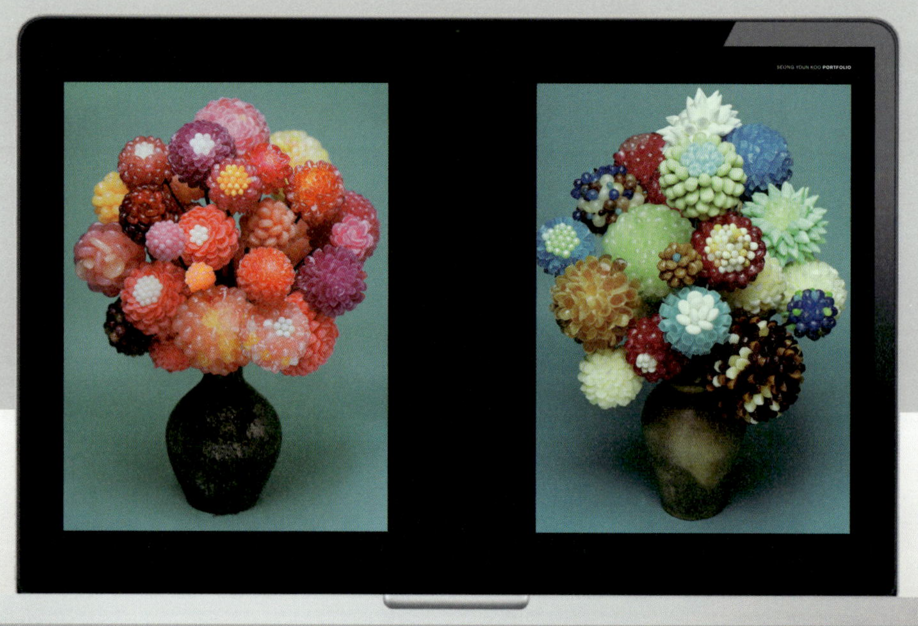

NOW ANYTIME,
ANYWHERE.

Other Edition.com

Art | Basel | Miami Beach

6–9 | Dec | 12

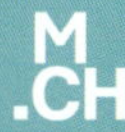

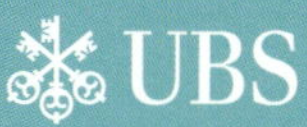